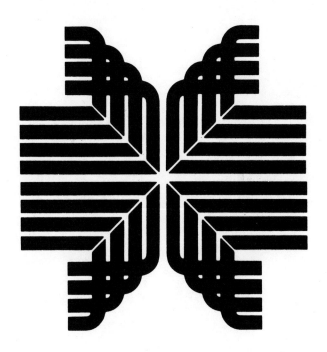

AUGSBURG SERMONS 2

*New Sermons
on
Gospel Texts*

AUGSBURG SERMONS 2

Gospels Series B

AUGSBURG Publishing House • Minneapolis

AUGSBURG SERMONS 2—GOSPELS—SERIES B

Copyright © 1984 Augsburg Publishing House

Scripture quotations unless otherwise noted are from the Revised Standard Version of the Bible, copyright 1946, 1952, and 1971 by the Division of Christian Education of the National Council of Churches.

Scripture quotations marked TEV are from the Good News Bible: Today's English Version, © American Bible Society, 1966, 1971, 1976.

Scripture quotations marked NEB are from the New English Bible, © 1961, 1970 by the Delegates of the Oxford University Press and the Syndics of the Cambridge University Press.

Scripture quotations marked Phillips are from the New Testament in Modern English by J. B. Phillips, © 1958 by J. B. Phillips.

The quotation from Psalm 41 in the sermon for Maundy Thursday is from the translation in *Standard Book of Common Prayer* copyright 1977 by Charles Mortimer Guilbert as custodian.

LCCC 84-72019   ISBN 0-8066-2095-1

Manufactured in the U.S.A.   APH 10-0534

1   2   3   4   5   6   7   8   9   0   1   2   3   4   5   6   7   8   9

Contents

Introduction

The first volume in the original *Augsburg Sermons* was published in 1973 to help pastors become familiar with the new Lectionary and Calendar prepared by the Inter-Lutheran Commission on Worship (ILCW). Ten volumes in all comprised the first *Augsburg Sermons* series—three volumes on the Gospels, three volumes on the Epistles, three volumes on the Old Testament Lessons, and one volume on texts for the Lesser Festivals. The widespread acceptance of the volumes is an indication both of the quality of the sermons and of the favorable reception of the Lectionary and Calendar.

One outstanding feature of the Lectionary is its use of a Gospel of the Year. Each year, one of the synoptic Gospels is featured, providing continuity to the reading and telling of the gospel story throughout the entire church year. This approach makes the uniqueness of each gospel stand out in all its clarity and richness. It also enables pastors to study the Gospel of the Year with greater thoroughness and to share their insights with their congregations in preaching.

Augsburg Sermons 2 builds on the momentum of the original series. This volume provides a fresh look at the Gospel of Mark, the basis for Series B. And it is offered with the confidence that the message of Mark will speak as clearly and powerfully to Christians in the 1980s as it has to all previous generations.

Guarding the House of God
Mark 13:33-37

I would like to talk to you this first Sunday in Advent, this new beginning of the church year, about gin.

That's right—gin—the intoxicating drink from which many a cocktail is mixed and in which many a person has sought to drown the sorrows of life.

Now, don't worry. I do not intend to spend my time arguing the evils of the three-martini lunch. This is not going to be a temperance sermon, although temperance—that is, moderation—is an admirable virtue, which we should all exercise and do not exercise enough.

No, I want to talk about gin because it can help us to understand better our text for this morning, in which Jesus commands us to be on the watch for the coming of the Son of Man: " 'Take heed, watch; for you do not know when the time will come' " (Mark 13:33). Jesus calls us to be vigilant, always prepared. He warns us that the owner of the house will return one day—we know not when—and the owner does not want to find us fallen asleep with the house unguarded and vulnerable. Listen to his words:

> "Watch therefore—for you do not know when the master of the house will come, in the evening, or at midnight, or at cockcrow, or in the morning—lest he come suddenly and find you asleep. And what I say to you I say to all: Watch" (Mark 13:35-37).

There is a menacing insistence in what Jesus has to say to us here. This passage comes at the end of a chapter in Mark where we have received not one but several warnings about God's holy will and judgment. These warnings are not to be ignored, even if they come in the midst of the hustle and bustle of the holiday season, when the mood of both our sacred and secular cultures is one of enjoyment, contentment, and celebration.

The House Unguarded

What do gin and our Gospel text have in common? The connection is made in a true story from church history about a group of Christians whose house was indeed unguarded, and the problem, or at least part of it, was gin.

17

It happened in England in the 18th century. At that time, England was not a pretty place. Although on the threshold of becoming a great power in the world, England was beset by problems of poverty, injustice, corruption, and drunkenness. The popular drink was cheap gin. Perhaps popular is too mild a word: over 11 billion gallons of the stuff were consumed in the year 1750 alone.

We can only begin to imagine what life was like then. We do have some help, however. The horrors of this fearsome social phenomenon of gin drinking are graphically portrayed by the great social commentator William Hogarth in "Gin Lane" and other pictures. They are striking and unforgettable.

To this situation the church was called to minister, to bring the gospel. To use Jesus' sharp image from our passage, the church was called to protect the house. But the church of the day had fallen asleep. It was not on watch. It is reported that the Church of England had more than 11,000 positions for clergy paid from state revenues. A full 6000 of these positions were occupied by men who did not even step foot in the parishes they were called to serve. These congregations were left in the hands of poorly paid and often alienated curates. What was operating was a corrupt system which put the clergy on the government dole. The absentee clergy lived luxuriously, some in London, some even on the Continent— as far away as they could get from the "house" they were called to guard and care for.

As you might imagine, chaos reigned. England was a spiritual desert. The church was the object of withering ridicule from leaders of the newly emerging Enlightenment. It was a time of judgment; the warning of Jesus to keep watch had gone unheeded.

The Problem of Success

Now our story takes a twist. In this terrible time in the life of a nation and of the church, John and Charles Wesley began their ministry. They were priests of the Church of England, but because of their emotional style they were not allowed to preach in the church. So they preached the gospel outside to the unchurched. They preached literally outside on the street, in the fields, in prison yards, and to the miners as they came out of dark holes in the ground.

The Wesleys preached the personal love of God for each precious soul. They preached the forgiveness of Christ. People listened in great numbers.

The Wesleys were ridiculed by the authorities in the church and by the sophisticated public. To add to the difficulties, John Wesley was a

18

man of frail health. But he kept at it, and the Methodist societies grew. Lay leadership in the church was fostered. Lives were turned around. The gospel became once again a powerful force in the land.

Now if you think I am about to conclude on a ringing note, praising John Wesley for guarding the house of faith, you are wrong. There is yet another twist to this story.

In a fairly short amount of time, Wesley's followers won admiration for their honesty, sobriety, trustworthiness, and their willingness to work. (Remember, this was a society wracked by the evils of drink.) The style of life of the Methodists led to considerable worldly success—so much so that old Wesley worried (he was ever the servant on the watch!) about a new problem: that success and riches might lead to the house of faith being unguarded again. As he reflected on what can only be called the irony of the situation of his Methodists, he had this to say:

> I fear, wherever riches have increased, the essence of religion has decreased in the same proportion. Therefore I do not see how it is possible, in the nature of things, for any revival of true religion to continue long. For religion must necessarily produce both industry and frugality, and these cannot but produce riches. But as riches increase, so will pride, anger, and love of the world in all its branches. How then is it possible that Methodism, that is, a religion of the heart, though it flourishes now as a green bay tree, should continue in this state?

And he concluded with a despairing question: "Is there no way to prevent this—this continual decay of pure religion?"

My purpose in relating to you this curious page from the annals of church history is not to offer you a proper blueprint for keeping watch and guarding the house of faith which is Jesus' command to us. On the contrary, what we have here are examples of temptations in both a failing church and a successful church! We are left with Wesley's question: "Is there no way to prevent this continual decay of pure religion?"

Guarding God's Church

It seems there is not. We always seem to fall short as God's church. But it is precisely in the realization that we fall short as witnesses to our Lord that his command to us be on the watch, to guard the house, is all the more a word for us as we enter this new church year. It is a word for us in two ways.

First, it can serve to remind us of the heart of the gospel. Remember Paul's words from our Second Lesson for today? God has promised us that we are his means, that we "are not lacking in any spiritual gift, as

19

[we] wait for the revealing of our Lord Jesus Christ; who will sustain [us] to the end, guiltless in the day of our Lord Jesus Christ" (1 Cor. 1:7-8). When Christ comes, when the Master returns, we will be ready, for he has made us ready. He has died for us that we might have life.

We do always fall short as God's church. We are ever in need of the mercy of God which he offers us in the depth of love which is his Son. Jesus' command to keep watch is made by a Lord who realizes full well who his servants are and yet does not turn away. He has saved us despite ourselves, and he uses us, weak as we are, as his instruments.

Second, knowing God's love and the freedom it brings, we can look at Jesus' command to us and how it applies in our church without flinching. The freedom Jesus gives us in his grace includes the freedom to be critical. Just like old Wesley who never put his guard down, even in the face of success, we can judge our actions as the church diligently, without having to hide anything and without discouragement.

"Watch therefore—for you do not know when the master of the house will come."

WALTER C. SUNDBERG JR.
Como Park Lutheran Church
St. Paul, Minnesota

SECOND SUNDAY IN ADVENT

A Revolution of Tears
Mark 1:1-8

Why did they go out to see him? John the Baptist was an unknown who came from the desolate areas of their country. He wasn't a president, coming with sounds of "Hail to the Chief" and bedecked with the aura of power and glory. He wasn't a star actor surrounded by adoring masses, glowing with popularity. He wasn't even rich, promising money to those who served him. Yet they went to him in droves. They piled out of Jerusalem, and they traveled from many miles away in the countryside, just because of rumors about him. Even today, hundreds of years later, we gather in churches all around the world to hear his words. What could be so important about him? Why would they—or we, for that matter—be interested in John?

But it's not the man; it's his message. That message runs gloriously counter to what the world has told us to believe. We have been taught in many ways that God either doesn't exist or doesn't care what happens to us. Even if God does care, it is only to preserve the status quo, to keep things the same, even if they are bad. God made the powerful, the smart, the privileged, the pious, and the irreligious. They are in charge; they are the elite; they are rightfully in control. And God is said to be a passive coparticipant in what the rulers of this world do. After all, God made the world, right?

And so we have religious art depicting the soft and gentle God who keeps the masses in line, peacefully calming them. God is seen as a soothing presence. Religious professionals speak for God in quieting words, counseling us to be good and to wait for eternal life. We have religious music, too, that helps us forget about the trouble in this world and leads us to the sweet by and by. And there are many who say they meet God in a quiet evening sunset on either the mountains or the plains. God is beautiful, kind, and harmless.

By this, our lives have been drained of hope. Isn't there anyone who can come and affect this world and its rulers? Isn't there anyone who has the authority and cares enough to change the world and put it on solid footing? Or are the confident rulers of our day, who control our thoughts and feelings, our only recourse, our only choice? Must we forever live under the bondage of evil in this world?

A Hopeful Message of Change

John's message—"God is coming"—is both hopeful and exciting, because it speaks of change. He quotes parts of Isaiah, phrases like "Every valley shall be lifted up, and every mountain and hill made low," and "The grass withers, the flower fades, when the breath of the Lord blows upon it." It is exciting to think of the spiritual hot breath of God laying waste the uncaring, evil, and destructive powers of this world. God does not then simply stamp "approved" on everything that is being done. God comes to make things right.

The air is electrified by John's message: "Get ready, God is coming to you!" The potential energy of the ages is breaking loose in those words. Massive doors are opening; time locks on great vaults are clicking. A spiritual windstorm approaches. And so the cry goes up out of our lips and hearts, out of our uplifted hands and through the still dead air of this world, "Justice, hope, and new life! Our God comes to us at last!" That is why they traveled by foot and oxcart so long ago, and that is why John's words are kept alive by reading them over and over again.

21

Such a hopeful message! There are so many ways that God could be helpful in our world. What if God came to you? What would you want? What would you do? What changes would you want to see happen?

Financial security would be first for many of us. This world is a jungle of people all trying to climb over each other. Oh, to have God come and give us a boost! And we could finally have the dreams we always wanted. We could quit work. No more struggles to buy that new car. No more worries about the energy bills. No more threat of creditors sending red-hot, blistering notices. We could take that dream vacation, finally resting in peace. This prospect makes John's message, "God is coming to you," very exciting.

Others of us would look for someone to come and give us power. We might like to control an enemy; it could be an unethical competitor, a relative, the bully down the street, or the Communist country across the sea. If God would come, we all might receive power to set right the wrongs of this world.

Or finally, out of a long list of possibilities, God could come and give you or me honor. We might introduce God as our personal friend. We could help people by saying "Would you like to be closer to God? Maybe I can help you make the connection, put you in touch through prayer." We could combat evil as God's honorable assistants, God's presence in the world.

And for those of us who would like to see the church grow, think of how we could pack the churches with these messages. It would be a Madison Avenue coup. We could proclaim on television, radio, and in the newspapers the message, "God is coming, and there are gifts for everyone. Be part of God's people and become prosperous. The more you give, the more you will receive back." Or, "Do you want more power in life to do the kinds of things that should be done? Do you want to set the world straight? Come and listen to God speak and become an assertive, powerful person." Or how about, "If you want to move to a higher position in life, a place of real meaning and responsibility, re-member, it's not what you know, but who you know"? God is coming.

God Demands Change from Us

But I must be honest with you today. All of these thoughts of pros-perity, power, and honor would be misplaced hope for our Advent season. It is unlikely that God wants to change everyone else and give you and me what we want. There is a small hitch in the Gospel text today, one little word, one little lingering doubt about our status. It is in the word *prepare.* That word has many implications. We often assume, just like

22

the world, that God is good, kind, and harmless. We have also assumed, just like the world, that God doesn't care what we do. God never comes, but even if God should come, there will not be any condemning or commanding directed toward us.

But the doubt about ourselves persists in that command, "Prepare." The potential reality may very well be that God doesn't like you or me. God could be coming once again to examine us like an IRS agent, going through our lives page by page. The time locks on the vault doors of heaven may be clicking, ready to open, but who or what lies on the other side? Are you sure God will give you what you hope for? Maybe God is looking for you and me with furrowed brow and fiery eyes.

And what would we say or do if God came to us? How could we prepare for the ominous royal guest? Would we say "Please have a seat," or "It's nice to see you," or "Could I get you something?" How about a quick smile, an endearing look, or even a respectful gaze? Maybe some quick promises would be in order. You or I could try that.

A poet wrote that God's personal presence among us, the Messiah, is "the still point in the turning world." Now it appears that this is all backward. It is not that "God is the still point in the turning world," but rather that God is the turning point in a still world. This is a world of stillness and death. A noisy still world that is really a despairing chaotic place, a world that only lives in God's shadow, a defensive creation looking in upon its helpless and hopeless self. God's messenger, John the Baptist, tells you and me that we must prepare; for the great Creator of all, the great spark of life and change in all the universe is coming to us.

Now you may say, "I've accomplished everything that should be done. I've gone to church, I've been reasonably good to my family and friends. I haven't done anything outlandishly bad. I'm preparing for a great Christmas." But that scary phrase keeps coming back: "You must prepare the way of the Lord" Who, me? Prepare God's way? One envisions a huge being with feet of steel who will come walking, and we are in the way. "Prepare the way, get God's path ready." And we think, "Run to the side, run to the side, somehow get out of the way of this fearsome being." Most of what we have done has been to prepare our own way, not God's way. And now God is coming.

How Repentance Works

The proclamation that "God is coming" first causes excitement over what God could do for us. It's much like being a child at Christmas time. Then we discover that we are to prepare for God's arrival. Finally, the worry sets in: What are you and I to do? How are we to prepare?

Our lives are driven by selfish desires, just like the world. We want God to serve us. We have been wanting our way all the time, while praising God and looking forward to the Lord's coming. The most noble words we have spoken are tainted by our own self-interests—interests in prosperity, power, and honor.

As we think about this text today, now is the time when something wonderful can happen in our lives. Right now, even as I have been speaking, you might find yourself tearful. I do most times when I think about John's words. No, the tears don't show on the outside; you and I are far too self-controlled to blubber like little children. But these tears are often present on the inside. It seems that there is a vast pool of tears inside all of us, waiting to be tapped by our Maker's words. And it is good that God comes to do this. There are tears of regret for all the wrong words we have said to those we love most. There are tears of bitterness for our persistent failures in some crucial aspects of our lives. There are tears of anger at how our lives are often out of control. And we wonder how we could be so careless with our lives and the lives of others. God addresses these issues with that word *prepare*.

God works in such wonderful and mysterious ways in your life and mine. For God really does want to change the world, starting with you and me. God wants to touch us where we most hurt. God is sending you this day a revolution for your life, a revolution wrapped in John's words. Not a revolution based on power, status, money, or honor, but a revolution based on your tears. This pool of repentance, this shedding of tears, is God's gift. We are opened up to life once again through a radical encounter with our need for God. Our defenses are softened, and God comes into us. Out of the deepest, darkest moments of your life and mine, when our souls are wrapped in despair, when we can no longer fool ourselves into believing everything is all right and we don't need God, when the word *prepare* has pinned us down, then, in fact, we are prepared for God's coming. And how we need God to come!

Surprise! God Is Coming to Comfort

Then comes the surprise. God is coming to us also with these words from our texts for today: "Comfort, comfort my people, says your God. Speak tenderly to Jerusalem, and cry to her that her warfare is ended, that her iniquity is pardoned, that she has received from the Lord's hand double for all her sins" (Isa. 40:1-2).

We are led once again to our God who really cares. God wants our world to be a good place for everyone, including you and me. God wants us to be together both on the outside and on the inside, and the only way that can happen is through tears. Today we are brought face to face with our own sin and with God who condemns and comforts. Exciting? Yes, with tears of happiness. Hopeful? Yes. God is willing to come for us. God is not passive after all. God's judgment comes in tears, but God's presence results in comforting hope. Have a good Advent, and let the tears flow. Now is the time, for comfort will soon follow.

R. Peder Kittelson
St. Andrew's Lutheran Church
Glenwood, Illinois

The Cost of Greatness
John 1:6-8, 19-28

You know what the Lord Jesus once said about John the Baptist? "He was the greatest." Quite a compliment! Now why would he say that?

What Made John Great?

Was John great quite simply because he didn't know he was? Would you have shocked and surprised John if you had said to him: "John, you are without a doubt the world's greatest person"?

So it would seem. Pointing to Jesus, John said: "That is the Great One over there. He is the Lamb of God who takes away the sin of the world. And you can't hardly get any greater than that."

Pointing to himself, John said: "I am not worthy even to untie the Messiah's shoes."

How beautifully, blessedly, and blissfully ignorant and unaware of his greatness John was. Is that what made him great—that he didn't know that he was?

Or was John great because the Lord Jesus said he was? Is greatness a gift that only Christ can offer and bestow? Some people strive, sweat, and labor all life long, courting and seeking the praise and applause of people, not realizing that there is only one whose verdict on our lives stands final and forever. And that is the one who pronounced John the greatest of all. If Christ says you are great, you are, even if no one else thinks so.

25

And so return to your Baptism and once again hear and treasure that affirming, approving word spoken over you by Father, Son, and Holy Spirit: "This is my beloved child in whom I am well pleased. He or she couldn't be better or more beautiful." That is the baptismal Word—the baptismal praise and applause, if you please—which sustains us when everybody tells us with justification how full of faults and failures we are.

Or was John great because his greatest concern was about the coming Christ? He did not continually ask, "What is coming? What will happen to me?" Not *what* is coming, but *who* is coming?—that was the crucial question of John's life. In other words, his was an Advent greatness because all he had on his mind was his coming Lord.

And what is on your mind this morning—everything under the sun but Christ the Coming One? Recall the words of Paul the apostle to the Philippian saints: "The Lord is at hand. Don't worry about anything." And so with John we make this the burning, crucial question of our lives. Not, "Dear me, what is coming? What tragedy, horror, or disaster?" That's not the question. *This* is the question: "*Who* is coming, coming constantly in Word, water, wafer, wine, and all those lovable and un-lovable people at my side, coming to challenge me, love me, comfort me, empower me, strengthen me, save and redeem me? Who is coming finally to free and liberate me from every jail and prison, even the one called casket and grave? And the answer is: "Jesus Christ."

Was John great because he knew how to live in the desert? That is the place where people learn two lessons. First, in the wilderness they learn how to deny themselves. You can't very well live the soft and self-indulgent life out there in the cruel, savage, bitter, and beastly hot desert. The desert disciplines you, makes you tough and hard and strong—the desert of trial, trouble, and temptation.

Second, the desert teaches us that we do not live by bread alone. Oh, we think that we do, that bread alone can fill and satisfy us. As long as the bread is there, plentiful and abundant—the bread of everything and everybody that is so precious, loved, and treasured—then we will be happy and content. Nothing else matters, nothing else is needed. But then it happens. The bread begins to go, devoured and consumed by some unexpected tragedy, accident, disease, or death. How shall we live, survive, and prosper without our precious bread? By the Bread of Life— that's how. By the Lord Jesus Christ whom death and hell greedily devoured on that first Good Friday but who then turned the tables and swallowed up death, hell, and the grave when he rose glorious and victorious at the crack of that first Easter dawn.

26

And so into the desert we go where God takes some or most of the bread away from us. And once again in the desert of some great sorrow, loss, or grief we relearn that we do not live and surely dare not die by bread alone. Rather we live and die by the Bread of Life, who, unlike all the other bread we love and cherish, never departs or disappears.

Or was John great because of his courage? What a rock he was! Why he literally lost his head rather than betray himself or be unfaithful to his divinely imposed mission. Nothing meant more to him—not even life itself—than his loyalty and devotion to his Lord.

Can that be said of us? Nothing means more to us—no money or pleasure or job or possession or person—than our commitment to the Christ of the cross and the conquered tomb? When that kind of unwavering loyalty begins to be our life-style, then we also begin to match and mirror the courage of great John.

Or was John great because he knew how to concentrate? He was indeed a single-minded man, devoted to only one task in life—getting God's people ready for their coming Messiah. He allowed nothing or no one to distract him from that goal.

We most certainly could use some of that single-mindedness, you and I who so often concentrate on many things and hence really concentrate on nothing. The fire, the fervor, the passion, the intensity just aren't there. Only the eternal apathy, indifference, lukewarmness, the pale neutrality, the middle-of-the-road mentality exists. Brill Cream Christians— that's what we are. A little dab will always do us. Vaccinated saints, injected with just enough of the serum of discipleship to give us that sick feeling of partial commitment, but not really consumed by the "disease" to the point where at last we begin to experience the joy and thrill of unbridled commitment.

Or was John great because he pointed people to Christ? By him, through him, in him the people saw their Savior.

Now that wouldn't be a bad epitaph: "By him, through him, in him people saw their Savior." It is not too late to make that epitaph a blessed reality for you. Your life still stretches before you with unlimited possibilities for you to point people to your Savior, both with your lips and with your life. What are folks reading these days in the "Gospel According to You"?

The Cost of Greatness

And so John was great. And it cost him to be so. His head was presented on a plate to wicked King Herod.

27

So it usually is for great people. They pay dearly for their greatness. Ask John. Ask the Lord Jesus, agonizing there in the Gethsemane garden, dying on the Calvary cross. Ask Albert Schweitzer, doing his doctor-healing thing in the steamy jungles of Africa. Ask Mother Teresa, giving her life away in the rat-infested, disease-filled slums of Calcutta. It is very costly to be a self-denying, cheek-turning, life-losing, cross-bearing disciple of Jesus Christ. And so, as the Master himself once warned: "Don't begin building the tower of discipleship unless you're sure you've got the resources for finishing it. Don't start a war with the powers of Satan, the demons of darkness, the hordes of hell, unless you're sure you have armies, resources, and weapons to finish it."

And you do, of course, have the resources in that crucified and risen One, that Savior Jesus Christ, who has already won the war for you by his death on the tree and rising from the tomb. His victory is yours in the gift of your Baptism. And now, as he supplies the strength and the power in gospel Word, in Communion bread and wine, in the love, support, encouragement, comfort, understanding, and forgiveness of all those loving people at your side, you battle all life long to win the war and build the tower of committed discipleship.

No doubt about the greatness of John! But he had an even greater cousin—Jesus Christ. And one day, after John's death, cousin Jesus said, "There is somebody even greater than the greatest, somebody even greater than cousin John, the greatest born of women. And that somebody is the most insignificant person in the kingdom of heaven. That somebody is you." Why? Because you have seen and beheld something that great John never did—Cousin Jesus dead on the tree and raised from the tomb to make us more than conquerors over Satan, hell, death, and the grave. Eyes on that slain and risen Savior, lips open to receive him in the Eucharistic meal, and God's power will be upon you, giving you the greatness of John—and then some.

HERBERT E. HOHENSTEIN
Unity Evangelical Lutheran Church
St. Louis, Missouri

A Song of Faith
Luke 1:26-38

There is a rhythmical pace to the Advent pilgrimage that includes a steady crescendo finding its ultimate expression in the celebration of Christmas. Each Sunday of Advent, Christians all over the world light a special candle, and with the passing of each week the light of the traditional Advent wreath becomes brighter.

The same rhythm is reflected in the Scripture readings of the season, beginning with the prophecies of Isaiah, then moving on to the work of John the Baptist, and finally focusing in on Joseph and Mary, who are the center of this Gospel text.

The story describes that moment when the angel Gabriel was sent from heaven to tell the Virgin Mary that she had found favor with God and that she would give birth to his Son, who would be named Jesus. And in response to that information, Mary made a statement that is nothing less than a song of faith: "Behold, I am the handmaid of the Lord; let it be to me according to your word" (Luke 1:38).

One might well wonder why the emphasis is on the Virgin Mary on this Fourth Sunday in Advent. Very little is said about her in the whole of Scripture. The Lutheran church is certainly not famous for exalting her position in the mind of the believer. We offer no prayers to her. We seldom even speak of her.

Perhaps it would be more appropriate to wonder why there isn't more emphasis on this significant lady. After all, she was the mother of the Christ child, and that is a fact we simply cannot ignore. And her words, recorded in the gospel of Luke, are a most beautiful expression of faith, a faith that is sincere and strong, a faith that validates Jesus' statement: "Blessed . . . are those who hear the word of God and keep it!" (Luke 11:28).

The motivation for such a song of faith has to be related to a particular understanding regarding the meaning of God and one's relationship to God. As the late Pope Paul once said, "Your song is your gift to God." And so it should be for the likes of you and me.

God Is Our Maker

At the outset, the possessor of such a song of faith must understand that God is our Maker. And that is to admit that you and I are dependent on him, that we can never ever be completely self-sufficient, that the creative power of God is at work in the midst of the reality of our daily existence, that he sustains the universe, and that the meaning of our daily living depends on his powerful presence.

For many people, this kind of dependence runs contrary to some of our deepest feelings. The word is out and around that the contemporary human being has a strong drive to be autonomous and self-sufficient. Of course, this is nothing new to history. But it is especially familiar to those of us who are a part of the current scientific age.

One of my friends describes it well when he says that "the simple fact of life is that we all want to be the boss, and to enter into any other kind of relationship with anybody or anything is done only with the greatest of difficulty."

However, if God is what the Scriptures tell us he is, then we cannot boss him. By definition he is supreme, all-knowing, all-powerful, everywhere present. The initiative is always from him toward us. And so when we think about our relationship with him, we have no right to try to be the boss.

You and I need to admit that God is God, and then we must let him be God. Along with that, we cannot expect to do just as we please or run our lives in any old way, and still expect God's help in becoming a more complete person. First and foremost we must accept the priority of God's will and purpose in our lives. And that includes the will to set aside false pride and self-centeredness, as well as the willingness to allow God to be at the center of our existence.

The Kinship Involved

We also need to understand that there is a friendship or kinship between us and the One who made us. You and I are made in God's image. That is to say, the deepest part of us, the most human part of us—in spite of all the dirt and grime—is our resemblance to God. We are made in such a way that the meaningful life for us is to subject ourselves to God's will for us. In fact, we will never be complete or satisfied or fulfilled as long as we insist on having our own way. To live a meaningful life means that we accept God's ways.

The Character of God's Will

Furthermore, we must understand that God's will is neither arbitrary nor spiteful. It is not against us. On the contrary, God wills only our good. In fact, the will of God is comparable to the rules of health. Such

30

rules are not intended to spoil our fun, but rather to help us maintain our well-being in such a way that we can enjoy life to the fullest.

In some ways, the will of God is much like the rules of the freeway. They are designed to increase the fun of driving, to make the use of the automobile and the road much safer for everyone concerned. The yellow line down the middle of the curve is not put there to inhibit the driver, but rather to enable the driver to safely round the curve and live to drive into the future.

When you and I discern what the will of God actually is, then our commitment to that will provides us with a significant pathway to a meaningful and complete life. To acknowledge the reality of God as our Creator and to recognize our dependence on God as well as our kinship with God constitute the motivation necessary for a song of faith like Mary's.

The Injury

Somehow we have managed to injure what was originally intended to be a good relationship with the one who made us. We are frequently arrogant, self-centered, independent, and even reluctant to acknowledge our kinship with God. And these characteristics easily spoil the good that God has always had in mind for us. Consequently, you and I have to learn to know God as our Redeemer—the one who restores and remakes us, repairs the damage that we have done to ourselves, and restores us to an effective and healthy style of living.

The Claim and Our Response

One of the great claims of the Christian faith is that God never changes in his attitude toward any one of us, no matter what we do to offend him. The Bible tells us that God consistently wills our good and that he patiently tries to win us back to the relationship with him that he had in mind from the very beginning.

Most of us find it very difficult to believe such a claim—and understandably so. We reason things out on the basis of our own experience in life. For example, if anybody treated us the way we are inclined to treat God, we would make life difficult for that person. In fact, most likely we would insist that the offender come crawling to us on hands and knees.

We project these same feelings on God. As a result, we are uneasy in the presence of the seemingly strange relationship that exists between us. Yet the Christian faith makes the startling claim that God never

31

changes in his desire for us to live a meaningful life. God never quits in his efforts to win us to that kind of life. He constantly holds out to the people of his creation the opportunity to establish a relationship of trust and obedience and love. And he does this by way of the gift of his Son, Jesus Christ, who lived and died and came to life again—all on your behalf, as well as mine.

When you and I accept God's offer of friendship, we begin to follow a new set of blueprints. There may not be a whole lot of dramatic, striking evidence to show for it, but so what? This whole picture involves a decision of faith. It's what the New Testament calls the "new birth" or a "new creation." At the very core of our being an adjustment has been made. No longer do we live for ourselves. Instead, we live as God's children. And God becomes our enabler, the one who helps us to become the kind of person we know we are intended to be, the one who makes it possible to live with some sense of fulfillment, satisfaction, purpose, and happiness.

Christianity claims that if you and I really want God's presence in our life, if we want God to be God—then we already *have* God's presence. We don't have to *argue* about it. We don't have to *feel* it. We don't have to *prove* it. We're just supposed to *live* it. None of us ever has to feel our pulse every minute of the day to be sure that we're still alive and kicking. If we're still up and around, we assume that the power of life is at work within us, and we enjoy it. In like manner there is no need to keep asking for evidence that God is present within you or me. God became a part of each one of us at the start of life and on the day that we were baptized into God's family. And when we honestly accept God and all God's promises, God is present within us.

The Implications of God's Presence

God's presence always supplies power, power that enables us to grow, the power that gives us the ability to understand ourselves more completely, the power that makes it possible for us to forgive, to care, and to hope. No one of us ever has to argue our body into growing. All we need to do is feed it the proper kind of food, and it will grow. Teenagers in a household never argue about growing. They simply feed themselves enormous quantities of food, and they grow.

And that's what the powerful presence of God will do for you and me—as long as we feed ourselves the proper diet of spiritual food. What might that be? Such things as disciplined thought, the reading of Scripture, kind and thoughtful deeds of love, time on our knees in conversation with our loving heavenly Father, and enjoying the blessing of Christ's body and blood—disciplines and practices that will nourish the power of God within us as God tries to lead us to that life of faith, a life such as Mary's, whose heart and mind contained a beautiful song of faith.

As we approach the celebration of Christmas, and the air is filled with beautiful music, perhaps we ought to ask ourselves the question: Is there a song of faith in me?

God is extending a hand to you at the manger in Bethlehem. God would like to help you to become what you have been created to be. You and I can join Mary in her song of faith: "Behold, I am the handmaid of the Lord; let it be to me according to your word."

DAVID L. ANDERSON
Trinity Lutheran Church
Moorhead, Minnesota

THE NATIVITY OF OUR LORD—CHRISTMAS DAY

God's Touchdown
John 1:1-14

For those who joined us or other Christian communities last night to herald the arrival of the Prince of Peace, who came as child of the manger, it was a time to sing and speak about shepherds and angels and that humble stable that became a maternity ward. But this morning, with last night's stardust mingled with the sandman's grains lingering in sleepy eyes, we are challenged by this text from the pen of the evangelist St. John. It may be presumptuous to tackle the rich diet of theological depth that is here while the visions of sugar plums still dance in our heads, but the effort promises to be rewarding. It is also necessary, I believe, if we are going to dispel the rich doses of sentimentality that we spread over the season and if we are going to come to grips with a proper perspective of the incarnation and its significance for you and me.

This is one of the great Christmas texts, but John doesn't deal with the historical facts of the familiar Christmas story. He doesn't write about Mary and Joseph and the baby Jesus, about shepherds and angels and mangers and smelly stables or swaddling clothes. Instead, John deals with the theological reality that lies behind the historical events, and sets them before us in such a way that we cannot miss what is happening in the God/human relationship, the Creator/creature relationship.

33

In the Beginning . . .

Two books of the Bible open with the words, "In the beginning . . ."—the book of Genesis and this gospel of John. And by using those words both writers seek to press back the curtain of time and speak of the time before the beginning. That's hard for us to understand, for you and I are locked in by the human limitations of time. It is hardly possible for us to think about a time when time was not. In the same way we cannot comprehend a future when there will be no time—when clocks and calendars are obsolete, mere relics of the time-life of our humanity. But before time was, there was God, and it is God who gave us the gift of time way back there when he said, "Let there be . . . ." It was at that moment of creation that time began. And John tells us that back there, before the beginning, was the Word.

And what does John mean when he says, "In the beginning was the Word"? In our print-oriented culture, it would be easy to assume that when the word *Word* is used, it means something written or printed. We place great value on the writing or printing of words. When something is written down, it takes on authority and power. But since we are dealing here before the time frame in which we are imprisoned by our humanity, the reference is not to writing or printing. Before a word is written, there is speech, and before speech there is thought.

So when John says, "In the beginning was the Word, and the Word was with God, and the Word was God," he is speaking of the mind and power of God—the strong, creative impulse of the Creator who speaks *things* into existence. It is this mind-power-speech-intention of God that John identifies as the *Logos*—the Word of God that formed and carried out the creative impulse of God. John goes on, "He [this Word] was in the beginning with God; all things were made through him, and without him was not anything made that was made" (vv. 2-3). This creative power, unleashed in the spacelessness and timelessness of eternity—the power that set the stars in their orbits and formed and filled the earth—is far beyond our power to comprehend. To try to wrap these events within the limits of human thought is so futile that we can only *suggest* in our language the mystery and transcendence of God. Our human consideration of this thought-mind-intention of God makes us feel so puny and insignificant in the plan of God that we are inclined to despair. And, if that's all there was—if God was only to be thought of as a master watchmaker who created the universe like a finely tooled timepiece and then set it on a shelf to admire from a distance—then we would be without hope, and God would be without grace.

The Word Became Flesh

And that's why the key verse for us in the Christmas season is this: "And the Word became flesh and dwelt among us, full of grace and truth" (v. 14). In this verse is the miracle of grace that Christmas is all about. This verse is the reason John wrote his gospel. This is the touchstone of all Christian theology: this Word of God whose hands spread out the heavens, whose mind ordered the universe, whose creative power established order out of chaos, this Word whom God chose to plunge into the arena of human life as you and I live it and take on himself the flesh and bones and blood of our humanity.

You and I know what that means, for you and I have lived with the limits of our humanity, and those grim limits of time and space continually remind us of the frailty of being human. We have known the exhaustion of trying to stretch the physical limits of our human flesh. We have known the heartbreak of being unable to overcome our frustrations. We have seen the limits of human flesh as every good resolve is tested time and again, and the spirit of our resolve so often loses the battle to the drag of sin. We know what it means to be weak, too weak to fight anymore. We know what it means to lose—to fail, to stumble, to blow it—and we know the hurt that loss costs us. We know what it is to lose someone dear to us, what it means to mourn and to echo the words, "My God, my God, why? Why have you forsaken me?" We know what it means to be hurt and stung by heartless critics who stand apart from us in our need, who shame us for our failures, and who cast suspicion on our motives and intentions.

The point of this verse, "The word became flesh," is that in the midst of our agonies in this life, we are not alone. For God chose in infinite grace to enter our flesh and share the reality of being human in our world that too often can be described only as inhuman. Into our world of tragedies, of broken dreams, of crushed hopes, and of merciless demands God came to tie our broken pieces of time back into eternity.

Deserve Has Nothing to Do with It

This event, the incarnation, is "God's touchdown." God was under no compulsion to touch down and live in the midst of the chaos we have made of his creation. God was not loved by some inner compulsion because you and I deserve better at his hand than the death our sins have earned. Deserving has nothing to do with it at all. God's touchdown into the affairs of his creation, his decision to live among the disorder created by his creature's sin, was prompted solely by his *grace*—not because we deserve or merit, but because his nature is grace, and his move to come among us stems from his mercy. He entered the end zone of our misery in the flesh as the child of the manger.

He came not merely to sample human life, to try to figure out what makes us tick and then retreat to heaven to file a report in triplicate about life among the sinners. God moved into the mess. He came to shoulder the burdens and bear the griefs, to carry in his own arms his exhausted children who had tasted and been infected with the bitter fruit of sin and death and destruction. He came not as an observer of the human scene but to give us power to become the children of God. He was born in that drafty stable in order that he might give us a second birth by faith. He was born in our humanity so that you and I who receive him will never die. He was born to give us a picture of the interior of the heart of God, a heart that throbs with a love only he can make known to us. And wonder of wonders, grace on grace, God shows us his love in the person of Jesus Christ. He doesn't come to offer an abstract description of love, to sit down and lecture us *about* love. In Jesus Christ, God touches down in our world to *be* love—alive and at work in our world. He puts himself within range of our senses.

In the beginning of his first letter, John tries in a rush of words that tumble from his pen to communicate just what that means:

> We are writing to you about something which has always existed, yet which we ourselves actually saw and heard; something which we had opportunity to observe closely and even to hold in our hands, and yet, as we know now, was something of the very Word of Life himself! For it was *life* which appeared before us; we saw it, are eyewitnesses of it, and are now writing to you about it. It was the very life of all ages, the life that has always existed with the Father, which actually became visible in person to us mortal men. We repeat, we really saw and heard what we are now writing to you about. We want you to be with us in this—in this fellowship with the Father, and Jesus Christ his Son. We must write and tell you about it because the more the fellowship extends, the greater the joy it brings to us who are already in it" (1 John 1:1-4 paraphrased).

It Was for You

Do you catch the wonder and the excitement of John as he describes his experience of being able to see and hear and touch the love of God in the person of Jesus Christ? He's saying this Jesus was the fullness of the love of God alive in this world. He came to wear the same kind of flesh and humanness that we wear. He was the victim of the world, vulnerable to the world. And we know the end of the story, the tragedy of what human sinfulness and pride did to that love. The shadow of the cross falls across the manger—not to dim our joy at Christmas time, but to make that joy complete. For Jesus chose to set aside the divine prerogatives that were his and submitted even to the death to show us to what lengths the love of God would go. This is grace: that God was not above the disgrace of the cross, not above the disgrace of being confined within the limits of human flesh. From the fullness of God's grace, John says, we have received grace upon grace.

The real miracle is that it was for you that he came—that he came to stay. It is a miracle of grace that in the midst of the worlds that you and I make for ourselves—worlds of confused and exhausting priorities, of aching bodies and torn and bleeding spirits, of heartbreak and loneliness—God still touches down with the assurance that Christ is not above your world. He is in it with you. He is there to be your support and stay, your shield and defense, your friend and brother, your Savior and Lord.

We have the assurance of his presence especially with us today, for he comes to us as the Word of God that says, "This is my body, given for you; this is my blood, shed for you." Actually, we can get no closer this side of heaven to the presence of Christ, to the wonder of the child of the manger, to the heartbreak of Calvary and the hope of Joseph's garden than we can as we share this blessed sacrament. For this presence of Christ with us in the anguish we make of our world is what we remember and proclaim and celebrate as we share this bread and cup.

Whether this Christmas is a good Christmas that brings you joy and fills your life with delight, or if this Christmas is edged with sadness and sorrow as you mourn the loss of those who have shared other Christmases with you, there is no better place to be this morning. For you are here to receive him who came to stay, to be with us in this special participation in his promised presence. The Word became flesh. He dwells among us. He offers himself to us once again today, and in that offering of himself he shares with us the holy meal of his presence right here, right now. This today is God's touchdown in the end zone of our despairing that wins the victory of faith for you and for me. Come to meet him. Come to taste the fruits of victory that began in a cattle shed in our world, but before that dwelt in the eternal heart of the Father's love for you.

PAUL K. PETERSON
Gloria Dei Lutheran Church
St. Paul, Minnesota

Behold, Your Salvation!
Luke 2:25-40

There are many moods and themes that we think about at this time of the year. By the calendar this weekend marks the ending of one year and the beginning of another. It is inevitable that we remember much of what has happened this past year and how it has affected us, and anticipate the beginning of a new segment of time. It is also true that only within the church does the full celebration of Christmas continue. For so many the festivity of the season has ended, and it is "business as usual." Yet for us within the church the celebration continues. Just as we heard the joyous good news that "to you is born this day in the city of David a Savior, who is Christ the Lord," so now we witness the moving testimony of two aged persons to God's promised gift of salvation. "Behold, your salvation!" becomes the theme not only of today's worship, but of our continued response to the gift of the child of Bethlehem.

In today's Gospel Luke continues with his story about the birth of Jesus and its immediate aftermath. The setting moves from Bethlehem to Jerusalem, as Mary and Joseph determine to fulfill their obligation to the Mosaic Law. They bring Jesus to the temple in Jerusalem to present him to the Lord and to offer a sacrifice to God. It is in this setting that Luke describes the wonderful vision of the two aged persons, Simeon and Anna. It is here that Luke proclaims Jesus to be the fulfillment of the Old Testament expectation; he is the one who is to fulfill both the law and the prophets.

Righteous Simeon

There is no attempt to identify Simeon fully; we have only Luke's statement that he was a "righteous and devout" man who had been waiting for the promised salvation of Israel. What is very significant is the importance of the Holy Spirit in bringing about this encounter. Three times Luke mentions the Spirit, the final reference being that Simeon was "led by the Spirit" to the temple. His encounter was not accidental; it was one prepared for by God. Simeon embraced the child Jesus, "taking him up in his arms" and speaking the words of blessing so beloved by the church, the *Nunc Dimittis*. In this well-known canticle, Simeon proclaimed that he now saw God's salvation, that this salvation was to be seen by all people, that this salvation was a light to the Gentiles and for the glory of Israel.

38

Salvation visible. Simeon saw with the eyes of faith God's promised salvation in the face of the child Jesus. Like Anna, Simeon had been waiting for this promised salvation. Now he realized that it had been fulfilled. "In the fulness of time" God had acted; salvation had come. Is there any news that is better than this? God has not left us alone but has chosen to enter our world, to share our humanity, and to reveal our destiny. Here it is to be seen in the face of the child: "Behold, your salvation!"

In the sight of all peoples. Most wonderful of all, this salvation is not to be limited to a particular people but is being revealed to all the world. The vision expressed by Isaiah in today's First Lesson is now fulfilled: God's saving act will not be limited but will be universal in its scope. Here is the news that God's salvation is intended for the whole creation, for all of humanity: "Behold, your salvation!"

A light to the Gentiles and the glory of Israel. The light which is the Christ will be a light both for revelation and for glory. In revealing salvation to the Gentiles and glory for Israel, the fulness of God's salvation is being seen clearly. It is a salvation that encompasses the whole of creation and reunites a broken and divided humanity into one new human community: "Behold, your salvation!"

With these moving and poetic words, the aged Simeon declared that with his "own eyes" he had seen God's salvation. What a wonderful gift God gave to Simeon! The waiting had not been in vain; Simeon's trust in the promises of God had been rewarded with this personal encounter with the Promised One. We can only imagine that there must have been tears of joy in his eyes as Simeon held the child Jesus in his arms.

Luke tells us that Mary and Joseph "marveled" at the words Simeon spoke. It seems strange, at first thought, that there would be any surprise at all. After the angel's visit before Jesus' birth and the visit of the shepherds following, we might imagine that nothing would have surprised Jesus' parents. Yet this meeting with Simeon in the temple startled them and caused them to wonder about another marvelous aspect of Jesus' birth.

Yet there was to be more. After Simeon blessed Mary and Joseph he spoke strange and disturbing words to Mary:

> "Behold, this child is set for the fall and rising of many in Israel, and for a sign that is spoken against (and a sword will pierce through your own soul also), that thoughts out of many hearts may be revealed" (vv. 34-35).

Simeon saw the opposition and rejection that Jesus would experience, and in this tragic vision warned Mary that there would be division because of her son. There have been many interpretations of this oracle, yet the one that seems most likely is that Simeon (and Luke) are referring to the division of Israel and of human families over the identity and ministry of Jesus. This theme is expressed later in Luke's gospel by Jesus himself:

"Do you think I have come to bring peace on earth? No, I tell you, but rather division; for henceforth in one house there will be five divided ... father against son and son against father, mother against daughter and daughter against mother" (12:51-53).

Simeon looked into the future and saw not only that Jesus would be a blessing to both Gentiles and Jews, but also the tragedy of so many rejecting Jesus—even within his own family. It is this reality that would pierce Mary's heart.

Waiting Anna

However, the presentation scene ends not with these words of tragedy but with the figure of Anna. Like Simeon, she was an aged person of great faith, whose worship, fasting, and prayer are wonderful examples of faith. Her words are not recorded, yet we are told that after seeing the child Jesus she "spoke of him to all who were waiting for the redemption of Jerusalem."

Luke thus ends the infancy story of Jesus as he began it: with two aged persons whose wait for the fulfillment of God's promises is rewarded. Simeon and Anna, like Zechariah and Elizabeth, knew the great joy of those who have experienced God's gracious presence.

Having finished their duties according to the law of the Lord, Joseph and Mary, together with the child Jesus, returned to their hometown of Nazareth. "And the child grew and became strong, filled with wisdom; and the favor of God was upon him" (v. 40).

What a marvelous scene is presented to us this day! The salvation of God has been revealed in the face of the child Jesus—and those who in faith waited for the Promised One declared him to be the one for whom Israel has waited. The vision of Isaiah has been fulfilled: "In the Lord all the offspring of Israel shall triumph and glory." With the eyes of faith Simeon and Anna saw in the ordinary event of a young family presenting their firstborn child in the temple the very salvation of God. While others saw only an infant and his parents, Simeon and Anna saw God's gracious presence in their midst. It was "in faith" and "led by the Spirit" that they were able to see the extraordinary meaning of such ordinary events. Here were two aged persons, whose eyes were no doubt dimmed by time, who nevertheless were able to "see" with a clarity unmatched by others the true meaning of what was before them. "Behold, your salvation!"

Our Salvation, Too

And what of us? We who this day continue our celebration of Christmas, do we have the same clarity of vision? Do we see God's salvation taking place in our midst? In the Word proclaimed and believed, in the meal of Christ's body and blood, the salvation of God is also taking place. Do we have the eyes of faith to see the "new thing" that God is doing in our world and in our lives?

In the apostle Paul's letter to the Colossians, we can discover our proper response to the event that we celebrate today. In that letter Paul reminded his hearers that God "has delivered us from the dominion of darkness and transferred us to the kingdom of his beloved Son, in whom we have redemption, the forgiveness of sins" (Col. 1:13-14). It is not simply a past event that we celebrate at Christmas but God's gracious sharing of our humanity and Christ's life, death, and resurrection that gives us the freedom and forgiveness of God's own children. It is not only that God is with us in our human world, but that we are now redeemed and are a part of "the kingdom of his beloved Son."

In today's Second Lesson, Paul tells us the consequences of that new relationship to God. He uses what is clearly baptismal imagery in saying that Christians, as God's people, are to "put on" (much as the newly baptized were robed in a new garment) the new Christ-like life and its qualities of compassion, kindness, lowliness, meekness, patience, forgiveness and, above all else, love. Having seen with Simeon and Anna the gift of God's salvation in the face of the Christ child, we are inspired and enabled by God's Spirit to "let the peace of Christ rule in [our] hearts," the peace of Christ that is beyond all human comprehension. The gift of God's salvation, seen and celebrated this day, leads us to lives of gratitude and thanksgiving. Our whole lives have been transformed. We are the baptized, forgiven, restored, spirit-led people of God who have been brought into the new creation that is the church to live out lives that witness to God's saving presence in our world. It is this new reality that leads Paul to the sweeping statement, "Whatever you do, in word or deed, do everything in the name of the Lord Jesus, giving thanks to God the Father through him" (Col. 3:17).

Is it possible for us to carry that sense of God's gracious presence with us as we return to a "post-Christmas" world? We have come together today to continue our celebration of God-with-us. With Simeon and Anna we have seen, in the face of the child Jesus, God's long-awaited

41

salvation. Having seen and believed, we are now empowered to go into the world with the good news of God's salvation come among us. We are "dismissed" as we leave this place and enter a world that does not yet believe. Yet we go knowing that God *has* acted graciously in the person of Jesus. We have seen our salvation and rejoice in it.

> Lord, now you let your servant go in peace; your word has been fulfilled. My own eyes have seen the salvation which you have prepared in the sight of every people: A light to reveal you to the nations and the glory of your people Israel. Glory to the Father, and to the Son, and to the Holy Spirit, as it was in the beginning, is now, and will be forever. Amen (*Lutheran Book of Worship*, pp. 93-94).

A. CRAIG SETTLAGE
Savior Divine Lutheran Church
Palos Hills, Illinois

The Birth of a New Family
John 1:1-18

Each year the week after Christmas seemed harder and harder for him. Before it had always been just a sense of disappointment, but this year he felt a bitter, biting depression much like the weather, chilling to the bone and numbing all of his senses. In his gloom he sat before the fireplace, watching the remnants of the small logs glowing in the darkness. The remains of Christmas morning were still scattered throughout the room: wrapping paper carefully folded, a small ribbon, the keycase he had received from one of the children, an unwanted scarf abandoned beside the tree. The tree itself looked grotesquely out of place now. The ornaments still sparkled as best they could to give off their artificial joy. The lights burned vainly to overcome the darkness of the room.

Each Christmas seemed more and more empty. It wasn't the same now that the kids were older. They wanted to open their gifts, and then they were off to see their friends. The best efforts to please them with some unexpected gift never quite worked. Gone were the bright eyes of anticipation on Christmas morning, the delighted squeals of excitement, and the warm embraces of gratitude. As the kids had outgrown that childhood thrill of Christmas, so the yearly routine had become less and less meaningful for him. *Maybe it's just because they're teenagers*, he thought hopefully to himself.

But it wasn't the same with the rest of the family either. Since their mother's death, he and his brother and sister had drifted apart. What fun it used to be on Christmas Eve to burst into his parents' home with his wife and children each bearing several gifts and joyful greetings. But the magnet that had drawn them each year to that same house was gone with the death of his parents. Sally's family was no better. Her sisters were each scattered thousands of miles away, and her mother was bedridden in a nursing home. *The family is gone*, he thought.

Christmas is supposed to be for the family! But what happens when your family is torn apart and fragmented? What kind of Christmas is there without family? His eyes searched the darkness above the mantel until finally he could make out the dim dimensions of the family portrait—Sally, the kids, mom and dad, and himself. *Those were better times*, he thought, *happy times, times of wholeness*.

The glow of the fire was nearly gone now and nothing lighted the room except for the Christmas tree bulbs, and somehow they seemed even dimmer than before. He reached down to where his coffee cup rested on the end table and lifted it to his lips—but nothing. It too was empty, even as he felt emptied. What good is a Christmas if there is no family?

The Failure of the Family

Perhaps some of you can identify with the feelings expressed in this short scene. Christmas is traditionally a family celebration—a joyous tradition rooted in the family, or so we have been told from our earliest years. And we try with all our might to make our Christmas celebrations warm and affectionate family experiences. The children come home; we visit in the homes of our relatives; we exchange gifts so that everyone in the family receives something. In short, our image of a successful Christmas is the happy family gathered together in one place.

The trouble is that it often doesn't work that way, in spite of our best efforts. The extended family is less and less a reality in our society, and the central hub of the family just does not hold us together as it once did. Moreover, there are the family alienations, the unsettled disputes, the hurt feelings, the old grudges, the broken promises. We live with them all year, but they are invariably more painful at the holiday season. So we find ourselves desperately trying by pretense to relive the Christmas experiences of our childhood.

43

Consequently there comes the depression and disappointment. Our best efforts at "being happy" too often end on the day after Christmas at the latest, and our spirits come crashing down and shatter to pieces like a Christmas tree ornament falling from its place on a limb. Then those who are honest with themselves may feel that Christmas is the most distressing time of the year—an occasion to mourn what is lost rather than to rejoice in what has been given. Suicides are common; the psychiatric wards are filled; and the counselors' schedules are booked solid. Let's face it! As a family affair, Christmas is often a *loser!* We admire the *holy* family in church on Christmas Eve, but we find little *wholeness* in our own families.

In addition to all of this, there are growing numbers of people who feel that they have no family—people who are widowed, divorced, or separated, orphans, single people, and others. Both by choice and by circumstance there are many of us who have little or nothing in the way of family. If Christmas is a family affair, where does that leave those who have no family?

The Christmas Family

While there are, to be sure, beautiful and joyous family celebrations of this season, the message of Christmas is not really about the human families of whom we speak. It is not essential to the heart of Christmas that it be celebrated in the context of the nuclear family. Instead, the Christmas message is about the creation of a *new* family. With the advent of the expression of God's love in human form, a new family is born. It is a family held together not by tradition or even blood. It is a family animated not by jealousy and egotism. It is a family not vulnerable to the passage of time and the diversion of interests. It is a family that cannot be shattered by death and separation. It is *God's family*, founded on God's love and held together by God's limitless grace. It is the family into which we have been adopted by means of our baptisms.

Concerning the results of the birth of the Word of God in human flesh, John says: "But to all who received [the Word], who believed in his name, he gave power to become children of God, who were born, not of blood nor of the will of the flesh nor of the will of man, but of God" (John 1:12). For John, Christmas meant the advent of a new family, the formation of unprecedented relationships among humans and between humans and God. Together those unique relationships constitute a new family structure. The good news of Christmas is that we do not have to depend on the frail and fragile relationship of our own families.

44

They can come, or they can go. We are still part of a larger family formed by God's act in Christ.

Feeling Powerless

Driving a car on an icy road can be a terrifying experience. You find yourself absolutely powerless to affect the movement of the car. You press the brakes, the wheels lock, and the car slides on as if you had done nothing. You turn the steering wheel, and, though your front wheels turn, the weight of the car pushes it on as if you had done nothing. You find yourself without any power to affect the direction in which you are traveling. It is the sense of absolute powerlessness to change your situation that strikes fear in the heart of us all.

It is that sort of powerlessness that we often feel in our personal lives and in family relationships. We feel helpless to do anything to reverse a situation or correct a direction in which we are moving. We are powerless before the reality of the death of a parent, a spouse, a child. We are powerless to rescue our loved ones from situations in which they have become entrapped—broken marriages, serious illnesses, emotional problems, financial crises, and addictive behaviors. We find at times that we have no power to shape our own lives, much less the lives of our families.

The Power to Become Children of God

It is that sense of powerlessness which the evangelist John addresses in this verse from the prolog to his gospel. The gift of Christmas, he says, is above all else a power to become children of God. Amid our helplessness, our utter inability to effect change in our lives and those of our loved ones, God gives us the power to become God's children. That's the present God bestows on us in this grand event of Christmas.

Where there is powerlessness and frustration, God gives the power to change. Where there is brokenness and alienation in our families, God gives the gift of a new family.

The tragedy of the weeks after Christmas is that many of us find ourselves sitting in a room with a Christmas tree, trying to understand why we are depressed and sad. The tragedy of the weeks after Christmas is that many of us find that our families are no longer the happy, joyous gatherings they used to be or that we always wanted them to be.

The good news of Christmas, on the other hand, is that we find ourselves embraced within the fold of a new family and given the power to become members of that family through the kindness of our heavenly parent.

It is that family that finally matters. It is that family on which we can depend. It is to membership in that family that God invites us this Christmas season.

ROBERT D. KYSAR
Lutheran Theological Seminary
at Philadelphia
Philadelphia, Pennsylvania

A Light Greater Than You Think
Matthew 2:1-12

A member of an urban congregation in the Midwest was vacationing on the East Coast and visited a church one Sunday morning in downtown Manhattan. She was thoroughly surprised, after telling a worshiper what city and congregation she was from, to hear him respond: "Oh yes, I know about your congregation. You have an outstanding youth choir. You sponsor several refugees from various countries. And your services are really alive—and a bit long at times." Little had the woman realized how brightly the light of her congregation had been shining over the past years.

The Epiphany of our Lord surprises us in much the same way. We know that Epiphany is the festival of light. The First Lesson in Isaiah 60 starts off with the resounding affirmation: "Arise, Jerusalem, and shine like the sun: the glory of the Lord is shining on you!" And as Epiphany Christians we recognize Christ as the source and the center of that light. But surprise! That Epiphany light is brighter and greater than you think!

We Often See Only a Narrow Beam

Actually, instead of expecting Christ's light to be dazzling and cosmic in proportion, we often see it as a narrow, flickering beam of light that illumines a few pieces of our lives from time to time.

That's about the way Joseph and Mary were undoubtedly tempted to look at Jesus at the time of the appearance of the Wise Men. The dramatic

46

events of that first Christmas night were fading into the past. The shepherds, with their astounding story of the angels' song in the heavens, had returned to their flocks. The curious Bethlehemites who had heard the startling story of the shepherds had likewise come and gazed and gone. Joseph and Mary and the Babe had moved from the straw of the stable to the warmth of a house. Things were undoubtedly settling down. Jesus was sleeping and crying and waking up in the middle of the night—just like an ordinary baby. So really, what is so extraordinary about this baby?

J. B. Phillips, the well-known British writer, wrote a whole book on how we Christians try to narrow down the scope of the Epiphany light of Christ. He titled the book: *Your God Is Too Small*. In chapter after chapter Phillips lifts up the images of God that we have carved out in our great effort to minimize and trivialize the impact of his coming. There is the image of God as the "tough sergeant" and the "sleepy grandfather" and the "pale Galilean."

We're a little like the chief priests and the teachers of the law in the story of the Wise Men. They certainly were knowledgeable about God. Clearly they were religious. They could even tell King Herod, on the basis of Old Testament prophecy, where the Messiah was to be born. But there is no indication that any of the teachers of the law were interested in following the astrologers from the East to behold and worship the King. As brilliantly as the Epiphany light was already shining—having drawn these learned men all the way from the area of Iran—the light still had made little or no impact on the lives of the religious leaders of Jerusalem. The only reaction reported by Matthew is that Herod and all of Jerusalem were troubled. Apparently the people—and the religious leaders with them—were concerned about the possibility of political changes and insecurity if a new king had appeared on the scene to challenge the unpredictable, but somewhat beneficent, King Herod. The possibility that the Messiah could have a deep, radical impact on their whole inner being had apparently not even crossed their minds.

And so it happens with us. Christmas and Epiphany may come and go in our lives, and our reaction so often is a broad yawn that communicates unmistakably the message that Christ's becoming flesh and blood for us barely causes a ripple in our mind and spirit. Certainly it does not light up our lives or dramatically change our thought patterns or radically empower us to reflect the amazing love of Christ.

So what is the problem? Does the glory of the Lord in the face of Jesus Christ shine less brightly today? Far from it! Our expectations are too low. The Epiphany light still is brighter and greater than you think!

47

Powerful Impact on Our Inner Beings

That light of Christ has the potential of making a powerful impact on our inner beings. The possibility of the birth of the Messiah moved the Wise Men to reflect deeply, to act boldly—setting out on a long and costly journey across burning deserts and strange terrain, and ultimately to kneel down and worship this little Babe with gifts of gold, frankincense, and myrrh and with the gifts of their own lives. What appears to be a strange fantasy is in fact the true story of how great is the Epiphany light! Somehow through Scripture and dreams and serious study, the Spirit of the Lord had shined into the minds and spirits of these learned men so that they were deeply changed—even before the self-giving, victorious life, death, and resurrection of Jesus had a chance to explode like a brilliant sun on the horizon of their searching minds and souls.

The Epiphany light is greater than you think! The eternal Son of God became a crying, kicking baby, then experienced our human joys and struggles, our progress and frustrations, and death itself so that the light of God's love and presence might be felt by you and me today, and so that we might experience deep inside our inner beings that penetrating, warming light that leaves no one's life the same as before.

The Light Keeps You Growing

That Epiphany light is brighter and greater than you think! It keeps you growing and changing and seeing something new and experiencing a fuller life.

The astrologers from the East were no shallow stargazers. They already had a deep theology. Their gifts to the Christ child bore silent testimony to the depth of their faith. Gold told of their belief that Jesus was king. Frankincense testified to their faith in Jesus as the great high priest who answers prayer. And the myrrh (used to anoint dead bodies) was mute testimony to their recognition of Jesus as one who came to die.

To be sure, the faith of the Wise Men was not full-blown when they bowed the knee before the Christ child. They had an amazingly mature faith in Jesus. But the Epiphany light was far brighter than they could ever have thought.

If the Wise Men had lived to follow Jesus from village to village as he made people whole, if they had lived to follow him to the cross and to the open tomb, then they would have discovered that the Epiphany light was far brighter than they ever had imagined. Bright enough to show the purpose of life to be that of touching lepers and eating with sinners and washing disciples' feet and struggling all night in prayer. Bright enough to show that pain and suffering can be redemptive. Bright enough to illumine horizons in the world to come, to affirm life after death, to show that the ultimate triumph belongs to love and truth. Bright enough to keep faith life growing from month to month and maturing from year to year.

Global and Cosmic Impact

The potential impact of the Epiphany light is still greater, greater than the depths of your being, greater than an ever-blossoming faith life. It even has political, global, and cosmic impact!

These global and cosmic dimensions of Christ's light must have profoundly impressed Mary and Joseph. It was some kind of astrological phenomenon—a flashing comet, a brilliant new star—some cosmic event of unusual proportion that announced the birth of the King. Joseph and Mary must have sensed that such a cosmic event connected with Jesus' birth had something to say about the cosmic reach of his kingdom and of the redemption he would bring.

If Herod was shaking in his boots, so should every ruler, authority, and star in the cosmos. For Herod it was threatening. For Mary, Joseph, you, and me, it is reassuring. To know and believe that Christ's rule extends to every land, to all things, to the universe is to be able to face all situations and to work for worldwide justice and peace with the assurance that Christ is the cosmic Lord of all, who has the power to handle all situations and the love and commitment to salvage all things.

Ethnic and Racial Dimensions

Probably more surprising to Mary and Joseph than the cosmic dimensions of the Wise Men's visit were the ethnic and racial dimensions of their appearance. Down through the centuries the church has recognized the Wise Men from the East as Gentiles. Later tradition goes even further and describes one as a swarthy African. Regardless of whether they were Iranian, Ethiopian, Greek, or Roman, there is no doubt that Mary and Joseph were dazzled and mystified by the brilliance of Christ's light that drew Gentiles to his brightness.

Paul, the apostle to the Gentiles, saw even more clearly what that Epiphany light of Christ really meant. Writing to Christians in and around Ephesus (in today's Second Lesson) he said: "By means of the gospel the Gentiles have a part with the Jews in God's blessings; they are members of the same body and share in the promise that God made through Christ Jesus" (Eph. 3:6 TEV).

The Epiphany light is brighter and greater than you think! Such brilliant light compels us and empowers us toward a truly inclusive church that affirms and encircles all people. Surely it was this Epiphany light that inspired Martin Luther King's dream that "Black men and white men, Jews and Gentiles, Protestants and Catholics will be able to join hands and sing in the words of the old spiritual: Free at last! Free at last! Thank God almighty, we are free at last!"

Such brilliant Epiphany light compels us and empowers us to global thinking and global concerns for justice and peace. Because of this boundary-shattering light we can no longer say that apartheid in South Africa is "their" business. We can no longer say that poverty and hunger in Central America and in the sub-Sahara region is somebody else's responsibility. We can no longer say that the mounting nuclear arms race that threatens all future generations to come is simply the concern of the politicians. It is ours. Christ's light melts boundaries and binds us all together in him.

The Epiphany light is brighter and greater than you think! Bright enough to renew your whole inner being. Bright enough to cause you to grow and grow and grow. Bright enough to impel you to a global consciousness that shatters walls and builds bridges. May you experience it, bask in it, celebrate it, and above all, be empowered by it this new year—because the light of Christ is still brighter and greater than you think!

JOSEPH W. ELLWANGER
Cross Lutheran Church
Milwaukee, Wisconsin

FIRST SUNDAY AFTER THE EPIPHANY

A New Name for Humanity
Mark 1:4-11

Our Gospel for this morning presents Mark's description of the beginning of our Lord's public work. Until the age of about 30, Jesus had been living a private life, unknown by the crowds which would later gather to follow him, a carpenter in an isolated village in Nazareth. Apart from the dramatic events of his birth and a strange incident at the age of 12, which are recorded by Luke, we don't know anything about him—who his friends were, how he looked, what his education was, what the formative influences of his growth were, or even whether he was a good carpenter. There are legends, of course, rather fantastic stories that were told much later, tales told by those whose faith needed to make Jesus a wonder worker and child prodigy.

Virtually the whole of what we know about Jesus refers to a three-year period that concluded in his death; and even of that interval we know very little. But until his baptism, no one seems to have had much reason to record his life; no one seems to have guessed what might become of his life; no one could imagine the words he might speak or the death he would die. It was after his baptism that people first began to take our Lord seriously, to think that his story might be important enough to remember. And his baptism is important not only because of something special it said about Jesus, but because of what John his baptizer was saying about us as human beings.

John: To the Heart of the Human

At the time of the baptism of Jesus, John the Baptizer was a far more notorious person than Jesus was. He was a ghostlike figure, a haunting man consumed with a desperate mission. Seeing him and hearing his words, we are drawn to an ancient past that returns to haunt its inheritors. He's not much like the New Testament apostles John, Peter, or Paul. John is more like something from long ago, something that belongs in the distant and dark recesses of the human mind.

If you or I were today to undergo psychotherapy, to spend a few years on the psychiatrist's couch recounting the hidden corners of our mind, we would discover in ourselves the message of John the Baptizer. For deep within us is the ancient form he presents, an image of ourselves as primitive, even violent, filled with deep and passionate longings. When we begin to sort through the pain and anxiety of life, the nightmares that cause us to sin and enforce our hardness of heart, we hear the words of John crying out in the wilderness. Although we may limit that feeling to those who are deeply troubled, it's not completely foreign to any of us. So few of our private rages and pains—our pleas with ourselves to begin again, to turn around and start from scratch, our lonely yearnings for something holy—ever rise to the surface of everyday thoughts and conversations. But if we could, many of us would recast the mold we call ourselves—clean it up, make it fresh and new.

Huge crowds followed John the Baptizer because they recognized in him and in his words this instinct, which is primitive in us all. They didn't follow him because he was a primitive freak, but because he was all too familiar. He represented in himself a part of the human race—

the ugly, angry, lonely, and longing part. In John the Baptizer Jesus has his public "coming out," his introduction to the world. From his baptism onward, the crowds and the limelight change from John to Jesus, from the man who symbolized the bad news about ourselves to the man who embodied the good news of God.

From Bad News to Good News

How odd it seems that God should introduce his good news for the world through the bad news of John the Baptizer! Jesus comes out of his silent and private life into the public arena of his profound teachings, wondrous acts of power, and ministry of love and compassion through the baptism of repentance, the washing of lives of regret and remorse. But that's not all John the Baptizer portrays for us. He also came with the burning hope, a hope based on a promise that was as ancient as humanity's sin: it need not be that way, it must not be that way, it shall not be that way with the human race; there is hope. In the midst of the bad news there is the good news promise: "After me comes he who is mightier than I."

In our First Lesson God declares, "I have called you in righteousness, I have taken you by the hand and kept you; I have given you as a covenant to the people, a light to the nations, to open the eyes that are blind, to bring out the prisoners from the dungeon, from the prison those who sit in darkness" (Isa. 42:6-7). The ancient promise is reconfirmed. John announces that after him God would break through the ancient darkness with the even more ancient promise. The promise is repeated not only with the ancient prophetic words, but with the new promise that after him the Holy Spirit of God would reside in him whom John promised with the ancient words.

The good news is the promise of the Holy Spirit. The Spirit of God will come to cleanse the painful spirits that enslave the human soul. It will cast out the ancient ghosts, cleanse, forgive, and recreate us. In that promise we will not be who we have been before. We will dare to see ourselves differently, dare to dream the dreams without the nightmares, dare to say that we are whole and human. The Spirit of God will come upon a man, human flesh and blood, in the body and blood, to cleanse with the purging waters of the deluge. As the Spirit of God hovered over the waters at creation, so now, in the water of baptism, the baptism of Jesus, the Spirit of God floods the earth and inundates it with grace. The bad news of the human race, which needs cleansing, is now flooded in a single man. Noah's flood of judgment bore the promise of cleanness; but Noah's descendants failed; they became unclean again. But now, in

Christ, the new deluge sweeps over the earth; and this time, finally, the earth is refreshed and renewed.

The Epiphany of Christ

Those who witnessed the baptism of Jesus knew nothing of the ancient connections with mankind's longings or Noah's promised renewal of creation. They may have heard the haunting words from heaven, "Thou art my beloved Son," but it would be three more years before a human being would look up at the corpse of Jesus and confess "Surely this man was a Son of God!" Jesus came from his private world into the public world very slowly. Who he was and why he came out, Mark repeatedly informs us, was a secret. Only when it was all over would people know what it was all about. The few who recognized in him the ancient promises were more confused than inspired by what they knew. But after his baptism, the life of this Jewish carpenter took on a certain unveiling, a gradual revelation, an epiphany. And even after the story was ended, after he had died and risen again and ascended to the Father from whom he came—even then for many years his disciples would try to put it together, to make sense of it, to explain what they had witnessed.

Epiphanies take a long time; they can't be rushed. The epiphany of Christ began, we are told, with a new star appearing to some astronomers of the East. It continued with a wisdom at which some sages marveled, with strange heavenly words, with wonders and signs, and finally with an incredible rising from the dead. But even after it was all over, the epiphanies continued—on a road to Emmaus or Damascus, in a room at Pentecost, in a prison cell, silently, unpredictably, as if a secret were finally being told.

We always look at the revelation of Jesus Christ from the perspective of its conclusion, after the witnesses to his resurrection and ascension had been assembled and their experiences had been shared. All that they wrote for us testifies to the almighty risen Lord of the church, the King of heaven and earth, the Savior of the human race. But none of that was known at his baptism, nor at any other single moment of his life. The most dramatic of God's revelations were largely hidden and unrecognized.

The Promise of Baptism

We too are hidden in our Baptism. Few of us can even recall the event, much less note any miraculous words which were spoken. Yet we are always epiphanous persons in our Baptism. Our epiphanies take a

53

long time, too. The Spirit of God which we were drowned with at our Baptism moves slowly and deliberately throughout our lifetimes. Nothing distinguishes us from others; few would recognize us for what we really are, yet something is being unveiled in us, a secret is being told, an ancient promise is being kept. Some may claim some dramatic moment in which the whole of God's glory was suddenly revealed. But even when this happens, it takes years to digest such heavy food. Nor are the epiphanies of our lives witnessing to some process by which we slowly become more enlightened. At any given moment, we continue to struggle with our wilderness, our darkness, the ancient haunting past. But at the same time we believe that something hidden is happening.

That hidden thing, that secret of God, happening at all times in our lives yet known only in faith, is the grace of God. It is that which continues to make us right with him, to make our lives holy, to make our service sacred, to make our lifetime journey a holiday (a holy day). The baptism of Christ repeats the ancient promise for us in our Baptism. It opens the eyes of the blind and leads the prisoner from darkness. It is a promise which is certain long after our heads have dried, long after we've forgotten the flood. It is silent, hidden, almost imperceptible, always confusing. Just when it seems most dead in us, it resurrects with alarming life. The epiphany goes on, the baptism of Jesus continues, the sacred story never ceases. You can count on it. It's a promise.

ELDON L. OLSON
Northern Rockies Institute of Theology
Helena, Montana

In the Midst of the Ordinary
John 1:43-51

Think of a piece of woven fabric. My wife has taught me that the color of a thread affects the way you perceive the threads around it. And the threads around it affect the way you see it. So if you have a thread of this color set in the midst of threads of these colors, that very setting will affect the way you perceive the thread's color, and it, in turn, will affect the way you perceive the color of those which surround it. Then, if you put that same thread over here, in the midst of another set of

54

colors, it will look different and the colors around it will also look different.

In a similar way we in the church are blended together. Each of us has an effect, an impact, on all of the rest of us. Where you've been this past week, at work or in your homes, what you have been and done and said as a citizen—in all of that, we all have been present, because you have been affected by our life together as the people of this congregation. So we have reached beyond ourselves through you into Exxon, Prudential, the gas station, the hospital, the high school, wherever it has been, because of the influence of our lives on you and your perspectives and your values.

For we are not just a group of individuals who happen to be together once in awhile. We are, rather, persons who have changed one another. We are not just woven together; we are blended. That means that where each of us is, all of us are—in a very real way.

Nathanael Who?

All of this is prompted by the Gospel for today, the story of Nathanael. Nathanael is mentioned only twice in the Bible and only in the Gospel according to John. He is never mentioned in Matthew, Mark, or Luke. Who was he? The best guess seems to be that Nathanael is the same person as Bartholomew. Bartholomew is mentioned in Matthew, Mark, and Luke, but never in John, and Bartholomew is always mentioned in the first three gospels where Nathanael is mentioned in John. So the best guess is that Nathanael and Bartholomew were one and the same person.

Nathanael was the fourth disciple. Andrew and Peter were called first, then Philip, and then Philip went and got Nathanael. Nathanael appears by name only twice in the Gospel According to John, here on the occasion of his call and later with the other disciples at one of the resurrection appearances of our Lord. Beyond that, Nathanael is blended in with the others. That's why Nathanael is like us. Note two characteristics of this man.

A Man of Hope

The first is that he is a man who was yearning. He was longing. He was hoping and searching. We know this because the account says that Jesus saw him under the fig tree. At that time most people lived in one-room houses. Often a fig tree was planted in front of the house—not just for decoration, or even just for food. A fig tree is about 15 feet tall,

55

and its branches could spread out to be about 25 feet in width. The branches were like an umbrella which created a space that was like a little private room. Thus, if you wanted to get out of the chaos in your house, you could come and sit not only under, but within, the fig tree. People often went under the tree to read Scripture and reflect and pray. It was the sign of a devout yearning, a longing and a seeking and a praying for God's living presence.

Isn't that why you and I are here? Why else are you in this room at this moment, if it is not because of a yearning you have, a longing, that you might taste the reality of the presence of the living God? We come together in this company, centered around Scripture and sacraments and prayer, in the aching hope to know the touch of the living God.

A Man without Guile

Nathanael is also described as a man who was not false, a man in whom there was no guile. He was a man who sought to be honorable, who sought to be decent. He was not a prominent person, but he was a good man, someone who tried to be a responsible participant in the community of which he was a part.

I think that describes most of you. I do not mean to dismiss sin and grace, our enduring need for repentance and for trust in God's forgiving grace. We will continue to need the Order for Confession and Forgiveness at the beginning of our services. At the same time, I know you to be much like Nathanael.

The Splendor of the Ordinary

There are two schools about writing history. The one is that you take the leading, prominent people and create a narrative that is just the linkage of these prominent people and where they led everyone else. The history most of us studied in school probably followed that pattern. The other school insists that the course of history is set more by movements of people, as they come to a conviction, as they move in a certain direction. Leaders just appear at the appropriate points, giving leadership to a parade that is already underway. (Consider the career of Winston Churchill. At times Churchill was in office and at other times he was out. Churchill became influential when and because he fit where the people were and what they needed at the time.) The truth is surely somewhere in between these two schools. Leaders do lead, but momentum and direction can also come from the people.

To discount the ordinary is to discount the significance of what we are and do and decide in determining the direction of our society. Our temptation is to discount the ordinary, and, if there is anything the gospel is trying to tell us to do, it is to be certain not to discount the ordinary.

Take Nathanael. We hear about him twice, and that's it. We are to see in him evidence of the gospel's emphasis that God does not roam across the human race picking out only the prominent people here and there. Neither the gospel nor God gives any preference for the elite over the ordinary. Indeed, the two chief reservations about Nathanael come for just that reason from Augustine and Gregory the Great. Augustine worried that Nathanael could not have been one of the Twelve, because he was too much of a scholar to be in that group. Gregory's concern was that Nathanael was too good a man to fit in with the commitment of Jesus to bind himself with sinners in order to make them new. For the gospel's everlasting and startling insistence is that in Jesus of Nazareth the living God has established himself at the absolute center of human nature and the human circumstance.

When Nathanael was confronted with the assertion that the Messiah had come from Nazareth, his first response was, "You've got to be kidding! What good can come out of Nazareth, a town equivalent to Nowheresville." Nazareth is never mentioned in the Old Testament. Neither is it mentioned in the Jewish commentaries of Talmud and of Midrash. Nor is it mentioned in the history of the time written by Josephus. "And you're telling me the Messiah is coming from there?" Nathanael asked.

But recall where the Messiah was born and the prophecy of Micah: "But you, O Bethlehem Ephrathah, who are little to be among the clans of Judah, from you shall come forth for me one who is to be ruler in Israel, whose origin is from old, from ancient days." Jesus was born in an ordinary village to two ordinary people, Mary and Joseph. All of which reaffirms the biblical message that it is in the midst of the ordinary that the presence of the living God may be found.

It is difficult for us to accept the full and true humanness of Jesus, that he was truly and fully bone of our bone, flesh of our flesh, mind of our mind, that he was truly one of us, that God would reach down into the midst of the most ordinary to make his presence known. Whether it's Nazareth or Nathanael or Jesus, God is in the midst of the ordinary.

At the end of this call of Nathanael, Nathanael said, "Rabbi, you are the Son of God! You are the King of Israel!" Jesus' response was, "Because I said to you, I saw you under the fig tree, do you believe? You shall see greater things than these." Then he said to Nathanael—and to us: "Truly, truly, I say to you, you will see heaven opened, and the angels of God ascending and descending on the Son of man."

These words remind us of the story of Jacob. When he was on the run and full of anxiety, he had a dream in which heaven was opened, and there was a ladder with angels going up and down on it. And God spoke his word of commitment. "Behold, I am with you wherever you go, and I will bring you back to this land, for I will not leave you until I have done that of which I have spoken to you" (Gen. 28:15).

These words also remind us of the witness of Stephen at the time of his death and martyrdom. Stephen declared "Behold, I see the heavens opened, and the Son of man standing at the right hand of God" (Acts 7:56). And the people counted him blasphemous and cast stones at him until he was dead.

Nathanael also had the experience of the heavens opening. After the death of our Lord he was with a group of disciples who found themselves in the presence of the risen Christ (John 21). The heavens opened, and Christ was alive again—not afar off, but in their midst.

Nathanael is one to whom we can relate. He is an ordinary person who yearns for the reality of God in his life and who tries to live honorably. But he is told, as we are told, that that is not where it ends. There's much more that God has in mind—so much more that it can be described only as the opening of the heavens and God coming to him, to us, to make his presence known in our midst. We and Nathanael are ordinary folk who discover that the extraordinary God has broken into our lives and by that has transformed them. There is a lot of Nathanael in all of us, and the message of Nathanael is for us all.

FRANKLIN D. FRY
St. John's Lutheran Church
Summit, New Jersey

THIRD SUNDAY AFTER THE EPIPHANY

This Disturbing Truth—the Gospel
Mark 1:14-20

Jesus once declared: "Do not think that I have come to bring peace on earth; I have not come to bring peace, but a sword" (Matt. 10:34). Those are disturbing words, although they do not mean our Lord abdicated his position as Prince of Peace. But he knew from the first what the result would be when he preached his message to the people. He knew the gospel would be a disturbing force in the world. He knew it would upset individuals and nations; it would change lives and bring new experiences to all who listened to his message.

And it is important that we too understand the revolutionary nature of the gospel. Dynamite is useful, but you have to know you're handling dynamite, not sand. The reaction of the world to Jesus sometimes shocks us and may even make us doubt our faith. So let's take a closer look this morning at *this disturbing truth—the gospel.*

It Upsets the Rulers of This World

Notice how our text this morning begins. "Now after John was arrested . . . ." John was arrested. Yet he had done nothing but preach the same message that Jesus did: repent and believe. But because he told the truth about Herod's wife, he was arrested and later put to death. And we know that the same thing happened to Jesus. His message disturbed those in power; they tried to silence him. And the chain of violence continued. In the text Jesus is pictured as calling four men to carry on his work. A long road was ahead for these men, but eventually three out of four of them also were executed for their witnessing. The powers that ruled the ancient world were upset by the gospel, and they tried to silence the original Christian witness.

And we are not speaking only about ancient history. For the governments of this world still oppose the gospel. Why should the communists in various lands proclaim atheism and try to stifle the message of love and forgiveness? Why do dictators feel they have to get the church under their thumb? Because the gospel is a disturbing force in the world. Even our own government officials sometimes get excited when the church speaks out on civil rights or on the issues of peace and war. But this should not disturb us. For we know the gospel has upset the rulers of this world from the very moment it was first proclaimed.

It Upsets Human Lives

But we don't have to paint on such a broad canvas. For the same upsetting effect occurs in the lives of individuals. I often wonder when I read this text what Peter's wife and his mother-in-law had to say about his chasing off after an itinerant preacher. And I wonder how old Zebedee felt when his two sons simply picked up and left their half-mended nets in the boat. I have an idea the relatives involved in this story weren't too pleased. But that's the nature of the gospel. It upsets people and disturbs relationships. Jesus' call to service can be a sharp sword, provoking controversy and trouble.

59

It hasn't been too long now since we celebrated the 500th anniversary of the birth of Martin Luther. Probably overlooked in that celebration was the reaction of Hans Luther, the Reformer's father. He intended that his illustrious son study law. Martin was to be the means of pulling the family up from their humble origins. Hans probably had dreams of Martin standing before kings. That happened, but not in the way the father intended. The gospel disturbed the relationship between Martin and his parents. It is a disturbing influence in the world.

I can remember a man who attended church when I was a pastor in Memphis, Tennessee. I urged him to join with us, and he said he would think it over. Then one day he came into my office, sat down and said, wearily, "I would like to join the church. But I have to live with my wife, and she gives me no peace when I talk church to her. I guess I'll have to wait awhile." He knew what the gospel can do in a household. It disturbs and upsets people. Perhaps some of you present this morning have experienced how Christianity sets husband against wife, parents against children, youth against age. The gospel is an upsetting message.

It Changes People

But that isn't all. The gospel also changes people. Once you meet Jesus Christ on the road of life, you are a different person. Those four disciples—Peter, Andrew, James, and John—were never the same after they heard the call. Even their vocation was changed. Jesus told them from that time on they would catch men, not fish. The secret is in two simple words—*repent* and *believe*. Once you have taken those two steps, life is never the same again.

Let's take a look at those two keys for a moment. First Jesus calls us to *repent*. For many people that means feeling sorry for what you have done—and then going and doing it again. But repentance doesn't mean that at all. It means a turning away, a change of direction, a new way of life. A popular evangelist once illustrated this in a striking way. He came down from the platform where he was speaking and walked down the aisle, chanting the words: "I'm going to hell, I'm going to hell, I'm going to hell." Halfway down the aisle he turned around and walked the other way, saying, "I'm going to heaven, I'm going to heaven, I'm going to heaven." That may have been a crude way to express it, but he was showing that repentance means a change of direction, a change of goal, a whole new approach to life.

Next, *believe*—have faith. That's the second part of Christ's call. And it doesn't mean simply nodding your head to the words of the Apostles' Creed. It doesn't mean listing your denomination as "Lutheran" on some application blank. It means trust and reliance and placing your whole life in Christ's hands. It's the leap of faith that Kierkegaard, the Danish philosopher, talked about.

Answering the call of the gospel will change you and me. If we repent and believe the gospel, we're different persons than we were before. There's no turning back. Jesus Christ makes a difference in a person's life, and that difference won't go away.

Oh, yes, a Christian may sin, may fall away, and may even renounce his or her faith. But life is never the same once you have met the man of Galilee. Peter knew that. He denied his master and escaped his accusers, but he didn't say, "I sure put one over on those people who were accusing me." He went out and wept bitterly. Recognize it, my friends. You can't turn back. You are changed, moved, turned in a different direction by the power of the gospel. Jesus Christ has a powerful influence in your life, an influence that you can't escape.

St. Augustine knew what the gospel could do. He had lived a rather dissolute existence before he became a Christian. Somewhat later one of the women who had been involved with him in his youthful sins spotted him on the city streets. She called, "Augustine, Augustine, it is I."

Augustine began to run from her, and as she pursued him he finally looked back over his shoulder and said, "But it isn't I." He was not the man he had been, the man she had known. The gospel had changed him. It changes all of us if we give it a chance in our lives.

The Christian is somewhat like a person who buys a new piece of furniture for the house and then finds nothing else looks right any more. Take Jesus into your heart, and you must get rid of other things. Out go your evil thoughts and your petty jealousies and your bad habits and anything else that doesn't fit with Jesus' presence. "Repent and believe" sounds like a rather mild suggestion, but don't you believe it! Jesus is a disturbing influence in life. He demands change, and nothing remains the same when you have given him a place. He shook up the lives of those four disciples. He will shake you too.

The Gospel Brings Blessings

I am aware that I haven't made the gospel sound very appealing as yet. We've seen that Jesus' message disturbs nations and individuals. It brings change into our life. And all that may be good or bad, depending on your point of view. But notice Jesus' call: "The kingdom of God is at hand." What does that mean? It means God's rule in the human heart. It means you can become a citizen living under God's control. And this is the good part.

Being a citizen of that kingdom means God is with you from this time on. Jesus promised his disciples that he would be with them and with us, to the end of the age. Just as those four disciples had Jesus with them as they walked the hills of Galilee, we can have him with us every day of our lives. You are never alone in life. When you go from this service, God goes with you. You don't leave him at the door. When you go to work tomorrow, God goes with you. You're a citizen of his kingdom, and he is not a Sunday friend. He's an every day, every hour, friend.

Moreover you have the assurance that because of God's presence nothing will happen that God will not use for your own good. Oh, being a Christian doesn't guarantee you won't get the flu or have business reverses or have to face unpleasant experiences. But even though you cannot see the reason behind all things that occur, you know you are a citizen of the kingdom, and the king will never forget you. Those four disciples are a striking example of what this means. They followed Jesus, and on a terrible Friday they saw all their hopes end in defeat. Yet on Easter morning they could change the name from Terrible Friday to Good Friday. They saw Jesus conquer the great enemy of human beings— death.

Jesus began his message by saying, "The time is fulfilled." It was. The gospel had come to this world. Hope and joy were alive again. But we know something more. There will come an even greater fulfillment ahead. There is the promise that Jesus will return, that life will go on for all eternity, that we will be with him. Surely this gospel is a great power. It shakes the nations. It disturbs lives. It changes lives. But above all it promises us eternal life with Jesus Christ.

A number of years ago the famous atheist lawyer Clarence Darrow was scheduled to speak at a church in Chicago, composed almost entirely of black people. When the meeting was delayed, some of the church members began to sing. Darrow, sensing a chance to score a point with the audience said, "With all your troubles, what do you black people have to sing about?"

From the back of the church came a voice, "We've got Jesus to sing about." Exactly! And we have Jesus to sing about too. We have the good news, the *good news* to sing about. Let's never cease praising God for sending his Son Jesus into the world and into our hearts.

WILLIAM A. POOVEY
San Antonio, Texas

The Lord Fights a Battle of Words
Mark 1:21-28

"Yakkety-yak, yakkety-yak. Turn down the lights. Put out the cat." More than once I've heard that song on the radio early in the morning. And more than once I've thought about those words at the end of the day. I've thought how those words were a prelude to what followed all day long: words and more words—yakkety-yak, yakkety-yak.

You know how it goes. Your day, like mine, is often filled with words: words from the radio, from the television, from the telephone, from clerks, from fellow workers, from sales persons, from neighbors, from everyone who gets into your day. You and I are inundated with words. We are so bombarded with words that sometimes we would like to muzzle the sender of words. Sometimes we try to do just that as we shout in words to a member of the family, "Can't you turn that TV off?" Sometimes one spouse shouts to the other, "Can't you stop talking and just let me be?" Sometimes a child puts words addressed to a mother into a song and its words become popular: "I'm moving out" because of the "yak, yak, yak, yak, yak."

Words! It seems that day after day it is nothing but a battle of words. So after an entire week of words, we grow weary. We long for some peace and quiet on the weekend. Then we come into a sanctuary on Sunday; and lo and behold—more words! On Sunday we even celebrate words. We celebrate the words of Jesus Christ, God's Word to the world. What's more, today we focus on the words which Christ Jesus used to fight a battle of words, as he engaged the forces of evil.

Yet, even though we focus upon more words, both you and I know these are the opposite of yakkety-yak, yakkety-yak. We have come to know the words of Jesus have power, power to bring healing and wholeness, peace and conviction.

So at the end of a long week, after hearing nearly 700,000 words from others and the media, you and I gather on the first day of the week to hear the words of Jesus Christ. For his words speak to our battered ears, battered minds, battered lives. His words speak to calm, direct, equip, and encourage us for another week of noisy life.

Arsenal of Words

Among the weapons our Lord uses for battling evil is an arsenal of words. He uses them and unleashes them whenever the forces of evil

63

attempt to sabotage God's desire for wholeness. One such victim of evil's sabotage was a man with a tormented mind.

⌐ The scene of this battle between Jesus and evil was a synagogue. The time was a quiet Sabbath. The place was a sleepy town tucked away on the shores of the Sea of Galilee. Jesus and his followers entered the synagogue there in Capernaum. The Master began to teach in words that were straight, direct, confident, and loaded with power. Those in the synagogue were amazed at such teaching. It was teaching with authority.

All of a sudden in this quiet Galilean village synagogue, the Lord encountered the enemy he had come to destroy. The enemy, evil, had entered the mind of a man who himself had just stepped into the synagogue. Speaking through the man's tormented mind, evil cried out: "What have you to do with us, Jesus of Nazareth? Have you come to destroy us?"

Jesus' words and actions were a resounding yes!" From his arsenal of weapons for battling evil, Jesus had a special arsenal of words. With words, Jesus issued a battle cry. Jesus flung the stern, authoritative word: "Be silent, and come out of him!"

With a shrill, agonizing cry the evil did come out of the tormented man. The loud scream reverberating in the synagogue gave evidence to the intensity of the battle and the magnitude of Jesus' victory. Jesus, God's Word, had thrown himself into the battle against the forces that seek to cripple, distort, and destroy human life; and he won the initial battle. In his battle cry, "Be silent, and come out of him," Jesus used those words as a warrior would use a sword to pierce the enemy to the heart. That's what was happening in this verbal battle. The evil which held the man in its grip was defeated. As Martin Luther put it in the battle hymn of the Reformation: "One little word can fell him" (one little word of God shall cause the Evil One to fall).

In that startling moment, the people in the synagogue began to realize that Jesus was announcing in no uncertain terms: "God has entered the battle, and he is in charge!"

Mark preserved this incident in our Lord's life because his generation of Christians felt defeated and powerless. Mark wanted them to see Jesus as the strong opponent of the forces of evil that attempt to paralyze human life. You and I also desperately need to hear this incident, preserved by Mark. That is why we gather after a long week of depressing and defeating words. We gather to hear the words of Christ Jesus on Sunday. For his words break into our lives and our world with assurance and confidence and hope and power. The words of Christ Jesus free you and me from all the evil words that try to enslave us.

So when evil whispers the words "It's no use; you can't do it," we turn to the arsenal of words in Scripture. There we hear the words of Jesus' servant Paul thunder in our ears: "I can do all things through Christ who strengthens me." When evil whispers the words "You're alone, there's no one but you," Christ's words assure: "Lo, I am with you always." When evil whispers the words "You'll always feel guilty about that," Christ's words empower us to carry on: "Go your way, sin no more; neither do I condemn you."

Authority of Words

With those words, our lives are steeled, because those are words of power and authority. When Jesus spoke, demons fled, storms ceased, the sick were healed, the opponents were silenced, the dead were raised, and the crowds were astonished. Those were words of authority and power because our Lord Christ backed up those words with action.

A poster showed a picture of a tough, 1920s hit man, with machine gun, big cigar, a double-breasted pin-striped suit. He was leaning against a dim street light on a deserted corner of New York City. The caption on the poster read: "If yas don't walk de walk, den don't talk de talk." Words alone aren't good enough. They must be accompanied by action if they are to have authority. Certainly the words of Jesus were accompanied by action.

Jesus didn't only "talk de talk"; our Savior "walked de walk" all the way to Calvary's cross. And when evil hurled the engaging word "Come down from the cross," our Savior stayed and took all the forces of evil into his pain-racked body. Then he shouted from the cross those victorious words: "It is finished!"

The gates of hell burst open, and sin, death, and the permanent power of evil were destroyed. As Luther trumpeted: "The devil is in chains!" For in that shout from the cross, there broke a voice more ringing and more authentic than any of the voices of this world. Like a bugle call across the ramparts of our lives, the words of our Lord sound from the moment of our Baptism. They are words of authority, because they are spoken by him who not only talked, but also died taking into the depths all the power the forces of evil could muster. Little wonder we practically shout the words of the hymn: "In the Cross of Christ I Glory."

Armor of Words

You know as well as I do that when we sing those words, we are not whistling in the dark. We are taking with us words. We are surrounding ourselves with words as we would surround ourselves with armor. Only this armor is not perishable like metal. Our armor is the strong, eternal word of Christ pierced and Christ risen from the tomb!

We said in the Prayer of the Day: "We cannot withstand the dangers which surround us." Of course we can't withstand them alone. Sickness, grief, pain, sorrow, and death itself confront us. As with the man in the synagogue at Capernaum, all these evil powers struggle to torment us. Therefore, as King Zedekiah asked of Jeremiah, "Tell me, is there any word from the Lord?" we too ask if there is any word from the Lord for our threatening situation.

And to that earnest question, raised from the daily battlefield of life, comes a ringing response: "Yes! There is a word about Jesus Christ—God's very Word to people on earth, born in Bethlehem, growing up in Nazareth, traveling through Galilee, healing the sick, forgiving the sinful, walking straight to Jerusalem, dying on a cross, rising on resurrection morning, defeating the powers of darkness, pouring out his Spirit upon his followers." That is the word you and I hear from the Lord. We hear the Word himself, alive and active in our world today.

Sense the exhilarating truth of it! Christ Jesus is on our side in the battle of life. We have the powerful word of Christ with us: the word that he abides with us so that nothing, nothing in death, nor life, neither the present nor the future, nothing in all creation will ever be able to separate us from the love of God which is ours through Christ Jesus our Lord.

So when life seeks to take us down into its shadows, we cling to the strong word of our Christ, who confronted the powers of evil, smashed them with the cross, and trampled them with resurrected feet. The strong word of Christ says to us: "Because I live, you shall live also." With that word, we too "shall win the battle! of words."

RICHARD REHFELDT
Windsor Heights Lutheran Church
Des Moines, Iowa

Christ Reaches out to Touch Someone
Mark 1:29-39

To Touch the Broken Body

The phone rang, and the voice on the other end in a numbed, muffled tone said, "My husband has had a stroke. They've taken him to the hospital. Will you meet us there?"

The entrance into the catacombs of the unit called "intensive care" has not become any easier for me after repeated trips over the years in ministry. It's not the vision of tubes and machinery that casts its haunting shadow across the room. It's the devastation that suddenly is seen in the body of a person. Last night he was a youthful 59. He loved choir rehearsal and added spirit to the group. He was one of those vigorous, stalwart, committed members. Today he lies ashen and unconscious. Your eyes sweep the room to see the miracle of machinery taking over some of the body's functionings so that he might rest and stabilize. The nurse touches the IVs, adjusts the tubes, and checks the readings. The family circles the bed, joins hands, the sign of the cross is traced on his brow. As we touch, we wonder what tomorrow will bring. Does death make its claim now? Will he undergo long treatment and therapy and one day walk away to live again? Can he sense the love of those close to him who want him back again? Does he know they want him to fight to live, to come home, to return to table, to family, and to friendship?

To Touch the Troubled Teen

The phone rings and a teenager is on the line. He's a bit nervous and jittery and wonders if he can make an appointment to talk. When he comes in, he makes every attempt to exchange pleasantries. Then it begins to come clear that there is something important on his mind. He really is bothered by something, and suddenly you find a combination of embarrassment and guilt and shame pouring out. You sense that you have entered the private confessional no matter how it may seem to be outdated as a relic of yesteryear's church. He recognizes the wrong he has done. There is no need to state law, for he sits there crushed by it. Quickly you pray that grace and forgiveness will come with simple and direct clarity so that this young life might live again. All he sees now is darkness and despair. Can the light be seen through you? He wants to be touched

67

by a grace that shares and acknowledges the grief while lifting and casting it off.

To Touch a Lonely Woman

She is an elderly parishioner who probably has never missed a Sunday in church in her life. Her face is radiant. It beams with a supportive smile that encourages you to speak the gospel and keep at it! It's been three years now since her lifelong partner has died. He shared the faith and the church pew. His life is forever etched in her being. When I speak a word about Easter and hope and eternal life, I notice that her face is affected by the telling of that old, old story. Occasionally I see tears that cause her eyes to glisten or her head to bow or a slight nod to acknowledge the hope and expectancy she hears in the gospel. Then I know that she is there in the gathering of God's people to be touched by a Word—a Word so full of grace that she wouldn't think of missing it for the world!

To Touch a Frightened Child

A little girl arrived nearly nine months ago from India. She is partially blind in one eye and hesitant and shy. She is taken into a family that is already international, into which a variety of children have come to be at home in an environment of love and care. Slowly learning English, she has expanded her boundaries from guarded corners of fear into a world of eager adventure. She listens to and loves music. She has discovered the story of Jesus with other children her age in Sunday school. When her parents called to ask if she could be baptized soon, she was excited about that special new birthday she would have in the church. She smiled when the baptismal candle was lit and endured the water running down her nose when the cupped hand touched her head. We presented her to the congregation and pinned a button on her that said, "One of the Family." A party at her home followed. The lesson that day began with the words, "and Peter opened his mouth and said, 'truly I perceive that God shows no partiality, but in every nation any one who fears him and does what is right is acceptable to him ....'" She helped us all to see the gospel's inclusiveness that day when she was touched with the water and the Word.

The Gospel Grasps and Gives

These vignettes in ministry parallel the Gospel from Mark appointed for this Sunday. In this account, Jesus enters the home of Simon and

Andrew to find Simon's mother-in-law ill with a fever. They tell Jesus, and now watch what happens: he takes her by the hand, lifts her up, the fever leaves her, and she serves them. Jesus' touch brings the gift of wholeness—then and now!

With broad brushstrokes on the canvas of his gospel, Mark puts together the portrait of the power and the preaching of the kingdom of God that are seen in this Jesus, a backwoods rabbi from Nazareth! What he says and what he does are so "together" that the world's darkened landscape is thunderstormed awake! His fame spreads. The people bring the sick, the diseased, and the demon-possessed to him. The apostles announce, "All the people are searching for you." The people press upon him around every bend in the road, realizing that the kingdom of God is at hand. This is explosive news! Pass the word!

These things that are retold to us in the ancient biblical accounts continue to be the same great, good news that is on the move in our times and lives. The compassion of Christ *is* his touch. Our God is the one who initiated the act of reaching out and touching someone, but not just anyone. He specifically touches you, me, and the persons to our left and right here today. In compassion and mercy, Christ touches us, and we are healed, forgiven, and restored. Christ touches, and we are made alive. We are empowered to serve. We are empowered to pray, praise, and give thanks. The touching was not left as a fragment of history to be remembered. The touching goes on today, because Christ lives and is present among us. He is the one who calls, gathers, and nurtures. His body, the church, lives in the world to exercise his touch. *Christ continues to heal.*

A Preparing Touch, a Promising Touch

One of my favorite stories as a child was a tale about Jack Frost. Jack Frost had a mission to dance his way through the fall season of the year. With a brush he would touch a bit of his frosty "paint" on this and that in order to prepare the world for its retreat into winter. The mission in the fairy tale is not so unlike the mission of the church, charged to touch The world not with a message to retreat from the coming winter, but rather a message to prepare for the coming kingdom. A world is to be made ready by the touch of Christ, preparing us to see his will being done and his kingdom to come, just as we pray for it in the Lord's Prayer.

The touch is to be seen in some predictable and expected places and in some places that are surprising and unexpected. The touch is the water on the head. The touch is a word in our ears. The touch is a tracing of the cross on our chest. The touch is bread in our hands and wine on our lips. The touch is in the unexpected places as well: in holding hands around a hospital bed in the intensive care unit and in the blessing on an unconscious person's head. The touch is in a word which frees and releases a troubled teenager. The touch is heard in a Gospel that assures us of the promise of Easter for a loved one who has died. The touch is the welcome embrace of an outsider and a refugee into a family's circle. The touch is known in the fingers and drill bits that scrape and pound into the dry earth, searching for water to supply a drought-plagued village. The touch imprints numerals and names onto a check, into an offering plate, and into the church's mission and ministry at home and around the globe. The touch is seen in a teacher's move to a shy child who needs an embrace. The touch comes through speaking a word of encouragement to someone who is depressed or discouraged. The touch is exercised in advocating social justice for the misused, the abused, the neglected, and the oppressed.

The gospel of Mark sees to it that the church has a record of how it was where Jesus went so that we might know today how it is where Jesus goes. Then and now Christ reaches out and touches people and they are made whole. He proclaims God's reign, and his people rejoice. He combines power with proclamation and sets his people free. His touch makes us *alive* and makes us *whole*. As we take his hand, he raises us to our feet. It is for this purpose that we, like Simon's mother-in law, might love, serve, honor, and obey him forever. May it be so!

JAMES G. COBB
Trinity Lutheran Church
Grand Rapids, Michigan

SIXTH SUNDAY AFTER THE EPIPHANY

Say Nothing to Anyone
Mark 1:40-45

The plight and delight of the leper captures us. His was the success story of the impossible turned possible. Appropriately documented, it is the story the press would want to pick up. It is the type of testimonial a healer, a church, or a denomination would like to have in its files. Magazines would run the story in their "Miracles Still Happen" column with striking before-and-after pictures. The leper was ecstatic. His miserable condition had changed dramatically to one of health.

The logic and tactic of Jesus tends to leave us cold. "Say nothing to anyone" made little sense in such a circumstance. The healed leper did what you or I would have done. He shared the good news with everyone he knew. Our public relations-conscious, Madison Avenue-oriented mentality suggests that Jesus is trying to pull a fast one on the fellow, assuming that some reverse psychology would encourage him to talk all the more about his healing.

Be Careful of Success Theology

That we think in these terms at all seems to betray our needs for success. In fact, our society is so success-oriented and we have so adapted to that kind of thinking—even in the church—that Christianity and our culture seem hardly distinguishable. That hard work added to sincere faith equals success has become cast as a "natural law." Our society accepts that. But we have gone further to embellish that kind of thinking with religious value. We create a "theology of glory," a religion of success. Everything must pay off. It must return dividends. There must be a glory road. There must be a trail that, even if it leads through the shadows now, must inevitably come to the end of the rainbow.

Our definition of healing does not involve pain and suffering. We want instant health, a magic injection. We want relief from pain, and we want it immediately. We want our extra pounds to erode away; we want a wonderful "new look" right now. The leper was on the receiving end of what looked like this kind of happy magic. And we can appreciate his joyful response. Jesus wanted to temper his reaction so he said, "Go through the channels. Pass inspection by the health authorities. *Say nothing to anyone* or you will be misled into a 'theology of glory.' You will think of me as Superman, as Wonderworker."

"Theology of glory" (success theology) grows from an improper messianic expectation. When you expect a Messiah on a white steed, you set yourself up for a theology of glory. If you think that you would get along better with God if only you would obey more, you are living with a theology of glory. Theology of glory is carrot and stick theology. The carrot is always out there on the end of the stick. Glory days are always just around the corner.

The Bible's Theology Is a Theology of the Cross

The Bible's theology is a theology of the cross. Victory is not around the corner. It is already here. Victory is not out there at the end of the stick. It is already accomplished. The cross is history. Calvary has happened. And resurrection is the proclamation of that victory. But it is not

71

necessarily victory spelled "success" or "health." It is not victory *over* suffering or *over* death. It is victory *in* suffering, *in* death. It is important that Christians understand the nature of their salvation and not be discouraged because their expectations are faulty. The godly happening in this miracle is the touch of care, not the sensation of now-you-see-it, now-you-don't leprosy. Fearing a misunderstanding, Jesus cautions, "*Say nothing to anyone.* Mine is a theology of the cross, not a theology of glory."

Theology of the cross is Martin Luther's name for the doctrine that our knowledge of God must be drawn from the cross, from Christ's suffering and death. Anything else is likely to be a product of human reason that misleads into a theology of glory.

We Are Called to Live the Cross

Our calling is to live the cross. Living the cross is not living in abracadabra land. Our Lord did not, with a magic wave of the hand, dispense with death and come down from the cross. He died. And he invites us to take up our crosses and follow him. What is that like? Look at Jesus and the disciples in the Garden of Gethsemane. It is not a brandishing of swords when the chips are down. Rather, it is "watching with him." It is not a pithy, "Cheer up!" when someone is down. It is, rather, a weeping together.

In a magazine article Betsy Burnham told about her experience in dying of cancer. People would say to her, "Cheer up. Things will get better." That, she says, "just doesn't do it." In contrast, she spoke of a friend who, she felt, "was actually trying to get inside my skin, to understand the intensity of my treatments." That is the process of "taking up your cross," of identifying with Christ (in this case, with a Christian sister) in his suffering. The theology of the cross does not look for cosmetic healing. It leads the Christian to identify with a sufferer in his or her suffering. It acts on the basis of loving your neighbor as you have been loved.

This is not an easy point to make, because the church itself is so caught up in glory-road standards of measurement. Criteria of success is often falsely gauged by the size of the worshiping community or the weight of the offering. Membership and budgets tend to tell the story. The theology of the cross finds its interest elsewhere—in carrying the cross, in being Christ—in whatever setting. It motivates Christ's people to feed the hungry, to visit the sick, to share another's joy, to bear another's burden. To *say nothing to anyone* confuses our sense of natural religion. It makes sense only in the understanding of Jesus and his theology of the cross. And it is critical that we do understand. We are fish swimming upstream against the tide of popular religion, glory religion, success

72

religion. We are not called to sell a product. Rather, we are called to *be* the product of Christ's redeeming.

NORBERT E. HATTENDORF
Grace Lutheran Church
Boulder, Colorado

New Life
Mark 2:1-12

The Man

Put yourself in the place of the man who was paralyzed. How would you feel knowing you'd never cross-country ski through a snow-covered forest, never take a quiet walk on a clear warm summer night, never run up and down a basketball court, or never skate across an ice-covered lake? How would you feel? No one knows how long the man had been paralyzed. Maybe since birth. He had probably tried many different cures. Perhaps there were even other "healers" who had tried to give new life to his dead legs. But it had never worked before. He'd given up. Why set yourself up for more disappointment?

The Friends

Then one day Jesus came back to his home at Capernaum. The friends of this paralyzed man had heard about Jesus. They had heard how "he healed many who were sick with various diseases, and cast out many demons" (Mark 1:34). Maybe *he* could help. So off they went to see their paralyzed friend.

"Guess what?" they said. "Jesus is in town. Surely you've heard about him. The rumor is that he heals illnesses—even casts out demons. We thought we'd take you to see him."

"Oh, great! That's just what I need. How many more times are people going to try to build up my hopes, only to see them all come crashing down? There's no hope. I'm paralyzed."

"But maybe this time will be different. This Jesus seems different. Even the way he speaks seems different. There's a real freshness in his preaching. Maybe this time."

73

"You guys really believe this will work, don't you? OK, but this is it. This is definitely the last time. A guy can only take so much."

So they set off down the road to the place where Jesus was staying—four men carrying the pallet that bore the paralyzed body of their friend, four men full of hope and faith, and one man barely hanging on to his last hope.

The Critical Moment

When they got there, they couldn't even get close to Jesus. They tried to push their way through the crowd. No luck. Now what? They'd come all this way, the poor paralyzed man bouncing up and down on his pallet as they walked. Now they couldn't even get near Jesus.

Never let it be said that these were mere fair-weather friends. If they couldn't get in the door, they'd find another way. "The steps on the side of the house! Let's try the roof!"

"Hey, you guys. These steps are steep. Careful. Don't let me fall. It's not bad enough I'm paralyzed; you guys want to kill me. Take it easy. I'm slipping. Whew! We made it."

The friends started tearing a hole in the roof made of mud and sticks. Soon it was big enough to lower the paralyzed man down into the house. (At least someone had thought to bring some rope.)

"Careful now, fellows. Do you think you could lower all four corners evenly? I just want Jesus to heal me, not raise me from the dead."

This must have looked like a sideshow at a circus, but there the man was in front of Jesus. Jesus looked at the four men on the roof. He saw their love for their paralyzed friend. He saw their faith in God's power to heal. Jesus looked at the paralyzed man. The man was filled with anticipation, anxiety, fear. Jesus spoke, "My son, your sins are forgiven."

"Oh, great! I came here to get my legs healed. My legs are what need the new life."

But no one heard him. Here was this poor paralyzed man lying there in front of Jesus. Up above, his four friends gazed through their new doorway to the sky. People in the crowd pushed and shoved to see what all the excitement was about. And what did Jesus do? He engaged in a theological discussion with the scribes!

"Why does this man speak like this?" asked the scribes. "It is blasphemy! Only God can forgive sins. Is he claiming to be God?"

Jesus perceived what they were asking. "Why do you ask such questions? Which is easier, to tell this paralyzed man that his sins are forgiven, or to tell him to rise up and walk? Only God is powerful enough to do either. To show you that I have the authority of God to forgive sins . . . ," and Jesus turned back toward the paralyzed man and said, "Rise, take up your pallet and go home."

The Result

Suddenly the paralyzed man felt something in his legs. He'd never felt anything in his legs before. He felt new life in his once-dead legs. Could it really be true? Could he really get up? Would he be able to walk? Would his legs hold him? He didn't take long to try. Immediately he rose. He stood up for the first time. He actually stood on his legs. He bent over. He picked up his pallet. He put one foot in front of the other—and again—and again. He could walk! He felt like that lame man that Peter and John healed in Acts 3, who went walking and leaping and praising God—for this new life.

And the people rejoiced with him. They were amazed. They'd never seen anything like this before. They glorified God. Perhaps they even recalled the words of the prophet Isaiah about the "new thing" God was going to do (Isa. 43:18-25).

The Message

Indeed, this was a "new thing." This was God. Jesus came into our troubled world, as he told the people of Nazareth, to preach good news to the poor, to proclaim release to the captives, to give sight to the blind, and to set free the oppressed (Luke 4:16-21).

Each of us has felt like that paralyzed man. Perhaps we've never experienced a physical paralysis, but we have experienced paralysis, nevertheless. We've known the paralysis of a spiritual poverty that is unable to find the way to God—the paralysis of captivity to our sin, captivity to our negative emotions, captivity to an uncontrollable urge, captivity to depression. We've had the paralysis of spiritual blindness, in which we turn away from God and the offer of healing. We've experienced the paralysis of oppression—an oppressive guilt that pins us to the wall and shoves death in our face. Yes, we, too, have been paralyzed. That's the way we were born.

But fortunately we've had some friends—friends with faith—our parents and sponsors, who, in faith, brought us to see Jesus. In faith they lowered us into his presence—into his name, into his kingdom, into the waters of Baptism.

Only this time there was no theological discussion. Just the simple command to rise up from the paralysis of our sin, to take up the cross of a life lived to God, and to walk in the words and promises of God.

Like the paralyzed man, we have been given new life—new life as the children of God.

And today we stand before him again. In the bread and wine of the Lord's Supper, God lifts us up out of the paralysis of our sin. As we hear God's Word, we are led into the new life God has prepared for us. So, like the once-paralyzed man, we go on our way from this place walking and leaping and praising God for this new life.

STEVEN H. DELZER
Trinity Lutheran Church
Northfield, Minnesota

EIGHTH SUNDAY AFTER THE EPIPHANY

What's New?

Mark 2:18-22

I have a friend who, whenever we meet, says to me, "What's new?" Most of the time he catches me unprepared with that question. Let's face it, some days there's not that much that's new. I get up, say my prayers, eat breakfast, go to the office, study for a sermon, make some hospital calls, have lunch with a council member, make some visits, counsel with a parishioner, go jogging, eat dinner, catch up with the others in my family, go to a meeting, and call it a day. What's new? Some days there just isn't that much that's new.

I have to admit he kind of bugs me with that question. I think there ought to be a good answer. But usually I don't have one. Today there is an answer. Jesus is saying to us through the Gospel: "There is something new. It's as new as fresh wine, fresh wine that you wouldn't put into an old wineskin because it would burst the skin and all would be lost—something as new as unshrunk cloth, cloth that you wouldn't use to patch your old, torn britches because when you wash your pants the patch would tear away and the result would be more of a problem than when you began.

What is it that is so new it has the energy of new wine and yet, if improperly applied, will shrink like cloth? What is it that is so new it cannot be contained within the old? What is this new energy that our Lord wants us to experience? What is it that is so new and exciting that

76

it calls for wedding-style celebration and renders fasting totally inappropriate? Jesus is talking about the power that comes to all people through the kingdom of God, and he is talking about the person who is redeemed by his salvation. That's what's new: the power of the gospel and the person who belongs to Jesus.

The Power of the Gospel

We are quite aware of the old. We often see the old powers unleashed these days—the powers that mutilate bodies, torture minds, destroy, and kill. Again and again we see the leaders of nations choosing to use military weapons to solve problems that could be solved in other ways. We've come to understand that while military powers sometimes shape events and may sometimes even be necessary, too often they do not solve problems. These are the old powers that humankind has resorted to again and again, only to see the issues that divide nations become more complex as the weapons become more and more threatening to all humanity. That is the old reality: the powers of evil are all about us, and we do battle with them.

The old is also seen in the ignorance and greed and fear that often divide nations and communities and neighborhoods. These elements have trapped people in every culture and sapped the energies that might have been used to enhance the quality of life. This was the case in the Middle Ages. As a young teacher of theology, Luther saw it all around him. But in his study of Scripture he began to sense the new. When he studied the epistle to the Romans, it hit him full force: "For I am not ashamed of the gospel: it is the power of God for salvation to every one who has faith, to the Jew first and also the Greek" (Rom. 1:16).

The power of God, the gospel, the new for a world under the dominion of the old! What's new? The power of the gospel is new. What is this power? What is this gospel? It's this:

> In many and various ways God spoke of old to our fathers by the prophets; but in these last days he has spoken to us by a Son, whom he appointed the heir of all things, through whom also he created the world (Heb. 1:1).

> In Christ God was reconciling the world to himself, not counting their trespasses against them (2 Cor. 5:19).

> If the Spirit of him who raised Jesus from the dead dwells in you, he who raised Christ Jesus from the dead will give life to your mortal bodies also through his Spirit which dwells in you (Rom. 8:11).

This is the power that's like new wine, like unshrunk cloth. This is what could not be contained within the old. Judaism, with its deeply entrenched forms of first-century legalism, symbolized in our text by fasting, could not contain this new power. So it broke through, and the New Israel, the church, was born. This also happened in the Middle Ages. The power of the gospel was released, and the worn-out forms of the church could not contain it.

This is God's world. "Though the wrong seems oft so strong, God is the ruler yet." He has released the one decisive power in this universe. While nations rattle their weapons, while this group and that group vie for power, we are called to believe that somehow under and through all of this the real power is at work. It is the power of the cross, the power of the crucified one, the power made known in weakness.

The New Person in Christ

So where do we meet this power? We are hardly able to see the hand of God behind the struggles of nations, even though we believe it to be there. Not many of us have had eye-opening, soul-jarring experiences like Isaiah, St. Paul, or Luther. We've heard the name of Jesus since childhood, and while that name means much to us, we have to admit that we don't find much power in our lives. Maybe we experience more weakness than anything else. Where do we meet this power?

We sometimes look for new life in the pleasures that life offers us. In Hosea's day pleasure seeking had lured the children of Israel away from God worship into Baal worship with its fertility rights and temple prostitution. In our day we are also tempted to believe that the temples we've erected in every major city—shopping centers and sports arenas and entertainment centers and casinos—will give life the zest and newness we desire. But for all the countless thousands of hours and dollars we spend on pleasure we have precious little to show for it in fulfilled lives.

Where then is the new? Where do we meet this new power that Jesus calls us to today? We meet it first in Holy Baptism. It is through the water and the Word that God makes us sons and daughters, new persons. It is through the water and the Word that the gospel moves into our lives. The infant child, totally dependent and totally open to new experiences; the new believer, excited about the gospel, ready for a new direction in life; the repentant sinner tired of old ways and old destructive habits—all these are ready for new beginnings. In them the Holy Spirit works the new birth by water and the Word.

A doctor recently told a woman suffering from heart disease in our parish "You must understand that from the time of your birth your arteries have been hardening." That's one way of viewing life. We come

78

crying into this world with a brand-spanking-new body, which immediately begins to grow old, to wear; finally it falls apart.

But there is another way to view life: from the time of our new birth in Christ, a new beginning. Day after day as we die to sin and rise to righteousness in Christ, the new moves in by the grace of God, and the old moves out. So we never really grow old and fall apart. We are ever new in Christ. Each day is a new beginning, each hour a new experience of God's rich grace. And through faith we await a new resurrected body and a whole new existence beyond the grave.

In the second sacrament, Holy Communion, we again discover the new. Isn't it amazing? Our Lord could have chosen to come with armies, conquering this land and that, making all persons bow down and worship him. Or having gone the way of the cross and empty tomb, he could have chosen to come among his believers through visitations—New York yesterday, Memphis today, your town tomorrow. Great crowds would come out and monuments would be erected to remember those visits forever. Of course, trinkets would be sold by the enterprising. But thankfully he didn't choose those methods to be among us. Rather he chooses to come through the very simple: the bread broken, the wine poured.

His body broken for you, this blood poured out for you, for the forgiveness of your sins, the renewal of your life—here is the new. It comes to us who are so often plagued by the old. It renews us from within as we bow humbly to receive the free grace of God, the living presence of our Christ. What's new? We are new. For, "If any one is in Christ, he is a new creation; the old has passed away, behold, the new has come" (2 Cor. 5:17).

A number of years ago there was a conference on healing ministries. Gathered were pastors, theologians, and church leaders to discuss prayer, healing, and related subjects. One afternoon a guest was brought to the conference, a little gray-haired lady in her late 70s. Agnes Sanford had spent a lifetime serving the Lord. The wife of an Episcopalian priest, she led a weekly Bible study for years. Later she found herself praying for people who were sick and found God using her prayers in amazing ways to heal them. Then she and her husband led schools of pastoral care to share their insights with pastors of all denominations. As she talked that day about her ministry of healing, one pastor asked her, "How do you know what to say when you are praying for a sick person?" Without batting an eye, yet very humbly, she answered, "He tells me." That is new life, the life of serving, healing, and blessing amidst the old life of sin, bondage, and death.

So our God, working through his new covenant community, sparks the new life for us. St. Paul was doing battle with those who wanted to drag the old into the church, the old issues of authority and power. Who really has the proper commendation for apostleship? They wanted to fight about that in the church of his day. He reminds his followers: we are "ministers of a new covenant, not in a written code but in the Spirit; for the written code kills, but the Spirit gives life" (2 Cor. 3:6).

To that new covenant community, that community which gathers at the table and at the font, the Spirit gives new life. There the old gives way to the new. There we gather for what can only be compared to a marriage celebration: "This is the feast of victory for our God, for the Lamb who was slain has begun his reign. Alleluia."

It is as that community freely gives itself to its Lord that new life is realized. "Behold, I will allure her, and bring her into the wilderness, and speak tenderly to her," says God of his Israel through Hosea in our First Lesson. And so he calls the church aside and speaks to it through the Word that it might know the new life. Even fasting then, not as religious requirement, but as devotional practice, can be God's way of giving new life to the community. Indeed the church, under the freedom of this gospel, ever seeks forms new and old by which it might place itself in the proper posture to receive the new life God offers.

What's new? In this old world it is the power of the gospel that's new. And you and I are new persons through Christ. Today we remember that we once came to the font and by coming to the table we celebrate what is really new in this old world.

NORMAN V. BRAATZ
Mount Olive Lutheran Church
Lake Havasu City, Arizona

THE TRANSFIGURATION OF OUR LORD—
LAST SUNDAY AFTER THE EPIPHANY

This Is My Beloved Son; Listen to Him

Mark 9:2-9

This morning, in the company of millions of Christians all over the world, we are making a journey to the Mount of Transfiguration. As we journey with our Lord, Mark provides us with a unique way of understanding both the Epiphany season, which this feast brings to a climax, and the season of Lent, which begins in less than three days.

We began this Epiphany season with John the Baptizer at the Jordan as Jesus came up out of the water more fully conscious of the ministry his heavenly Father was placing upon him that day, a ministry of helping and healing. It was to be a ministry of messianic deliverance, a ministry that had God's own stamp of divine approval, signaled by the voice from heaven, "Thou art my beloved Son; with thee I am well pleased" (Mark 1:11).

Manifesting Messianic Ministry

And for the last six Sundays we have been following that ministry through the eyes of Mark, watching Jesus perform the signs of the messianic deliverer: the lame made to walk, the leper cleansed, the evil spirit cast out. We saw Jesus speaking with a power and an authority no one before him could claim, the power to get at the root of our human problem and help us there where it really counts. "Which is easier to say . . . 'Your sins are forgiven,' or to say, 'Rise, take up your pallet and walk'?" (Mark 2:9).

And now today at the end of the Epiphany season Mark takes us within months of the climax of Jesus' earthly ministry. It was the end of a busy day, and in the company of Peter, James, and John the Lord decided to journey up a mountainside to pray. The choice of the three companions was not accidental. Seven or eight months later the same inner circle of the disciples were to be the companions of Christ as he went into the olive grove of Gethsemane. As on that awful night which began Christ's redeeming passion, so on this night also, they allowed their weariness to lull them into drowsiness.

The night passed, and Christ continued to pray. Suddenly in the early hours of the morning they saw the Lord transformed as they had never seen him before. And they saw Moses and Elijah appear and engage with Christ in conversation about his imminent death for the redemption of a world that had broken the commandments of God and rejected the witness of God's prophets. Then a luminous cloud enshrouded them, and out of the cloud the heavenly Father spoke. His words were identical to those spoken at Christ's baptism, although this time they were directed specifically to these three disciples, and through them to the first-century church, and through the New Testament to every succeeding generation, so that today they are addressed directly to you and me. "This is my beloved Son; listen to him" (Mark 9:7). These words are the heavenly Father's endorsement of everything that Christ had said and done during his ministry. They are the divine declaration that everything Christ was yet to do has the Father's complete blessing.

81

Implementing Messianic Ministry

What a sight that must have been there on the holy mount when for a moment Christ's full and complete identity as the Messiah of God was fleetingly revealed to those three amazed and terrified disciples. "How good, Lord, to be here! Your glory fills the night," the hymn declares. Yes, indeed, but the path of glory and light is not to be what those disciples expected. Moses and Elijah talked with Christ about his coming shame and defeat and death on a cross.

There on that mountain of glory Jesus was made to face the meaning and purpose of his ministry. God sent him to be our helper, and the greatest help he could give was to be ours only through suffering, pain and death, a death made necessary by the righteousness of God, which demands both the accountability and judgment identified in today's psalm (50:4-6).

Who would know that better than Moses? When God summoned him to the top of Sinai, his face shone with such splendor that the Israelites could not endure the sight. Yet Paul said the glory of that covenant made in stone fades by contrast with the covenant that Christ is making with God on our behalf (2 Cor. 3:12-18). Who could better witness to the faithfulness and trustworthiness of the promise of God than Elijah? He was that bold prophet who would not tolerate placing one's trust in the empty promises of any false god (2 Kings).

Empowered by Messianic Ministry

How important it is that we profit from the disciples' example and not let the dull drowsiness of the sleep of our earthly cares and concerns or the brightness of the cloud that excites our expectation of the supernatural keep us from realizing what is happening here on this holy mount! We are looking at our messianic deliverer. We are peering into the very mind and heart of God. We are catching a glimpse of God's own plan for our rescue as it moves toward its final hour. Our own relationship with God, our own most precious hopes and highest goals for life are all wrapped up in that mountaintop experience. The transfigured Lord is taking all of our concerns, all of our needs and problems into himself as he prepares to go to Jerusalem on our behalf.

As he prepares to walk the way of the cross, listen to what he says. He is none other than the beloved Son of God taking the judgment of our sins and guilt upon himself. He is delivering us from the intolerable burden of them. He is making it possible for us to trust him, wholly and completely. And what he says is bound up in the very promise of God himself. "This is my beloved Son; listen to him." Listen to him!

Trusting the Messianic Word

When you are tempted to believe that you can manage quite satisfactorily on your own, when your lives remain untouched by the daily tragedies that sadden so many homes, you can profitably recall the words the Savior spoke when they brought to him word of the Galilean nationalists whom Pilate had slain at the very altars of the temple on the annual Feast of Dedication. "Do you think that these Galileans were worse sinners than all other Galileans, because they suffered thus? I tell you, No; but unless you repent you will all likewise perish" (Luke 13:2-3).

When you are tempted to believe that the right relationship with God is the automatic reward of a normally decent life, it is well for you to listen to his words to a man of impeccable morals and untarnished probity: "Unless one is born of water and the Spirit, he cannot enter the kingdom of God" (John 3:5).

When the allurement of seeking other ways to God becomes strong, he warns you: "I am the way, and the truth, and the life; no one comes to the Father, but by me" (John 14:6).

When you are inclined to attach yourself too strongly to your loved ones, and forget that your love for them must be sanctified by a greater love toward God, he reminds you: "He who loves father or mother more than me is not worthy of me; and he who loves son or daughter more than me is not worthy of me" (Matt. 10:37).

When the cares of making a living, your fears for your family's welfare, and the difficult task of making ends meet oppress you, he says: "Therefore do not be anxious, saying, 'What shall we eat?' or 'What shall we drink?' or 'What shall we wear?' For the Gentiles seek all these things; and your heavenly Father knows that you need them all. But seek first his kingdom and his righteousness, and all these things shall be yours as well" (Matt. 6:31-33).

When the burden of your disappointments becomes too heavy to bear and the mere task of living overtaxes your courage and your strength, he speaks to you personally: "Come to me, all who labor and are heavy laden, and I will give you rest" (Matt. 11:28).

When you take seriously your allegiance to Christ and find that the price of obedience to God is persecution, when loyalty to Christ evokes not admiration but resentment and ridicule as it has for so many Christians in other parts of the world, you should remember that he told you it would be so: "You will be delivered up even by parents and brothers and kinsmen and friends, and some of you they will put to death; you will be hated by all for my name's sake. But not a hair of your head will perish" (Luke 21:16-18).

When bereavement deprives you of a friend and companion in whom a very part of your life was bound up, and the days ahead seem filled with gloom and frustration and empty loneliness, you must listen to him and believe him when he says: "I will not leave you desolate; I will come to you" (John 14:18).

"This is my beloved Son; listen to him." As Christ came down from the holy mount, he was strengthened to carry out God's great plan for our salvation. And now through that very passion and death of Christ the Spirit strengthens us so that in the living out of our lives we discover that the word of the Savior is indeed *yes* and *amen*. Now the Spirit bids us come down from the mountain of glory to face whatever it is that will unfold in the coming days, trusting firmly in the promise that at the end of the journey, we, too, shall be like Christ, transfigured in our resurrection garment, shining resplendent in the reflected light of God's eternal presence.

JOHN S. DAMM
St. Peter's Lutheran Church
New York, New York

That the Wicked Foe May Have No Power over Us
Mark 1:12-15

The world we live in is not only a "fallen world"; it is not just passive like a Humpty Dumpty, lying there in bits and pieces, challenging all the king's men to put him together again. It is also an enemy-infected world, one of fear and threat, a "wilderness" where Satan (the Enemy) and wild beasts try to separate us from the love of God in Christ Jesus our Lord.

It was in the wilderness that God's grand experiment of making a people out of no people, a people both free and obedient, seemed to bite the dust. They who heard the divine voice left Egypt under the leadership of Moses; yet they failed the test of the temptations of the wilderness. God swore that they would never enter his rest—those who used their newfound peoplehood and freedom to provoke, rebel, and be disobedient.

84

That is why God's Son, Jesus, was driven into the wilderness—to recapture that desolate, lost territory, that geography of human experience which seemed to be in the control of the enemy Satan.

In the process, however, Jesus was put to the test. "Although he was a Son, he learned obedience through what he suffered; and being made perfect he became the source of salvation to all who obey him" (Heb. 5:8-9).

The biblical idea of temptation is not first of all one of "seduction." It is to make a trial of the person, of putting one to the test. Such a test may have beneficial goals as well as a more devious intent of showing up weaknesses in order to trap and condemn. Trials can make you either a "better person" or a "bitter person," suggests an old proverb. Better, if you keep your mind and heart on the promise of God. Bitter, if you are instead overcome and led by the trial and test into unbelief, despair, shame, and all those other things that inhabit the wilderness experience. God's intent is that "the genuineness of your faith, more precious than gold ... tested by fire, may redound to praise and glory and honor at the revelation of Jesus Christ" (1 Peter 1:7).

Temptation after a High

Temptation often comes just after something "divine" has happened to you, and you are feeling high. Take Abraham, for instance. Abraham had become a somebody! He was no longer an impotent old man without heirs or a future. His immortality was assured in his "son of the promise." In that son all the nations of the earth would be blessed. Abraham was riding high on that divine experience. That high became his vulnerable spot. The test came: Would he still fear, love, and trust in God above all things—even his beloved Isaac? Would God indeed provide a lamb for the offering? Or would Isaac be considered like a sheep to be slaughtered?

Where are we with our divine experience of naming and Baptism and being God's son or daughter? Can our hearing of the voice that names us, who has promised to guard and keep us, survive in the wilderness experience of deprivation and threat? Is God for us also in *those* experiences, or do we succumb to the temptation and believe that we have been deserted and the Enemy is in control?

Jesus had just had a magnificent spiritual experience in his baptism. It is from that "high" that he is driven into the wilderness for the test.

The Enemy comes to us, too, with his accusations and condemnatory judgments. Who do you think you really are, Mr. and Mrs. Christian, with your high title and claim to belong to God's friendship? Didn't I just see you try to put a questionable tax shelter to work for you to avoid paying taxes to whom taxes are due? What about your "shadow self"

85

that seems to be so friendly with the shadows of "wild beasts" in the desert? What about other enemies that attack from the outside? What about tribulation and distress, persecution and famine, nakedness and peril and sword? Temptation comes in the troubled towns of America where fast changes lead to joblessness, where deprivation eats away at self-worth and dignity, where there doesn't seem to be a "future" for most, where many become wanderers in a "wilderness" asking, "*Is the Lord among us or not?*" (Exod. 17:7). *Is he Lord of the wilderness* too? Does the promise stand up there too? The goal of the Enemy is to turn wilderness experiences against us and break faith with the divine naming experience. Temptation is not so much sexual seduction or the enticement of the bottle as it is the struggle to keep faith, to maintain hope and love and faith in the face of threatening loss and impending defeat and humiliation. That is why we pray that God would guard and keep us, that the Evil One, the world, and our own flesh may not deceive us, shaming us into the wilderness of unbelief, despair, shame. *What we have as gift, what we possess as a grace, is never that fixed or secure that we need not hold on to it for dear life in the face of threat and attack*—and hold on with God's promise!

Temptation Is Not Sin

Temptation is an arena where a struggle takes place, where faith wrestles against unbelief, where God-forsakenness and death are like a wasteland, a no-man's land, where God would once again establish his presence and power and promise. Temptation as such is not by itself sin. We glory in our Lord Jesus Christ, "who in every respect has been tempted as we are, yet without sinning" (Heb. 4:15).

A boy once answered an ad to work in a hardware store. He wanted to work at the cash register and was really disappointed to learn he would start out in the basement. The first day on the job he was given the dull task of sorting a large box of bolts, screws, nuts, and nails. It was tedious and uninteresting—a wilderness experience. But the boy kept at it. After a few hours of sorting he came across a wadded piece of paper. As he unfolded it, he saw that it was a $20 bill. What should he do? Pocket it? Trade short gain for the long wilderness journey? On impulse he rushed to the store manager to report the discovery. The employer looked at the bill and at the boy and said, "You may keep the money, son. You have passed the test!"

"What test?" the boy asked.

"Well," answered the manager, "I hid the money in the box to test your integrity. Three other boys failed last week. But you have passed the test, and now I know you can handle the work upstairs at the cash register."

Temptation in the biblical sense is only for those who have been called. When God acts in our lives to call us by the gospel and enlighten us with his gifts, be ready for the test—exposure to new possibilities of good, growth, and maturity, or evil, self-seeking, and failure. Temptations are indeed Satan's work, but we must remember that Satan is God's servant and tool as well as foe and enemy (Job 1:11f; 2:5f). The wilderness experience may indeed be from God, but the actual desire which drives one to sin is not God's but our own, and it is fatal to yield to it as James suggests (1:14f). It becomes either an opportunity to grow on, trusting God in the face of crisis—or a long fall and failure. The stumbling block of the moment becomes either a stepping stone up or a stone that makes us stumble and fall.

The Wilderness

In biblical thought the wilderness was the traditional haunt of demons and the Evil Spirit. Are the "wild beasts" mentioned in Jesus' experience mentioned to heighten the awful threat and loneliness of the desert? Or do we have the suggestion that in Jesus' presence they have become docile, tamed, and subject (Job 5:22), that the mouth of the lions have indeed been closed? This may suggest that the Messiah tames the wild ones, and that with his victory we will indeed live in the "peaceable kingdom" (Isa. 11:6-9). A world gone wild and uncontrollable is tamed by this one, who redeems and makes the wilderness safe.

The Messiah came to "destroy the works of the Evil One" (1 John 3:8). People were amazed that the demons were subject to him. Early in his ministry Jesus was confronted by a man with an unclean spirit and Jesus with authority rebuked and tamed the evil spirit (Mark 1:21-28). This authority and power had been tested and made genuine in Jesus' own wilderness experience, where Jesus himself knew for sure that nothing can separate us from the love of God. The wilderness experiences of life have been tamed.

It was a long struggle and a continuous struggle. The 40 days recall the long 40 days of Noah's desolate and lonely experience, the long arduous struggle of Israel in the wilderness (Deut. 29:5), and Elijah's wrestling with his wilderness experience when Jezebel threatened his life. The wilderness experience was a life-threatening, faith-wrenching struggle. Could Jesus still believe what the divine voice had said? We hear Jesus' awful desert cries, how "in the days of his flesh, Jesus offered up prayers and supplications, with loud cries and tears, to him who was

87

able to save him from death, and he was heard for his godly fear" (Heb. 5:7). He was heard, for he believed against the odds, hope against hope, that the last word would not be abandonment and separation, but that even here, especially here, God's power would be made available in weakness.

That is why we pray, *"Let your holy angel be with me, that the wicked foe may have no power over me."* That is why messengers of God, the holy angels, whisper God's promise in our ears in the face of all enemies: *"Fear not, I am with you!"* That is why we sing "Though devils all this world should fill, all eager to devour us, we tremble not, we fear no ill, they shall not overpower us." If God be for us, nothing can be against us—not even the "no things," the "no bodies" of life have the power any longer of sucking away our vitality and life and joy and confidence of being "somebody," called and named "son, daughter of God!"

Good News Wins over Bad News

So it was that even in the face of the bad news of John the Baptist's arrest Jesus came from his wilderness experience and victory both optimistic and confident. "The time is fulfilled, and the kingdom of God is at hand! Repent and believe the gospel." The first word Jesus heard after leaving the wilderness was of the arrest of John. No matter. The wild beasts had been tamed. Their power to control and move us to despair are over. The kingdom of God means just that—that the kingdoms of this world have become the kingdom of our God, and he shall reign forever. *Repent* then means to turn away from defeat, despair, and shame and face the Son who has replaced all the *nos* of life with a divine *yes!*

The gospel of the kingdom prevails. It calls us to believe again and turn away from the temptation that suggests, "God is not found nor is he a protective presence in the wilderness experiences of life." For now we know that if God is for us in the wilderness *especially*, then who or what can be against us? The wilderness too has been redeemed and tamed. Thanks be to God *that the wicked foe has no power over us!*

NORBERT E. KABELITZ
Redeemer Lutheran Church
Oklahoma City, Oklahoma

88

That We Might Live
Mark 8:31-38

The late Vice-President Hubert H. Humphrey is reputed to have said, "I don't care what people say about me, just so they talk about me." He was more than flippant; he was realistic. Popularity wins votes.

Jesus was popular when he had this meeting with his disciples. We read that he asked them, "Who do *people* say that I am?" There was an abundance of interest and a wide variety of answers. He did not seem to be disturbed by the popular answers, wrong and distorted as they may have been.

But then he asked his disciples, "Who do *you* say that I am?" Peter spoke for them all when he responded, "You are the Christ." This was the right answer, but it disturbed Jesus deeply. "Keep still about it," he said. "Don't tell anyone."

Why does the correct answer receive such a rebuff?

Jesus is popular today. Gospel songs are being sung on secular programs by high-priced artists. Religious broadcasts abound, with a wide assortment of interpretations of the meaning of Jesus, and they are well supported by their listeners and viewers. "Jesus talk" is in. Jesus is popular. And most of us who call ourselves his disciples are glad about this.

It is Jesus' treatment of Peter that disturbs us. Can it be that as we church people gather in our churches and confess our faith with the words, "I believe in Jesus Christ, his only Son, our Lord," that Jesus might be saying to us "Don't tell anyone"? What a disturbing thought.

Shouldn't we tell the world about Jesus? Shouldn't we rejoice that there are miracles today, that illness often succumbs to his name, that many people are finding peace to surmount their tensions in him? Shouldn't we be excited about the fruits of the gospel?

Of course, but since Mark has told this story to give us directions for our lives today, and not only to inform us about how it was when he was on earth, the rebuff seems meant for us, too. Why?

The Centrality of the Cross

We are being discipled by his words about the cross. The well may run dry if the source is neglected. Part of the reason for our worship is to be conditioned by the gospel so that the gospel may continue to bless the world. We are in boot camp; we are in training camp. So we let him lead us to the source of life itself. The source, says Jesus, is in the cross: "The Son of man must suffer and die."

89

Must. There is no other way for God to enter our lives and reshape them, reenergize them, redeem them. The Son of man must suffer and die so that we may see God. The cross is central to God's plan. If we are to be delivered from suffering, he must suffer with us. If we are to be rescued from sin and death, he must endure sin and guilt and death with us. There is no other way.

He must suffer and die because the stakes are so high. What is at stake? Life itself, says Jesus. Jesus did not come to make life a bit more bearable, to ease the pain a little, and to give us that warm feeling we all want. He came to give us much more. He came to give us life—life that cannot be crushed by sin or guilt, or ended by death.

Life is at stake.

"Consider," he asks us, "if you gained the whole world but lost your life, what have you gained?" A father and mother were in the grips of despair because their child had let himself get so tangled in wrongdoing that prison was unavoidable. A friend saved them with the simple reminder, "But your son is still alive, and so are you. That means there is hope."

Since physical life is so pivotal, certainly one wants this physical life to throb with purpose and meaning. You do want to live before you die, don't you? And you do want a life that death cannot end, I'm sure.

"My mission," says Jesus, "is to give people life." But this life doesn't just drift down from above. It comes into your lives in the same way it came through his: "Take up your cross and follow me."

Following Jesus

We find life by following him, and he went to the cross. We take up his cross, since ours are so trivial by comparison. We take up his cross, and as we follow we are given our own crosses. And it is then that we know what it is to be alive. The way to life for all of us, Jesus says, is through death. "Whoever would save his life will lose it, and whoever loses his life for my sake and the gospel's will save it." This is not *an* option, not *a* way; it is the only way.

We shudder. We are puzzled. Many of us are offended. After all, we do know something about mental health, we of this 20th century. Isn't it sick, even bordering on the masochistic, to say that life can be realized only through suffering? What sort of a Savior is this? Shouldn't a Savior release us from suffering? Haven't we been told that a Savior binds up our wounds, frees us from our prisons? Didn't Jesus himself say that he came to give sight to the blind, to help the lame to walk, to raise the dead? Isn't it in these gifts that we see the true evidence that he is the Christ? Life is cruel enough as it is. We want that peace beyond understanding, the healthy self-image, the hope that tomorrow will be a better day.

And even if there is some truth in what Jesus says, how do we go about it? Must we seek suffering for its own sake? No, that is sick! Jesus does not say that we should seek suffering. He says we should take up the cross. There is a vast difference. The stakes are high.

It shouldn't be so difficult to see why the cross is so essential to life. Rome used it to punish criminals. Like all empires, Rome was nervous about people who thought for themselves, met in small groups to foster their beliefs, and then refused to bow the knee to Caesar. So Rome often crucified "thought" criminals.

The state always offers life. It offers life on its own terms, and these terms often become totalitarian. In one way or the other, political power tends to become ultimate and gets nervous when people don't accept this. So where is life? With the God who suffers with us—or with the state that seeks to control actions and thoughts? Christ's followers have no choice. If they would be his disciples, they must fight that which would usurp the place of God, whatever it may be. And that means a cross.

We Americans have in our lifetimes emerged from such a cross experience through the sacrificial life of Martin Luther King Jr. In various ways we are being challenged to protect the right to life of the people of our day. Jesus says, "I befriended the outcast, the derelict, and preached the message of hope to the poor. You do it too. And don't say the times are different. The poor you have always with you. Work for justice for the poor, a future for the children, equal opportunity for all."

But there will be a cross you say? Ah, yes. Jesus offers his own. He doesn't say we have to do it all. We carry his and work in his achieved victory.

Life from the Cross

The stakes are so high. At stake is life itself.

We know that moral decay destroys life. It happened in Jesus' day; it happened in Rome; it happened in Europe; it is happening to us. Somebody must say no to the insidious self-gratification that corrupts us and makes a mockery of moral commitment. The onrushing wave of pornography, of chemical dependency, of dishonesty in business, of exploitation of the poor, cannot be allowed to continue—or we lose life itself. But is there any other way than the cross? More police power is powerless against inner corruption. Prisons are full, and we are not improving. From somewhere there must come a rebirth of the will. And this is so easy to say, and so hard to accomplish.

91

The cross appears instantly. Loss of popularity, misunderstanding, scoffing, and ridicule come easily. Jesus says, "Carry mine." If we do, we are forbidden the luxury of self-righteousness and smugness. We see how ridiculous we are when we sit in our self-righteous corners and say with Jack Horner, "What a good little boy am I!" Jesus says, "Carry my cross." He broke the power of sin.

And what of the poor, whom Jesus loved so much? What of the sick, the unemployed, the unemployable, the powerless? If God has chosen to give himself—God, the world's Creator—for these "unproductive units" of our society, is it too radical to expect that we, his followers, not only share our wealth and health, but also work to make the power structures more sensitive to these hurting ones? There will be a cross. It is inevitable. We will be attacked by the strong as enemies of the economic system and by the poor for not doing enough. It is too often a no-win situation. But, "never mind," says Jesus. "Carry my cross."

If we try to address life on these three levels—government, morality, and economics—we will inevitably come to the point where we realize our weakness, our helplessness. We will become painfully aware of our moral and spiritual bankruptcy. In graduate school I was often with a young idealistic man who was going to give himself, he said, to working with the poor of his own minority group. He believed he would be sustained by his own goodness of heart. He needed nothing so useless as faith in a loving God. He went out, and the next year he was back in school.

"What? Why are you here?" we asked.

"I couldn't take it," he said. "Nobody said thank you."

Very few do. And perhaps then we see the ultimate reason for the cross.

We find we do not love as we ought. We are more self-indulgent than disciplined. We resent the needy. We want success and approbation. We lust, we covet, we slander, we ignore God. We seem to be in the grips of an evil power. We are dying. We cry out to God.

"Good," he says. "Finally. Let yourself die. Your sins are forgiven if you just let it happen to you." Jesus must suffer and die that we might live. Because he died, we are alive. How beautiful this world is after all! And it is just the prelude to something we call eternal life. We stay close to the Jesus of the cross that we may live.

ARNDT L. HALVORSON
Luther Northwestern Theological Seminary
St. Paul, Minnesota

The Wrath of Love
John 2:13-22

One day a delegation of Greeks came to Philip, one of Jesus' disciples, and said, "Sir, we wish to see Jesus" (John 12:21).

What image does the name *Jesus* conjure up in your mind? Is he the babe of Bethlehem laying peacefully in a manger of straw while an adoring Joseph and Mary gaze down on their wonderful son? Do you see a lad of 12 astounding the learned doctors in the temple with his knowledge and wisdom of the prophets? Perhaps your mind captures the mighty prophet standing on a hill preaching to a multitude who are mesmerized by his proclamation. "No one ever spoke like this man!" they exclaim. It may be the miraculous Lord who calms the angry sea or makes a blind man see. Or it could be the crucified Christ suffering a horrible death on the cross while his accusers stand beneath jeering at him. Maybe it is the resurrected Lord and the ascended Christ who comes to mind, and we know that he shall come again to judge the living and the dead.

But how many of us pictured an angry Jesus who takes a whip in his hand and drives the money-changers out of the temple with the shout "Take these things away; you shall not make my father's house a house of trade"?

Most of us have a concept like that of the poet William Blake, who penned these words:

> Little Lamb, who made thee?
> Dost thou know who made thee? . . .
> Little Lamb, I'll tell thee,
> Little Lamb, I'll tell thee:
> He is called by thy name
> For He calls Himself a Lamb.
> He is meek, and He is mild;
> He became a little child.
> I a child, and thou a lamb,
> We are called by His name.
>   Little Lamb, God bless thee!
>   Little Lamb, God bless thee!

We suffer in our day from a concept of a weak Jesus who is so meek and mild that he would not lift a finger to correct the errant sinner. The ethereal, almost effeminate, paintings of Jesus you see displayed in homes belies the true nature of a rugged Christ who marched across the hills of Palestine, slept under the stars, and confronted his adversaries. This prophet of Nazareth was a person of strength, character, and outstanding courage. It was said of him, "Teacher, we know that you are true . . . and care for no man; for you do not regard the position of men" (Matt. 22:16).

However, a rugged and wrathful Jesus does fly in the face of many concepts of Scripture. "Do not resist one who is evil. But if any one strikes you on the right cheek, turn to him the other also (Matt. 5:39). Paul said "Repay no one evil for evil, but take thought for what is noble in the sight of all" (Rom. 12:17). And remember those words of Paul to the Ephesians: "Let all bitterness and wrath and anger and clamor and slander be put away from you, with all malice, and be kind to one another, tenderhearted, forgiving one another, as God in Christ forgave you" (4:31-32).

How then do we explain this picture of a wrathful Jesus driving out the money-changers with a whip? Doesn't it contradict all that Scripture teaches?

The Wrath of Love

We must come to grips with the wrath of God. Even though today we often hear that God will always say, "I forgive," the truth is that God will not stand by helplessly and watch his children destroy themselves.

Israel had to learn that lesson over and over again. In many ways God permitted their enemies to attack them and lead them into captivity in order that Israel might be brought back into a faithful relationship with Jehovah.

That is what the author of Hebrews tells us, "My son, do not regard lightly the discipline of the Lord, nor lose courage when you are punished by him. For the Lord disciplines him whom he loves and chastises every son whom he receives" (12:5-6).

I am convinced that Jesus knew about his impending death. Those who plotted against him were the religious leaders of the nation. They had polluted and corrupted the temple and the worship life of the nation. In a furious rage he took a whip and cleared the temple of those who misled people in their worship.

Last year I had an opportunity to visit the People's Republic of China and see several churches and church leaders. I was thrilled and amazed at their faithfulness, commitment, and devotion. The Protestant church has tripled in size since the missionaries were chased out in 1949. Through the long years of suffering and persecution that took place during the

Cultural Revolution, those Christians grew in their devotion and dedication to their Lord and his church.

One night in Shanghai, we listened to Dr. Kiang Wen-han. He was an old man who had been trained at Columbia University and Union Theological Seminary in New York.

He was 60 years old when the Gang of Four took control in 1964. He and his wife lived in a three-room flat in Shanghai. They were told that they had to move all of their things into one room so two other families could move into that apartment. For 15 years 11 people lived in the cramped corners of those three rooms. The only way he could communicate with his wife was to whisper in her ear as they lay in bed at night.

We asked him how he survived and managed during those years. "It wasn't easy," he said, "and we learned great patience. One thing I now know: suffering and persecution will never destroy the faith of the church."

The intense faces of Chinese people listening to sermons or bowing in prayer have caused me to raise the question, "What has happened to American Christians?" We are so relaxed and indifferent about our church relationship. Could it be that we have had it too good for so long that we have become soggy in our faith?

Pearl Buck tells about a Chinese warlord who was conquering village after village. The mayor of one village did not want his beautiful community to be destroyed. So he took a different strategy. Rather than resisting the warlord, they welcomed him as a conquering hero. They put up beautiful silk tents to house him and his men and fed them their finest foods and drinks.

Soon they became like fat cats and lost their fierce will to fight. Then the villagers fell upon them and destroyed them. The conquerors were conquered by their own lusts.

We Americans fear suffering as much as anything in life. "This is a land of plenty and no one should suffer," we boast. However, we may experience God's wrath in our future and discover many meaningful lessons that we have forgotten.

God disciplines those he loves, and our sinfulness and disobedience may be the source of God's wrath toward us.

Zeal for Thy House Will Consume Me!

There is a great lesson to learn about our Lord's concern for the worship of the temple. The money changers were profiteering by selling pigeons, oxen, and sheep and corrupting the purpose of God's house. In

95

Luke's gospel Jesus shouts, " 'My house shall be a house of prayer'; but you have made it a den of robbers" (19:46).

It was after this event that his disciples remembered that it was written of him, "zeal for thy house will consume me." Don't you wonder what has happened to the zeal we have for God's house? Worship attendance has been falling among mainline Protestant churches for some time. The growth of the church has been stymied, and we appear to be losing the battle to win our world for Christ.

It isn't that way in other parts of the world. People living under repressive governments seem to have great zeal for the faith of the church. One commentator said that there are more people worshiping on a given Sunday in the Soviet Union—where Christianity is repressed—than in all of England and Scotland, where worship is free.

In a book entitled *Households of God on China's Soil*, Raymond Fung tells a story of an elderly woman who went to her first church service after a congregation was opened in her community. "So I went to church. It was heavenly. My heart was full of blessings and my eyes full of happy tears. I shamelessly clutched the arm of an old man sitting next to me, wetting his jacket with my tears. I was so happy I had a headache. My heart beat fast every time the congregation sang and the piano played. It was too much for me. Now I can only remember the sermon title. It was 'Jesus the Shepherd.' "

"Zeal for thy house has consumed me."

The Sign of His Resurrection

Finally, the Jews asked Jesus a question: "What sign have you to show us for doing this?" Jesus answered them, "Destroy this temple, and in three days I will raise it up." The Jews were confused, "It has taken forty-six years to build this temple, and will you raise it up in three days?" But he spoke of the temple of his body.

It all hangs together, doesn't it? Jesus became wrathful and drove the money changers from the temple, because they were polluting and corrupting its worship. He told them that it was not the edifice that was important but the spirit and presence of almighty God whom they seemed to ignore. Jesus said to the woman at the well, "God is spirit, and those who worship him must worship in spirit and truth" (John 4:24).

Too many of us forget the true reason for our worship. We focus on the building and get caught up in the economics and the politics of the church. The result is that the spirit of the resurrected Christ passes through our midst without our recognition and adoration.

I wonder how often Christ weeps over us. Will we feel the wrath of his love as he attempts to drive the corruption from our lives and to bring us into a living relationship with him?

Luther comes to mind. Pope Leo X had sent John Tetzel into Saxony to sell indulgences in order to collect funds for building St. Peter's Basilica in Rome. Tetzel beat a drum and shouted this tune: "As soon as a coin in the coffers rings, a soul from purgatory springs."

People thought you could buy indulgences that would release a soul from the agony of purgatory. Luther saw this as a money-making scheme. He shouted "I'll put a hole in Tetzel's drum!" and he did this with his attack on indulgences. The result was a counterattack by the pope.

This caused Erasmus to say, "Luther is wrong on two accounts. He has tampered with the belly of the monks and the treasury of the Pope."

We do not like to see our worship disturbed and our sins confronted. Many times the preaching of the gospel can be like a two-edged sword that cuts and unsettles. However, we must remember that this is the wrath of his love. He disciplines those who are his sons and daughters and reaches out to restore us in a living faith-relationship.

I became acquainted with a wonderful Christian gentleman. Although he was old and wore very thick glasses, he had a lively step and an energetic faith. We traveled across the state one night, and he shared his story with me. In mid-life he had an accident that made him blind. For three years he was forced to sit in darkness. He became despondent and bathed himself in self-pity. His wife left him, and his children couldn't stand to be around him.

Then a preacher of the gospel started to visit him regularly and shared with him the love of Christ. The blind man came to a living faith, and his life was transformed. Through a miracle of surgery his sight was restored. "I thank God for my blindness," he said. "God made me sit in darkness so that I could truly see."

Many of us have experienced suffering, disappointment, and struggle in our individual lives and in our corporate experience in the household of faith.

However, the truth of this gospel is that in spite of the difficulties we have encountered, there is a mighty resurrected Lord who has redeemed us.

It is as St. Paul says, "The sufferings of this present time are not worth comparing with the glory that is to be revealed to us" (Rom. 8:18). Even when we experience the wrath of his love, we know that it is a gracious Saviour who works good for those who love him. Let us live in that faith with expectancy and comfort.

PAUL M. WERGER, BISHOP
Iowa Synod—LCA

The Light of the World . . . on a Tree

John 3:14-21

Jesus is the Light of the world. Who among us would deny that? Certainly not the author of the Fourth Gospel who uses the word *light* to describe our Lord more than all of the other Gospels put together.

Turn out the Light

We like light. We don't like "being left in the dark." We bask in the warmth and brightness of a warm sunshiny day. And yet there are times when light can be blinding, times when light can expose our blindness and nakedness, and we feel most uncomfortable. There are still some private corners of our life that we want to keep hidden in the dark shadows. And what if the light does illumine those corners? We explode. We attack or excuse. We accuse or rationalize. "Shine the light elsewhere, on someone else," we say. "Expose the other person, who is surely worse than I." Or we say, "It's his fault," or "She made me do it."

The Light shines in a dark world of nuclear insanity, abject poverty, and ecological madness. And we shout, "Turn out the light. I only do what I'm told. If it's wrong, it's the fault of those who give me the orders." Or we say, "The poor are poor because they are not ambitious. I work hard for what I earn." Or, "If I don't look out first for myself and mine, no one else will." Or, "It's the government's fault. You can't fight city hall." "For God's sake, turn out the light." No, not for God's— for my own.

In today's Gospel we are told: "The light has come into the world, and men loved darkness rather than light, because their deeds were evil." If our eyes are so sensitive to the light, it is only because they have been wrapped in darkness for so long. And darkness can, for a short time, be comforting. We can avoid facing the cluttered corners of our life. They look a lot cleaner in the shadows.

Turn up the Light

The Light came into the world not to condemn but to bring life. It is only as those dark, private corners of our life are exposed that we can

98

be helped. If the cancer is not detected, it cannot be treated. Without illumination the surgeon cannot cut it out. It's painful—but therapeutic.

The Light came into the world not to bring condemnation, but salvation—not to rub our noses in those dark corners of the soul, but to bring healing and reconciliation. The gift is freely given.

This light may be painful at first to those eyes accustomed only to the dark. Indeed, as Plato said, we may not even be able to look directly at the light, but in the beginning, only at the shadows dancing on the wall.

But then the warmth and brightness of the light enable us to see the darkness of our prior existence and the possibilities for the present and future. "Come," says the Light shining through our baptismal waters, "You are my daughters, my sons. Come and enjoy the illumined, the enlightened, life I offer. You are forgiven. You are accepted. Come and enjoy the light and the life. Bask in the warmth and beauty of the sun— the Son." "For God so loved the world"—and that means you.

The Light Lifted Up

None of this comes easily. God's love for us may be free, and it certainly is freely given. But it cost God much. The gift is free for us, but it comes at great cost to God—God's Son. It meant the raising up of that Light of the world on a rough-hewn cross—*for* the world. Jesus talks about this in the Gospel and uses an analogy from the First Lesson: "As Moses lifted up the serpent in the wilderness, so must the Son of man be lifted up, that whoever believes in him may have eternal life."

In John, the height of the Light's glory is on the cross. Later on in the Fourth Gospel, Jesus refers to his suffering and death, "Now is the Son of man glorified" (John 13:31). Strange words here. But in John's gospel the proof of who Jesus is, the pinnacle of his glory, is not the virgin birth or the ascension (not even mentioned in the Fourth Gospel). It is not even the triumphant resurrection. The pinnacle of our Lord's *glory* for John is when Jesus is lifted up on the cross. God is most glorified, Jesus is glorified, in that supreme act of giving himself in sacrifice for others. That is why in John's gospel the Last Supper does not occur on the Passover as it does in the other Gospels, but prior to the Passover (John 18:28). Good Friday, according to the author, was the Day of Preparation for the Passover, when the lambs were slaughtered (John 19:31). In John, Jesus *is* the Passover lamb who was slain for us, and his glory is found in his suffering and death.

How different from the way we view things. Glory in suffering? No way! We glory in power, prestige, wealth, success, fame. We love it. We strive for it. We yearn for it. And not just as individuals, but also as

99

congregations, denominations, and other institutions as well. Have you ever wondered why there are so many awards shows on television? We have Miss America, Mrs. America, Miss Universe, Miss Teenage America, Miss Jr. Miss America, and just you wait, one of these years a Miss Junior Preadolescent America. Or, look at the plethora of different country hits awards shows. Why are there so many of these? Because so many people out there in "viewer land" watch these programs. Why? Because these millions of people dream about their own day in the sun when the person at the podium will say: "And now the envelope please? . . . And the winner is . . . Al Neibacher." And the auditorium explodes with applause.

But the gospel of John implies that true glory does not come from prestige or power, fame or wealth, but from the supreme sacrifice—for others. (Maybe that's why we all know who Mahatma Gandhi or Martin Luther King Jr. were, but we cannot name three Miss Americas from the last 20 years.) In the Fourth Gospel nowhere does the light, the glory, shine more brightly; nowhere does the grace come through more clearly; nowhere does the love burn more deeply than on the tree—the cross.

The Light of *The Giving Tree*

There is another tree, *The Giving Tree*, which is the title of a book by Shel Silverstein. If you don't have a child to whom you can read this book, go out into the highways and byways and compel one to come in. Young and old alike will benefit by this book.

The story is about an apple tree who gives a little boy her apples to pick and her branches to climb. The boy and the tree love each other and are happy in their life together. As the boy grows older, however, his interest in the tree wanes.

The tree is very lonely until one day the boy returns as a young man. The tree offers her apples and branches, but the boy claims that he is too old to climb and play. He is more interested in money. "Can you give me some money?" he asks the tree. The tree has no money, but she does have apples. Why doesn't the boy pick the apples and sell them, and then he will be happy. The boy does this—and the *tree* is happy. But then the boy stays away an even longer time and the tree is sad.

Years later the boy returns. The tree is overwhelmed with joy as she invites the boy to swing from her branches. But the boy is too busy to play. What he really wants is his own family and a house to keep him warm. Can the tree give him a house? No, but the boy can cut her branches and build a house with them, suggests the tree; then he will be happy. The boy does this, and the tree is happy.

Many years pass before the boy, now middle-aged, returns. The tree, overjoyed, invites the boy to play. But now the boy is too old to play. All he wants is a boat which will take him far away. "Can you give me a boat?" The tree invites the boy to cut down her trunk and make a boat so he can be happy. The boy does this, and the tree is happy—but not really, for now only a bare stump remains.

When, years later, the boy returns, he is a hunched-over, old man. The tree apologizes for having nothing to offer any longer, no more apples to eat or branches to climb, only an old stump. But the old man says his teeth are too weak for apples, and he is too old to climb. All he needs is a quiet place to sit and rest, for he is very tired. "Well," says the tree, straightening herself up as much as she can, "An old stump *is* good for sitting and resting. Come, boy, sit down. Sit down and rest." And the boy does. And the tree is happy.

Oh, the *grace* of "the giving tree" which gives even to one who always takes—"by grace you have been saved through faith; and this is not your own doing, it is the gift of God" (Eph. 2:8). Oh, the *love* of "the giving tree" which gives sacrificially for the one loved—"But God, who is rich in mercy, out of the great love with which God loved us, even when we were dead through our trespasses, made us alive together with Christ" (Eph. 2:4). And this giving of self, even unto death, is also God's greatest glory.

Learn from the giving tree and from the one who was given on the tree of the cross, the Light of the world, the Light *for* the world.

ALBERT L. NEIBACHER JR.
Christ Lutheran Church
Minneapolis, Minnesota

I Only Asked for a Single
John 12:20-33

During his first year in Little League baseball a young boy never hit the ball. After each game he would tell his father, "My Sunday school teacher said that Jesus promised to help us if we asked him. I asked him to help me hit the ball." Father and son had long talks about prayer. On the opening night of his last year in Little League, the same boy went up to bat with the bases loaded. He hit a home run. On the way home, with the home run ball clutched firmly in his hand, the boy said to his father, "I only asked him for a single."

We often remember our prayers to which God says no. Sometimes we easily forget the times we ask God to help us get to first base and instead we hit a home run.

We Want to See Jesus

This pattern of asking for a little and getting a lot happened to some Greeks who came to Jerusalem to celebrate Passover the year that Jesus Christ was crucified. Naturally these people from a far country soon heard about Jesus. He was the chief topic of conversation in the Jewish city. A short time before, he had gone to the grave of his friend Lazarus, who had been dead for four days. Jesus acted as though the grave was the man's home, and he called, "Lazarus, come out!" And the man who had been dead four days came out to see him. Naturally this had caused a lot of excitement in Jerusalem. Those who loved Jesus were filled with joy. Those who hated him were filled with anger. And the rest were eager to see what would happen next.

The visiting Greeks shared the excitement. They wondered if the story of a dead man coming back to life was true. So they found one of Jesus' followers with a Greek name, Philip, and asked him, "Sir, we want to see Jesus." They thought they would know more about the man if they looked at him. We all like to look at other people. We want to look at the people we buy from, vote for, and listen to. We want to see how they hold their bodies when they stand and walk. We want to look into their eyes. We want to see how they hold their jaws and see the lines of smiles and frowns. We can understand why the Greeks said, "Sir, we want to see Jesus."

In today's world Philip might have given the Greeks an autographed picture of Jesus and sent them away. But he couldn't do that 2000 years ago. So he teamed up with Andrew and they went to Jesus with the Greeks' request. Listen to the next part of the text carefully: "Jesus answered them, 'The hour has now come for the Son of man to receive great glory. I am telling you the truth: a grain of wheat remains no more than a single grain unless it is dropped into the ground and dies. If it does die, then it produces many grains'" (John 12:24 TEV).

That doesn't sound like an answer to the request made. When the boy prayed to hit the ball, he wanted to hit the ball. He didn't want a lesson on theology. To the Greeks it was a simple request: "Let us take a look at you." Yet Jesus answered by telling them the time had come for him to receive great glory and then something about seeds.

If a Grain Dies

Jesus told the Greeks to hang around and watch what was going to happen. Don't just look and run. Wait, because the time has come for him to do something great. Stay and see the glorious thing that is about to happen.

Jesus explained his answer. If you look at a grain, you see only a grain. What you see is what you get as long as the grain stays a grain. But if the grain is planted in the ground, it rots. As the grain loses itself in the ground, a new plant grows and produces many more grains. From the grain that is planted, you get a lot more than what you first saw.

If we could look at Jesus and see what the Greeks saw almost 2000 years ago, we would see an interesting man. If that is all we would see, that is all we would get. But if we stuck around to see Jesus receive his glory, we would see and receive much more. We'd see him die as a grain dies in moist soil. A tragic loss? No, a marvelous gain! Because as the sprouts come up to produce many grains, Jesus died and came back to life to give life to all who believe in him. Jesus invited the Greeks to see more than *himself* in Jerusalem. He wanted them to see him in the *people* of Jerusalem and in the *people* of Greece. In the glory of the resurrection they will see him in the lives of people wherever the gospel is preached and believed.

There's Still More

By now the Greeks had received more than they'd requested. They'd rounded second and were heading for third. But that's not all. Jesus said, "Now my heart is troubled—and what shall I say? Shall I say, 'Father, do not let this hour come upon me'? But that is why I came—so that I might go through this hour of suffering. Father, bring glory to your name!" Then a voice spoke from heaven, "I have brought glory to it, and I will do so again" (John 12:27-28 TEV).

They asked to see Jesus—and they heard God speak from heaven. It was a home run. God the Father verified what Jesus said. Jesus would give his life to die for the sins of the world. But the act of violence and shame would bring great glory: a glory that God gave in the past when he came to be with his people, a glory that he will continue to give, because the Christ who dies will live again and remain in and with people forever.

You can imagine the little group of Greeks standing in the crowd. They heard Jesus explain his death and resurrection. They heard the voice of God speak from heaven with a promise of glory for people. One must have elbowed another and said, "But all we asked was to see him."

Now let's parallel this story in our lives. In seven days we will begin the week we call holy. In 14 days we will celebrate the resurrection of Christ from the dead. We are like the Greeks who came to worship. You came here today with a request. You will return to the special Holy Week and Easter services with the same spoken or unspoken request, "We want to hear about Christ's death and resurrection." And you will hear it.

But could it be that you will get more than you ask for?

My Servant Will Be with Me Where I Am

When Jesus told the Greeks to stick around and see more than just how he looked at the moment, he also spoke beyond the time of his death and resurrection. He tells us who hear the story of how he died and rose again to stick around to see what happens to us because of what he has done. Listen to his words: "Whoever loves his own life will lose it; whoever hates his own life in this world will keep it for life eternal. Whoever wants to serve me must follow me, so that my servant will be with me where I am. And my Father will honor anyone who serves me" (John 12:25-26 TEV).

At first that answer must seem remote from our annual request to hear of Christ's death and resurrection in our Lenten and Easter worship. But notice: Jesus is telling that what he did affects your life. He gave his life as a grain is planted to produce more grain. His death gives life to us because it removes our guilt and eternal death. He tells us that if we try to protect our own lives, we cannot receive the new life he has given us. Don't just listen to what Jesus *has done!* Listen also to what he *is doing!* He has invested his life in ours. He now lives in us.

When we ask to hear the story of what he has done, we hear not only of his death and resurrection. We also hear that he loved, forgave, healed, strengthened, comforted, and taught. The Greeks could have watched him do those things. But when we hear about them today, he tells us to stick around and see how he shows his glory today. He is still doing those things. He does them through us! When we forgive others, heal others, strengthen others, comfort others, and teach others, we are following Jesus. When we follow him, we are with him. When we are with him, God the Father honors us. We ask to hear a story of what happened long ago. As we hear the story, the past turns into the present. We are with Christ and share in his work. We have rounded second and are headed for third.

The Voice Speaks for Our Sake

But that's not all. Remember Jesus prayed, "Father, bring glory to your name!" A voice from heaven said, "I have brought glory to it, and I will do so again." Jesus explained, "It was not for my sake that this voice spoke, but for yours."

God spoke from heaven to assure the people around Jesus that what Jesus was doing was being done by God. Those who saw Jesus, saw God. Those who followed Jesus, followed God.

That same voice speaks to us today. Through the words and actions of Jesus Christ we have seen and heard God. We ask to hear again what *Jesus* has done for us, and we hear what *God* has done. It's a home run.

When you walk out of the Easter service two weeks from today, you will have completed the trip from Bethlehem to Calvary and to the empty tomb. I pray that while on that trip you will have seen and heard not only what *has happened*, but what *is happening* in your life. I hope you see how others are giving you the blessings of God because Christ is in them. I hope you see many opportunities for you to give the blessings of God to others because Christ is in you.

And I hope you can say to someone who worshiped near you, "And to think, I only asked to hear how he died and rose again."

ELDON WEISHEIT
Fount of Life Lutheran Church
Tucson, Arizona

Never a King Like This!
Mark 15:1-39

Something new and extraordinary is going on in each of the scripture lessons for this Passion Sunday.

In the Old Testament lesson we hear a prophecy about a victorious king, who rides humbly into Jerusalem on an ass. Of triumphant and victorious kings, we have heard plenty in our world's history. But of a humble king who rides in lowly majesty we have scarcely heard, if at all. Something new and extraordinary is going on here.

In the Second Lesson we encounter one who was in the very form of God, but who nevertheless emptied himself of this divine glory and took upon himself the form of a servant and died in utter humiliation on a cross. Yes, something new and extraordinary is going on here.

Now consider and look at the Gospel text for this Sunday. Six times the central figure is addressed as "King of the Jews," a royal and revered title. But this "King of the Jews" is scarcely treated like one, and all that happens to him defies everything that we would expect of a kingly figure. Truly, something strange and extraordinary is going on here, for there never was a king like this, never before, and never since.

It is up to us to try and understand something of the paradox of this king who doesn't fit the mold of kings, of the king whose rule comes to an end with a crown of thorns and a cross for a throne. The whole story of this king, in fact, is a paradox of the greatest sort—so much so that both we who are so familiar with it, and those who are not, cannot help but be drawn into it in a way that once heard and felt will never leave us at peace.

Let me share with you this new and extraordinary story as Mark tells it, and then let St. Paul interpret for us something of what it all means. First, Mark's story in five scenes.

Mark's Story

In *Scene One*, Pilate asks Jesus, "Are you the King of the Jews?" The Sanhedrin, the ruling council of the Jews, had already met and accused Jesus of claiming to be a king, one who wanted to usurp the authority of Rome and replace it with his own rule. Whether they actually believed this or not, it was the right charge to bring before a Roman court if one wanted to catch their attention. And by beginning with this question,

Mark raised the issue for his readers: "Who is this Jesus? What kind of king is he, anyway?"

Jesus' response to Pilate's question is the ambiguous reply, "You have said so." Does this mean yes or no? Not even Pilate is certain, so he seeks another reply from Jesus. But we are told that Jesus makes no further response, and as the story unfolds Jesus does not speak again until he cries out on the cross. Pilate meanwhile wonders what it all means.

And you and I are left wondering too. Is Jesus the king of the Jews? How do the events of his passion, these recollections of the last frightful hours of his life, add up to anything that can be called *kingly* or *royal* or even *divine*? How could these events establish Jesus as the royal ambassador of God?

In *Scene Two*, Pilate asks the crowd, "Do you want me to release for you the King of the Jews?" The choice is between Barabbas or Jesus. Barabbas was an insurrectionist, a guerilla fighter in the deadly struggle against imperial Rome. The cause was a popular one, especially among the poor people of the land, and for good reason. The Romans were bent on exploiting their power with excessive taxation and brutal force.

When Pilate seeks for an easy way out of his dilemma over Jesus, he gets caught in his own game. The crowd asks for Barabbas' release, and finally ends up demanding death for Jesus. Pilate surrenders to the pressure and delivers Jesus the King to be crucified.

An insurrectionist goes free, and one who claims a royal title dies in his place. Something is wrong. The roles are getting reversed. Oh, it is true that kings and rulers have been deposed by popular rebellions, and often for a good cause. But that's not the case here. This Jesus has not joined the ranks of authoritarian and oppressive dictatorships that have become so familiar a pattern in our world's history. They may call him King, but if anything, he was on the side of the people, the friend of the poor and oppressed. Yet he was different here too, for he never took up arms to incite a rebellion, or a sword to kill and destroy. This king simply does not fit either side, and maybe that's why he was put to death. At any rate, a murderer and insurrectionist goes free, while a king is crucified, a king like no other.

In *Scene Three*, this king is unmercifully mocked: "Hail, King of the Jews!" The soldiers must have their sport too. After all, theirs is a violent life, hardly given to humane and noble sentiments or building of character. When you deal with brutality and bloodshed too long, you get coarse and hard. You've got to in order to survive.

So they play king with this Jesus—a purple cloak, a crown of thorns, and the mock salute, "Hail, King Jesus!"

It gets a little out of hand with some hitting and spitting, but this is only one of many victims they have seen. The outburst of violence soon subsides, and they're on the way to the place of execution.

This victim is a king, however. But how can you tell? Where are the signs of his royalty? How could the poor soldiers know any better? In a world of violence and cruelty and innocent slaughter, of which our generation is a worthy heir, where does this king fit in? And won't all of his followers, those who seek to follow his different way in a rough and tumble world, simply end up as mocked fools and innocent victims as he? Where is the power and glory in this king with a crown of thorns?

In *Scene Four*, this king is crucified with the inscription of the charge against him reading, "The King of the Jews." But of course this is nonsense, only a cruel joke. He couldn't even carry his own cross to Golgotha. And Golgotha means "the place of the skull," an all-too-fitting name for the place where one of the most horrible forms of execution humankind has ever devised was carried out. No wine mixed with myrrh can deaden the pain, nor does this king seek relief. He's not alone, but the two others are robbers or insurrectionists, while he's a king.

But how can he be? Where's his royal power? He's accused of claiming he will destroy the temple and then rebuild it in three days, but he can't even save himself. Where's his glory? He's accused of claiming to heal the broken and sick lives of others, but he can't finally save even his own life. This broken figure is the Christ, the King of Israel, the King of kings? Come on now! As long as he hangs on that cross, there is nothing to see and believe. All his claims to be a king sent by God come to nothing.[1]

What else can one conclude from a crucifixion? Reserved only for the worst of wrongdoers, there is no way it can be prettied up or lied about. It's a horrible way to die, and no human being should have to endure it, much less an innocent victim, much less one who came in the name of God. Either the whole scene is one of the cruelest jokes ever played, or there is something going on in this scene that only the eyes of faith can see and believe.

In *Scene Five*, the royal figure on the cross utters his final words, "My God, my God, why have you forsaken me?" It is a dark moment in every way. The whole earth shudders in darkness from noon to three. But even greater is the agony and despair of the one who pierces the darkness with his cry, "My God, my God!" Here is the darkest night of the soul, that moment when we seem to stand utterly alone and naked with our terrors and dreams. Only here is one who claimed to know God as no one before. Here is the one who dared to speak and act in his Father's name as no one else, and with his full authority. Here is the

108

one who even dared to pray "Abba, Father," as one person who knew God so intimately that he could even call himself the "beloved Son." This is the *one* who cries out in the dark night of his soul from the cross, "My God, my God, why have you forsaken me?" This one who knew God like no other, and trusted him like no other, this is the one who feels himself utterly alone and abandoned by God at the hour of his deepest need.

Is it not absurd to think of this despairing, abandoned, dying figure as a king? If so, he is suffering the worst humiliation a king could ever suffer. No throne but a cross, no kingdom but death. And so the curtain falls on this once noble life. He utters a loud cry too great for words, and breathes his last. The King is dead. His rule is done.

Or so it would seem. But Mark is not quite through with the final scene. He tells us the curtain of the temple was torn in two, from top to bottom. This curtain separated all but the high priest from the presence of God in the Holy of Holies. Now, however, the curtain is gone, and the way to God wide open. And then there is the Roman centurion, the captain in charge, a veteran of war, crime, and violence. He sees something else than the others in the death of Jesus. No cursing, no reviling, no rage, no clenched fists of defiance or shouted obscenities. Only acceptance, pain, sorrow, and the cry for help to the heavens, once uttered in words and once without. And as he looked on that one who had saved others but not himself, his eyes were opened, and he began to see and believe. And from the lips of this outsider and sworn enemy of the King of the Jews, poured out the confession of faith, "Truly this man was the Son of God." The crucified King has been transformed by the eyes of faith into the royal Son of God!

That's Mark's story of the crucified King. But what does it all mean?

Paul's Story

Let Paul unveil its meaning in the ancient hymn he preserves for us in Philippians 2. This is a hymn about a King, Christ Jesus, the same king Mark wrote about. Only now we get the full picture.

This King Jesus was once in the "form of God," equal with God. But in the fullness of time, this Jesus emptied himself of his divine glory and entered our human race and human history in the form of a servant. And in servant form, he emptied out his life for others. But this led to his humiliating death on a cross, as the obedient servant of God.

Yet death was not the last word. The very God who sent him heard his agonized cry from the cross, "My God, my God," and raised and exalted him as Lord over all. Now this servant Jesus reigns again in the

109

form of God and will reign until the whole creation confesses him as Lord to the glory of God.

Why did this King Jesus empty himself so? Why this incredible reversal of roles, from the Lord of the universe to the humblest servant of all? While the hymn does not tell us explicitly, the meaning is ready to burst forth from this hymn. Why does he empty himself so? *For us*, and *for the whole creation!* There is no other reason why. He takes a servant form among us and goes the way of death so that you and I and all humanity might live and confess him as Lord. He goes from riches to rags to express in unmistakable manner God's unbounded love for us. That's the secret of it all. Paul summed it up with his usual eloquence in another letter, "You know the grace of our Lord Jesus Christ, that though he was rich, yet for your sake he became poor, that by his poverty you might become rich" (2 Cor. 8:9).

And what should be our response? Gratitude, of course. But more. The Lord who took upon himself the form of a servant *for us*, calls us into a life in the form of a servant *for others*. The goal of the Christian life and the goal of the Christian community is faithful service to Christ in the world. This is done by proclaiming the gospel of God's forgiving love in Christ and by practicing that love toward others. It is taking upon ourselves the form of a servant. And in this servant form, we the people of God must be prepared to bear the marks of the servant.

Today we enter Holy Week. This week we remember the divine self-emptying of the King of kings. The story of Jesus' passion dramatizes as no other his obedience as God's servant, even to death on a cross. Already, as we saw, the Old Testament Lesson had alerted us to the strange news of a lowly King who brings peace and justice. Jesus fulfilled that prophetic promise as he entered Jerusalem riding on a donkey. Triumph through humility, power through weakness, victory through suffering, greatness through service—these are the paradoxes that this week sets before us. And they are the paradoxes to which this King who was like no other calls us, as we seek to follow him as Lord of our lives.

WALTER E. PILGRIM
Lutheran Institute for Theological Education
Tacoma, Washington

110

Treason at the Table
Mark 14:12-26

Jesus was not surprised. He knew what was about to happen. That last night of his life, lying—as was the custom—on couches around the table, Jesus abruptly interrupted the ancient ritual of the Passover meal. "One of you will betray me," he said. The apostles—at least 11 of them—were surprised, and each objected, "Surely it is not I?" But Jesus knew. "It is one of the twelve," he said, "one who is dipping bread into the dish with me."

No Surprise

Jesus knew what was happening. He knew it first of all because of his careful and constant study of the Bible. In various places the Old Testament made it clear, to those with eyes to see and with ears to hear, that the one by whom the Messiah was to be betrayed would be one of his most intimate companions. Jesus loved the Psalms and often quoted them, even when he was on the cross. This last night at supper again he seems to have had the Psalms in mind. Surely as he pondered the situation, verses like this from Psalm 41 must have been going through his mind: "Even my best friend, whom I trusted, who broke bread with me, has lifted up his heel and turned against me" (*BCP*). An intimate companion would betray him.

But it was also because of Jesus' marvelous ability to see, his supernatural insight, that he knew what was about to happen. Even the most realistic, down-to-earth portrayals of Jesus in the Bible from time to time contain certain disturbing passages in which Jesus is shown to be more than a man. He was fully human, like us, to be sure; but there is more. There is that uncanny ability to know what was going on, to see through events to the heart of the matter, to see beyond the present into the future and know what was about to happen. The outline of his life was clear to him. He was never surprised, for always he *knew*. So this night he knew Judas even better than Judas knew his own heart. Jesus foresaw Judas' treachery. But the apostles could not believe it.

A Willing Sacrifice

Knowing clearly what was about to happen, Jesus gave Judas a stern warning and *freely accepted* what would happen. He willingly embraced

111

that unpleasant future, because he understood it to be in accord with the will of God. It was, he was convinced, what the Father wanted, and it was surely what the Scriptures had revealed. All of the history of Israel had been moving toward this night; the whole experience of his people had been converging on this moment and on this man.

The course of history therefore was not haphazard, and the impending death of the young Prince of Glory was not a meaningless tragedy. It had significance. His death was part—it was the centerpiece—of "the definite plan and foreknowledge of God," as St. Peter was later to testify after the apostles had seen and experienced it all (Acts 2:23). It was in fact *necessary* for this man freely to give himself in sacrifice, submitting to the intention of the Creator of the world. He who came to do the will of God, had come to do this. Despite all of his natural reservations and fears, he willingly—even gladly—offered himself as the sacrifice because that was what the Father desired.

Who Was Guilty?

All of this, of course, does not excuse Judas the betrayer, for Judas' act was his own responsibility, and the guilt was his. So we condemn and reject and denounce Judas, calling him the betrayer, the traitor, the one rotten character among the 12. The apostles did so too, finding biblical passages of cruelty and brutality to describe him. Before Matthias was chosen to replace Judas, Peter applied Psalm 69:25 to him: "Let his habitation become desolate and let there be no one to live in it," and from Psalm 109, "His office let another take" (v. 8). It is easy to say bad things about Judas.

It is too easy, in fact. As we meditate upon this Gospel, we move out of the past and into the present, and we see the old story in terms of modern events. "Woe to that one by whom the Son of man is betrayed," Jesus warned. The betrayer *then* was Judas. But who is the betrayer now? The betrayer is a repressive government, anywhere in the world, that binds and blinds and controls its people. The betrayer is a state or local government in our own country that will do nothing to relieve the suffering of the poor, the ill-housed, the unemployed. The betrayer is a health care facility that refuses to serve those sick who have no money or that gives them second-rate care. The betrayer is even within the church, just as Judas was one of the Twelve. The betrayer is a pastor who is unworthy of the high calling, who uses the office for self-aggrandizement to exercise control over the lives of lonely, desperate, or insecure people. The betrayer is any member of any congregation—this congregation—who does not live always the life God expects of each of his people. The betrayer now as then may be one who has eaten at the Lord's table with the Lord himself. Each of them and all of them have betrayed the Savior of the world and the Lord of creation.

And what about us? What about our role in the unfolding drama? Jesus makes it clear that Judas could not escape the guilt of his act of treachery that he was about to do, but the Gospel also makes it clear that we cannot avoid the guilt of what we do by passing it on to another. The blame rests not on someone else but squarely on each of us, on me, on you. I crucified him.

No Escape

At the beginning of the Great Thanksgiving tonight, as always, the pastor will invite us to "Lift up your hearts," and we will willingly respond. We want to do just that. We want to leave behind the conflicts and ugliness and sordidness of the world and our lives and the mess that we sometimes make of it all and lift at least our hearts above this world toward heaven, where, we like to think, we will be in a simple and pure place beyond all trouble. If only we could. But the Bible seldom lets us so escape from reality.

Look at the order of things in the Gospel today. The betrayal and the Last Supper are set side by side, and that is disconcerting. Surely the institution of the Holy Communion in that upper room must have taken place above the sordid meanness of our lives and this world. It was an *upper* room, above the mud and grime and dirt of the room below where people lived. It must have been a place apart, separate and above, in which this holy and blessed sacrament was first celebrated and which we commemorate and reenact tonight. But look at the Gospel again: the betrayal and the Holy Communion are side by side.

In fact, the Holy Communion is sandwiched *between* Jesus' prediction and Judas' act of betrayal. The Lord's Supper is surrounded by treachery. The meal begins with Jesus knowing what will soon happen: "One of you will betray me . . . one of the twelve." Then we hear the holy words of Jesus that we have come to know and love so well, "This is my body . . . this is my blood." Finally, this Gospel ends with Jesus and the Twelve going out to the Mount of Olives, to the Garden for prayer and for the betrayal. Between the Lord's scrutiny of Judas and the Lord's submission to the will of God and to the act of Judas, we find the Lord's Supper: the Lord's scrutiny, the Lord's Supper, and the Lord's submission; Jesus' prediction of betrayal, the Holy Communion, the act of treachery.

113

So it was then, so it is still, and so must it always be in this mixed and contradictory world. The Holy Communion has for its setting this world, this world we know so well, with its conflict, stains, and shame. In a world like this, Jesus takes the elements of a common meal and transforms them into a sacrament of his presence. He takes bread and wine and makes of them his body and blood. He gives us a meal and makes it be himself.

There is no escape from the world, for all its shame. Jesus does not come to take us away from all this; instead, we find him, like the setting of the meal, between the prediction and the act of betrayal. In the meal itself, Jesus joins himself to the innocent victims of the world, the persecuted and betrayed of all times and all places, and makes himself one with them and makes them one with him. He shares their sorrow so that they may share his triumph.

The Mandate: Love

The overarching theme of Maundy Thursday is love: God's love for us and our responding love for God and for other people. The odd word in the church's name for this day, "Maundy," comes from the Latin *mandatum*, the mandate we have from him, the new commandment that Jesus gave to all who belong to him: "Love one another as I have loved you."

Each failure to love is an act of betrayal, a turning away from our calling to live as people for whom Christ died. But to strengthen us in our commitment to that way of life we have the gift of Holy Communion, the sacrament of God's self-sacrificing love for the world. In this meal we are joined to God and to one another.

We have moved tonight from the past into the present, from Judas' guilt to that of our world and of us. We have moved from the Last Supper to the Lord's Supper, from then to now, from that night to this night. Finally, this Holy Communion points us beyond the present, into the future. Then the union of Jesus and his disciples and the union of his disciples with one another will be completed and perfected in the kingdom of God.

In the meantime, he has given us his body and blood as our food and his love as the model for our lives. While we wait for the fullness of the kingdom, we have his meal to eat and his commandment to obey.

PHILIP H. PFATTEICHER
East Stroudsburg University
East Stroudsburg, Pennsylvania

114

Our Redeemer through Suffering
John 19:17-30

This is the church's service of worship in which it ponders the death of Jesus Christ. Why should we have that custom? Our altars have crosses standing on or hanging over them. Officiants at our services make the sign of the cross at various moments in their procedures. Many of our people make the sign of the cross before and after prayer. Why should a whole sermon and service emphasize the cross of Jesus Christ? More: we say in our creeds that we believe that Jesus Christ died on the cross for our sins. Do we need special reminders? We believe that several days after the crucifixion he rose from the dead. Is the cross really that important by comparison with the joy and wonder of his rising from the dead?

More than that: in our services of Holy Communion we say that we receive the body and blood of Jesus Christ, and that reminds us of his death. In our Baptism we are buried with Christ into his death. Why another whole service about it?

One reason is that the very frequency of mention may make the cross mean less to us Christians than it should. When we say we believe that Jesus died on the cross for us, we may be making the cross a matter of teaching with which we agree rather than medicine or food that we take for our health. All of us can use help to be able to say with St. Paul: "But far be it from me to glory except in the cross of our Lord Jesus Christ, by which the world is crucified to me, and I to the world" (Gal. 6:14). The cross means that Jesus is redeemer, savior, helper, rescuer— the only one that we have, and that he is all of that through suffering.

More Than Sympathy

The cross is a symbol of worship. We wear it as an ornament in jewelry. But we have to think twice to realize that it was a fiendish instrument of torture, so evil that it is seldom employed in our present world. Our text from John's gospel spares no detail to reinforce the horror of the cross of Jesus Christ—its injustice, the jibes of prestigious opponents, stolid executioners gambling for the clothing, the howling mob yelling for blood, the grieving mother beneath the cross. When we take time to think about this horror and pain, we may find ourselves moved to pity. The piety of the church has made much of "the sacred

115

head now wounded." Our Lenten devotions have helped us to focus on this pain and to respond with sympathy.

But this means that we have to beware of the satisfaction with the feeling of sympathy as the aim of the whole story. Many centuries of Christian piety have conspired to create that impression: "Be moved to tears and fear by the horror of the cross and then you are a bit closer to God." But that idea has come out of the opinion that God is vengeful, that God is interested in making people suffer, beginning with his own Son. That means that the aim of our own life has to be somehow to escape that determination of God to make us suffer the way the Son suffered. But when we surrender to that opinion, the whole Christian gospel and its plan of life goes down the drain and is nullified, and so it actually has done for many people. A simpler response to that opinion is going on in our own time, namely just not to think about God at all. This is a grotesque perversion, a defeat, of the story of Christ's cross.

God Wills the Suffering

Having said that, we have to make sure that we are not removing God from suffering altogether—Christ's and our own. "He couldn't be that mean"—how often we have heard or even thought that view of God in order to make trouble more comfortable or understandable.

The psalm for this service is Psalm 22. It is the cry of the believing worshiper and child of God for his help out of the extremity of suffering. Both Matthew's and Mark's accounts of the crucifixion of Jesus put the first words of that psalm, in their original language, into the lips of the suffering Christ: "My God, my God, why hast thou forsaken me?" When we first heard that cry from the cross we may have wondered whether Jesus was actually succumbing to littleness of faith, as we are apt to do from time to time under our own suffering. It helps us therefore to read on in the psalm: "I will tell my people what you have done. I will praise you in their assembly. . . . He answers when they call for help." The story of the cross is depicting our Lord at the climax of three hours of sub-mitting himself to God for death in life, and God goes on to raise him from that dreadful death.

Can we find God's purpose in this puzzling account? In our Second Lesson the writer to the Hebrews searches for an answer: "Although he was a Son, he learned obedience through what he suffered" (5:8). God had a program before Jesus Christ. The way of suffering and trouble had begun in the manger stall in Bethlehem; it went on in the flight into Egypt; it led through years of poverty, misunderstanding, and rejection; it only climaxed on the cross. All the way this was the plan of the loving Father. How can this be? What is loving in that?

We begin to get an answer in that word about Jesus in Hebrews: *obedient*. People are cruel to us when they make us do something against our will. But Jesus is in on the program. Hebrews 10 uses Psalm 40 to voice that accord of Jesus Christ with the Father's will: "How I love to do your will, my God! I keep your teaching in my heart . . . . Lord, I know you will never stop being merciful to me. Your love and loyalty will always keep me safe" (Ps. 40:8,11 TEV). Do we still have questions about the cross, and about that obedience of Jesus?

The Cross Is for Us

If we had only the story of the crucifixion in the gospel of John we might be in trouble on this Good Friday. But we have the whole gospel. It brings the story of how God gave his Son into the world to be the Word of his help to the human race—and to us right here. The Second Lesson puts it this way: "He became the source of eternal salvation to all who obey him." In the cross God is reaching out not just to his Son, but to us. "He gave him up for us all"—that is the plot to this amazing story. Christ is priest, high priest for us all, in God's plan. We are the aim, the purpose, that God had for us all when he gave up his Son into his death.

But God reaches out to us not from a distance, or from the manner of an indulgent parent, but as the helping Father. The Lord disciplines the people whom he loves (Heb. 12:6). And it is the story of Christ's cross that brings the way of God home to us. For here God is taking the whole human race to himself. What he is doing on the cross he is doing for us all. The dreadful scene of the crucifixion is the loving Father at work not only to his Son, but to us all. A few hours before the event of our text Jesus in the upper room said to his disciples: "In the world you have tribulation; but be of good cheer, I have overcome the world" (John 16:33). He would signal that overcoming when he would rise from the dead on the third day. But Jesus made clear that he had already done the job. He did it when he came into the world as a baby, when he walked the pathways of Palestine as a religious teacher helping and feeding and healing even when people were ready to shout, "Crucify him."

What in the world is going on here, that this way of help is the way of sorrows, his and ours? Two great facts work together in this process, and we have to keep them together to understand them at all. They are that God forgives, and that we accept that forgiveness by faith.

In the Cross God Forgives

On the cross Jesus cried out with a plea for the very people that were executing him: "Father, forgive them; for they know not what they do" (Luke 23:34). There is nothing else in the world that is quite like God's forgiveness. For it means that God forgives. God does not hold our sin against us, even though we thwart the plan for which we were put into the world. God forgives.

How does the cross of Jesus Christ have something to do with God's forgiving human failure? Religious teachers have struggled for words to describe this. They have called the work of Jesus Christ on the cross *substitutionary*; Jesus takes our place. Or it is *forensic*, as though he paid a price that balanced out our wrong. Or it is an *example* for us of the way we ought to forgive people who wrong us; it has a moral influence. But God's forgiveness is probably deeper and bigger than any words that we find to describe it. It is altogether the work of God. God does it all; it does not depend on us; it comes out of God's own nature and reaches down to us altogether out of God's own grace.

But that is true also of the other component of God's goodness through the cross, namely that we take hold of that forgiveness by faith. We have been saying that faith is more than simply accepting a truth or agreeing with a doctrine. When we believe, we are reaching out for help from God, a help that we can get nowhere else, a help that is there for us only as we take it. We are helped and saved by faith, we like to say; but we have to remember that even that faith is the gift and work of God in us.

In the Cross God Helps Us to Believe

Here comes the great gift of Good Friday to us today: God's Son went to the cross so that we are able to believe. No matter how much we have heard about the cross, no matter how many crosses abound in our lives, the one big need remains that we find Christ's death the way of God's forgiveness to us, and we have to find in the word of that cross the constant renewal of our faith. At first sight this might seem offensive, that God would use the spectacle of human weakness and cruelty to help us trust in him and give us the power to grasp forgiveness. But that is exactly what God is trying to do: to have us give up any confidence in human goodness and power, least of all our own goodness and piety,

118

but simply find in his Son, given up for us all, the gift not only of forgiveness from God but even of faith in God.

Reflect for a moment on this method of God's love. God is putting the weight and stress not on our ability and excellence and piety, but on the work of the Son. God is reaching not into our own excellencies and piety but into our handicaps and weaknesses, and into our very death, as the Son undergoes death for us all. What is great about the cross and its story is not simply that it is so different, such a once-in-history act by which God brings help, but that in one sweep God reaches into all the corners of our lives, into their darkness and death itself, as giving up his Son for us all.

That's why we call this day Good Friday. Here the act of God makes all the difference. God reaches down into our hearts over and over to give us, right where we need it, the forgiveness of our sins and the will in our hearts to trust in it for life. God forgives our sins, he makes us his own, and keeps us all the way to the life that is to come.

Yes, indeed, we call this Friday Good!

RICHARD R. CAEMMERER SR.
St. Louis, Missouri

THE RESURRECTION OF OUR LORD—EASTER DAY

Christ's Resurrection and Our Deepest Needs
Mark 16:1-8

Jesus was nailed to Calvary's cross at nine o'clock on a Friday morning. Six cruel hours later his body and the bodies of the men who were crucified with him were hastily cut down from the rough beams on which they died. The sun was lowering in the Judean sky. Jewish law decreed that an executed criminal had to be buried before sunset on the day he died (Deut. 21:23). Also, in a few hours the Sabbath would begin. For Jews, no burials could take place on that day. The Romans who were in charge of the crucifixion had no such laws. In other places they often let bodies hang on crosses for weeks as a warning to others. But the Romans were sensitive to the religious customs of the Jews, especially during this holy time of Passover, and so the bodies of Jesus and his companions in death were removed from their crosses that same Friday afternoon.

119

The bodies of the two malefactors were probably thrown into crude graves. Jesus, at least, was buried in a proper tomb. Joseph of Arimathea, a wealthy member of the Sanhedrin and a secret disciple of the young Nazarene, arranged with Pontius Pilate to have Jesus' body taken to a peaceful garden. There the body was wrapped in linen and placed in a new tomb which Joseph had prepared for his own eventual use. The tomb was sealed with a large stone. Because of Joseph's caring, Jesus' body was treated with more respect than was usually given to that of an executed man.

But there were three women who wanted to do more. Mary Magdalene, Mary the mother of James, and Salome wanted to wash and anoint the body with spices according to the custom of their people. There had been no time to do that in the haste of Friday afternoon. The women waited through the Sabbath. And then, very early on the first day of the week, they set out with ointments in hand to care for the body of their beloved teacher and friend.

Their journey to the tomb would result in a heartpounding ride on an emotional roller coaster. Within the space of a few minutes their attitudes would change from determination laced with concern, to amazement, to fear. But the experience these women had on that first Easter morning point us to the source of the strength we need to live our lives more fully, the promise we need to live our lives more hopefully, and the confidence we need to minister more faithfully.

The Strength We Need to Live More Fully

The two Marys and Salome were determined to complete the job they set out to do. We can admire their spirit. Knowing that a large stone blocked the entrance to the tomb, and aware that they didn't have the strength to move it on their own, they might have decided to stay home. The body would have to remain as it was. But their love for Jesus wouldn't allow them to do that. They had to try. But we should also admire their grasp on reality. As they made their way to the tomb, they said to one another, "Who will roll away the stone for us from the door of the tomb?" As determined as they were to complete their task, they recognized that determination alone wouldn't be enough. They would need someone to help them. They knew that soldiers had been posted at the tomb by the chief priests. They feared that Jesus' body would be taken away by his disciples, who then might claim that he had been resurrected. Perhaps the women hoped that the soldiers might be persuaded to help, or would allow a gardener to help them move the stone.

They would need only a brief time to wash and anoint the body. The women knew they would need help.

Many people, especially Americans, never like to admit that they need the help of others in any significant way. In 1893 at a meeting of the American Historical Association, Frederick Jackson Turner delivered a seminal lecture on "The Significance of the Frontier in American History." In that presentation he agreed with a report of the superintendent of the federal census that by the year 1890 the American frontier had closed. From coast to coast the United States was a settled land. But as Turner pointed out, the long existence of an unsettled frontier had shaped American culture in multiple ways. More than nine decades later, our thinking continues to be influenced by our frontier past, particularly by our admiration for the pioneers' "rugged individualism." But that esteem is based largely on legend. Some pioneers were loners. But most of them, interested in building communities, cooperated with each other for defense, for barter and trade, for the maintenance of order, and for the establishment of schools and churches.

Our 20th-century world has become an interdependent "global village." The more complex our society becomes, the more dependent we are on others for goods, services, and social cooperation. We can't do everything ourselves. Acknowledging that basic truth is a step in breaking down the pride that sometimes prevents us from reaching out for help. To be sure, the gospel constrains us to be inner-directed in terms of living out the Christian values we profess. But none of us is so strong in character that we don't need the support of other Christians in being inner-directed. That's one of the reasons we come together for corporate worship—supportive fellowship. We should not selfishly manipulate people to stroke our often inflated egos, to accept the blame for our weaknesses, or to tell us that we are OK when we aren't. But we should responsibly seek and gratefully accept help to strengthen our lives. Nonetheless, many people with emotional or relational problems limit their lives by refusing to seek help from a pastoral counselor, psychologist, or psychiatrist when they ought to do so. They feel it would be a sign of weakness to admit that they can't solve all their problems on their own. Pride is their real weakness. Others limit their lives by turning aside the caring support offered to them by family and friends, or by declining to build mutually supportive relationships on a daily basis in the giving and receiving of Christian love.

Jesus was the most inner-directed person who ever lived, and he never manipulated people for any reason, but he was not the kind of "rugged individualist" who felt he should or could live his life alone, or carry out his mission by himself. At the beginning of his ministry he called

121

12 men to be his disciples. He gave thanks for them in his high-priestly prayer. Sometimes they failed him when he needed them most: during his fiery trial of the spirit in the Garden of Gethsemane he found them sleeping. Yet, after his resurrection, he entrusted the future of his ministry to them in the great commission. But above all, he reached out to his Father God. It was in God's Word that he found the resources to withstand the tempter's power in the wilderness. Sometimes he spent whole nights in prayer. He relied on his Father to provide the strength he needed to confront the Pharisees, to bear rejection, and to go to Golgotha to die.

We need the help that only God can provide to live our lives fully. The responsibilities, cares, sorrows, uncertainties, and moral ambiguities of daily life deplete our spiritual resources. We need those resources steadily renewed by meeting God daily in disciplined prayer and Bible study, and by opening our lives regularly to the energizing power of God's Word in preaching, teaching, and Spirit-filled corporate worship. The three women who went to the tomb knew that determination, no matter how rugged, wouldn't be enough to move the stone. They knew they would need help. We too need help to move the stones of moral confusion, relational concerns, and despair that block our way to fuller authentic living. We need to reach out to others for support, especially the support of fellow Christians. But above all, we need to reach out for God's undergirding strength. And so we sing to our gracious Lord: "I need thee every hour, In joy or pain; Come quickly and abide, Or life is vain" (*SBH* 479). He is able to meet our hourly need of him because he is a living Lord. Except for a messenger, the tomb was empty!

The Promise We Need to Live More Hopefully

When the women arrived at the tomb, the help they knew they would need had already been provided. The stone was rolled away. But more than that, there was no dead body. The young man who met the women inside the tomb declared "Do not be amazed; you seek Jesus of Nazareth, who was crucified. He has risen, he is not here; see the place where they laid him." "Do not be amazed," he said. But of course they were! Who wouldn't have been?

In 1685 when King Charles II of England lay dying, the best physicians from throughout the realm were brought to the king's bedside to save the monarch's life. They made a valiant effort. But the king was a dying man, and the king died. Abraham Cowley, a poet of the time, wrote a verse upon the king's death: "Let Nature and Art do what they please, When all is done, Life's an Incurable Disease." Truer words were never written. No one ever gets out of life alive. The two Marys and Salome knew that. They also knew that the dead remain dead. Those are immutable facts of nature. But in the resurrection of Jesus Christ God reversed the natural order. One of the world's most ancient and poignant questions is Job's: "If a man die, shall he live again?" (Job 14:14). Nature's answer is a cold and absolute no. But God's answer is a resounding yes! Jesus' glorious promise is this: "I am the resurrection and the life; he who believes in me, though he die, yet shall he live, and whoever lives and believes in me shall never die" (John 11:25-26).

There are times when death comes mercifully into a person's life—when a person is no longer able to experience life consciously or to relate meaningfully to other human beings. Since death is not the culturally taboo subject it used to be, more people are accepting it as a natural part of life. But, elementally, death remains "the last enemy" (1 Cor. 15:26).

With each passing day, hour, and minute each of us is moving closer to the time of his or her death. As I approach the half-century mark in my life, I am increasingly aware of that reality, and of the pressing certainty that I won't have time to read all the books I would like to read, to meet all the people I would like to meet, to see all the places I would like to see, to do all the things I would like to do. The gospel constrains me to keep growing, but I increasingly realize that, as a limited human being, I won't ever preach or write as clearly as I would like, express my caring to others as fully as I would wish, face my lack of caring as squarely as I should, or understand as much about the knowns and unknowns of our human existence as I would desire. My life is limited by time. "The last enemy" is waiting for me.

The truth that death is the last enemy is felt the most desperately when we stand at the head of an open grave which is about to receive the body of a beloved mate, parent, or child. We cry out inwardly for, at the very least, one more day, one more hour, one more minute to say "I love you," to take back what we wish we hadn't said or done, to say what we left unsaid, to do what we left undone. Just one more word. One more touch. The natural reality of death always answers no. That's all there is. There will be no more.

But thanks be to God for the victory that is promised us through the resurrection victory of his Son! Our disappointments about the limits of this mortal life will be wiped away by the marvelous truth that belongs to every Christ follower: "What no one ever saw or heard, what no one ever thought could happen, is the very thing that God prepared for those who love him" (1 Cor. 2:9 TEV). By God's grace that promise will be completely fulfilled on the other side of heaven's line. And although we will be parted for a season from our loved ones, God promises us that ultimately there will be the opportunity for much more than one more touch or word. There will be the gift of much more than one more minute, hour, or day; there will be the reach of all eternity. God promises us an infinitely joyous reunion with our loved ones and all the faithful in the kingdom fully come, and that all of our relationships will be more secure than anything that we can imagine on this side of heaven's line. But even now—and especially now—living by the strength of God's resurrection promise brings security to our lives by casting out our fear that "the last enemy" will defeat us and our loved ones forever, and constrains us to care about the security of other people's lives beyond our family circles.

The Confidence We Need to Minister More Faithfully

After declaring that Jesus was raised from the dead, the young man at the empty tomb told the women, "Go, tell his disciples and Peter that he is going before you to Galilee; there you will see him, as he told you." At that the women's amazement turned to fear. Here is the original ending to Mark's gospel: "And they went out and fled from the tomb for trembling and astonishment had come upon them; and they said nothing to any one, for they were afraid." The ending Mark wrote to his gospel seems to be a "downer." We are left with three persons too frightened to speak. We can understand why, in later years, others felt moved to provide a more "upbeat" ending to Mark, and did so in what older versions of the Bible present as verses 9 through 20. But modern versions end where Mark did. Good enough! Because, in being true to Mark's original ending, there is a lesson to be learned. Of course the women were frightened. In the space of two minutes or so they were trying to adjust to the young man's declaration that Jesus was alive. After all, his story was too good to be true. But it was and is the story too good *not* to be true! The other Gospels, the history of the church, the whole Christian message make clear that eventually the fear the women experienced at the empty tomb was overmatched by the responsibility they felt to tell Peter and the others what the young man had told them: "He is not here, he is risen. He is in Galilee, he is in the world. You can see him there. Go, look." And the resurrected Christ did meet his disciples in Galilee, in Jerusalem, in the world.

We have almost 2000 years of Christian history to help us grasp the truth that Christ is risen and alive. Yet sometimes in the face of the suffering that fills this world we fear he isn't. But look with clear eyes in the light of his own declaration in the parable of the sheep and goats that he will be in the world with those who suffer. Where was the living

Christ while nine million Jews and Gentiles were being systematically murdered in the death camps of Nazi Germany? He was there suffering with the victims, crying for mercy and for an end to the vicious moral disease of anti-Semitism and all twisted views that demean the worth of human life. Where was the living Christ during those long centuries when black people were held as slaves in this nation and degraded by segregation? He was in the slave markets and on the freedom marches in Selma, Birmingham, and Chicago, crying for justice. The living Christ is alive today with sufferers in Lebanon, in Central America, in the ghettos of this nation. He is crying for peace and for us to love one another because he has first loved us. He is in the world. You can see him there. Go, look.

Every Christian generation is called to provide a positive ending to Mark's gospel—not by adding to the text, but by seeking and serving the resurrected Christ, who is alive in this world calling us to serve where he already is. He provides us with the confidence to overmatch our fear and minister faithfully to him and those whom he loves in our giving, serving, and witness.

The resurrected Christ meets our deepest needs. He is the source of the strength we need to live our lives more fully. He proclaims the resurrection promise that we need to live more hopefully. He provides us with the confidence we need to minister more faithfully. And so the risen Christ declares: "Go therefore and make disciples of all nations, baptizing them in the name of the Father and of the Son and of the Holy Spirit, teaching them to observe all that I have commanded you; and lo, I am with you always, to the close of the age" (Matt. 28:19-20).

LARRY L. LEHMAN
Lutheran Church of the Holy Trinity
Lancaster, Pennsylvania

The Resurrection Difference
John 20:19-31

"I've never seen such a crowd in church," the woman exclaimed. I didn't know her, but apparently she was impressed by the number of people here for Easter worship. Then, as she was shaking my hand and moving toward the front door, she added, "Do you suppose it will make any difference?"

I held on to her hand so she couldn't get away. "What do you mean?" I said. "Will *what* make a difference?"

"Easter," she shot back. "Will *Easter* make any difference for all these people, or will life tomorrow be the same as it was yesterday?"

Will Life Go on "As Usual"?

Will it make any difference? The question has stayed with me all week. This resurrection business that we celebrated last Sunday with so much gusto—with such magnificent music, with a record crowd—will it make any difference? For the throngs of people who worshiped last Sunday, will life in this church or elsewhere, go on "as usual," as this unknown person asked, or will life in some way be different? Will it make any difference?

Even a quick glance at today's texts reveals that the resurrection *did* make a difference in the lives of the apostles. The difference wasn't that everything from this point on was now wonderful for them. As we get into the Acts of the Apostles, we read about the intense opposition encountered by the apostles. For Stephen, faith in the resurrected Christ meant a barrage of stones and death. For Paul, it meant jail. And for Peter, as legend has it, faith in the resurrected Christ meant his own cross. So the resurrection difference wasn't an end to life's difficulties and disappointments, but for those followers of Jesus there was a difference. And the words of St. John, in today's Gospel, outline for us this resurrection difference.

God Is Alive and Well and Here

The resurrection difference was knowing that they were living in the presence of the living Lord. "On the evening of that day . . ." wrote John, "Jesus came and stood among them."

A couple of days before, they had thought he was dead, that God had abandoned them, that Jesus—this one for whom they had given up everything to follow, this one on whom they had pinned all their hopes—was dead. They had seen him hanging on the cross. They had seen him breathe his last. He was dead. There was no question about it. But now, here he was—among them.

So God wasn't dead after all. God hadn't removed himself from their world, or from our world and our lives. Even though there are days when that seems to be the case—when we wonder where God is, why

126

God doesn't do something about this mess, why evil seems to have the upper hand, why God remains silent in the face of our tears and prayers—the resurrection difference is that God is alive and well *and here*, with us. God *still* is at work in the world.

Peace That Frees

The resurrection difference also meant a profound sense of peace. "Peace be with you," Jesus said to those frightened disciples. Then he said it again, "Peace be with you."

The peace which the resurrected Christ imparted to his apostles was not the tranquil and serene life; neither was it the absence of conflict. The story of the early church reveals just the opposite. Rather, the peace of God is an inner sense of well-being; it's the deep conviction that everything is right between God and me, that everything is OK, that my life is in order and in God's hands, no matter what.

The story is told of a little boy with a terminal illness. Although it had never been discussed with his parents, this boy knew—as do most dying people—that he was dying. So one day he asked his mother, "Mom, what's it like to die? Will it hurt?"

As the mother mustered up her composure, she searched for an answer her child could relate to. "Charlie," she said, "do you remember when you used to play with your friends all day? You'd be so tired that when we'd sit around and watch TV after supper, you'd fall asleep in the chair with your clothes on. Well, that wasn't where you belonged. But in the morning, you always woke up where you *did* belong—in your own bed in your own room. Dad had carried you up the stairs, into your room, and tucked you into your own bed where you belonged.

"Charlie," she continued, "I think that's what death is like. It's like waking up some morning and finding ourselves in another room—in the place where we belong—safe in the strong, loving arms of Jesus."

That's the peace that the resurrected Christ imparts to his people—the knowledge, the conviction, the comfort, the confidence that we belong to him, that no matter what happens in this life, on this earth, we belong to God.

It's that peace—that sense of well-being, that sense of *shalom*—that sets a person free to live for others, to risk his or her life for the sake of the gospel. It's that peace that freed Peter to boldly proclaim the truth, as we hear in today's Second Lesson. It's that peace that freed Paul from the fear of public opinion, from the fear of Caesar, and even from the fear of death. And it's that sense of peace—that confidence that a person belongs to God no matter what—that freed Dietrich Bonhoeffer and

Kai Munk and Martin Luther King Jr. to risk their lives for the sake of the resurrected Christ. It's the peace that frees us, too.

A New-found Purpose

The resurrection difference, you see, means life marked with purpose. "As the Father has sent me," said Jesus, "even so I send you."

When someone asks that age-old question, "What's life all about?" we don't tell them to do their own thing, to get all the gusto out of life they possibly can, because they only go around once. We tell them the story of Jesus and his resurrection. We tell them the story that gave birth to the Christian church, the story that turned a small band of disillusioned disciples into people of hope, into a band of world-upside-down-turners. We tell them the story that tells us that we're more than poor players who strut and fret on an empty stage, but that we're here to be God's servants, to tell the story of God's love to the world, to be advocates for the poor, to be seekers of justice, to be the salt of the earth, the leaven of society.

When ordered to hold his tongue, Peter, a different man because of the resurrection, boldly replied, "We are witnesses to these things" and "we cannot but speak of what we have seen and heard."

Power to Get the Job Done

Finally, the resurrection difference is power. "When he said this," John wrote, "[Jesus] breathed on them, and said to them, 'Receive the Holy Spirit.'"

God not only gives us a job to do, but God gives us what we need to get the job done. God gives us the Holy Spirit, and that's all we need, for it was the power of God's Spirit that raised Jesus from the dead. It's that same Spirit the resurrected Christ promised and gave to his disciples and the same Spirit who still today injects the same resurrection power into dry bones to give them new life, to renew our broken spirits, and to restore to us the joy of salvation. It's the same Spirit who produces in us the gifts of love and joy, of peace and faithfulness and goodness. It's the same Spirit who gives us courage and strength to cope with the crushing circumstances too often confronting us in life.

"Receive the Holy Spirit." That's the power of God—resurrection power and resurrection difference—given to you.

The Risk of Faith

The resurrection of Christ—Easter—made all the difference in the world for those apostles. There's no doubt about it. But the question is still before us: Will it make any difference for those people who celebrated the resurrection last Sunday? Will it make any difference for us? For you and me? That *is* the question, isn't it?

It can, of course. The resurrection can make the same difference for us as it did for the apostles. We can go through life as they did—knowing the presence of the resurrected Christ, living in his peace, plunging into life with purpose and power, with the same reckless abandon, afraid of nothing, secure in the knowledge that we belong to the resurrected one, to the one who has power even over death.

Life *can* be different. And *we* can know this resurrection difference, too, just as they did, and just as Thomas finally did, when, in spite of his reluctance and scepticism, he took the risk of faith—when he fell down on his knees and blurted out in faith, "My Lord and my God."

LESLIE G. SVENDSEN
St. Philip's Lutheran Church
Fridley, Minnesota

THIRD SUNDAY OF EASTER

The Resurrection Today
Luke 24:36-49

Jesus was crucified, dead, and buried. Those who had followed him were cast down in gloom. In their time together they had come to love Jesus, and at his death they suffered the grief that is always felt when a loved one dies. But there was more here than the normal grief in the time of death. They had followed Jesus with the high hopes that he was the Messiah, the Christ, the one sent from God to free the people of God from their oppressors. But when Jesus died, it seemed the final proof that their hopes had been in vain. A dead Messiah could never set them free.

Some of the women who had followed Jesus went to the tomb to pay their last respects and found the tomb empty and heard the good news that Jesus was not dead but risen. But the men brushed aside the women's testimony as an idle tale. Later, two of the followers were encountered by the risen Jesus on their way to Emmaus and they hurried home to tell the good news to the others. And, as the Gospel of the day tells us, even as they were telling their story Jesus appeared in their midst.

129

Inevitably, they were startled and afraid. They took the risen Jesus for a ghost. And so Jesus showed them his hands and his feet and he called on them to feel him for themselves to see that he was in fact real. And, to clinch it, Jesus ate before them. At last the followers were ready to believe, and Jesus began to interpret the resurrection as the fulfillment of the Scriptures.

The One-Dimensional Age

I doubt that any of us today can hear this passage of Scripture without feeling a keen sense of envy for the people who had the opportunity to see and feel the reality of the risen Jesus. We tell ourselves, "Oh, if only I could have an experience like that, my doubts would flee and my faith would be strong and unshakable. But, alas, it is so different today! Jesus seems so far away, so long ago, that belief is not easy."

A few years ago the philosopher Herbert Marcuse described our age as being "one-dimensional." That is, he charged that we live our lives and do our thinking in the one dimension of this space-time world in which we find ourselves. For us reality is limited to this world that we experience. Someone has summed up the one-dimensional age by saying that, if we cannot see, feel, hear, taste or smell it, if we cannot make a profit with it or kill somebody with it, we say that it does not exist. We are an age of doubt, because we want the proof of our religion in terms that can be confirmed within this one dimension of our life.

I recall hearing the well-known preacher, Donald Soper, tell of a conversation that he had with the famous Christian scholar James Hastings, who at the time was in his nineties. Soper asked him what were the major changes he had seen in his long ministry. Hastings answered, "When I began to preach, the one thing that you could be sure of was that everyone in the congregation was aware of a problem of guilt. But today the only thing that you can be sure of is that everyone before you has a problem of doubt." I think that those words are still relevant today. In religious matters we do tend to be an age of doubters. That is why the Gospel of the day fills us with envy. Those present on this occasion received concrete proof of seeing and touching the risen Jesus.

A one-dimensional age seeks to overcome its doubts by finding concrete proofs for its religious beliefs within the one dimension in which it lives. We hear the stories of how accepting Christ has brought material wealth to believers, miraculously cured illnesses, and so on. We grab hold of such stories because they seem to be affirming the truth of Christianity within that one area of experience that we accept as being really real.

130

The Need for the Holy Spirit

At first sight, our Gospel of the day may seem to confirm the one-dimensional age. Jesus gave his gathered followers the concrete proof of his resurrection in terms of seeing and touching. But when we read further, we find that Jesus tells them not to set forth on their mission of telling the good news to the world "until you are clothed with power from on high." Clearly this is a reference to the coming of the Holy Spirit at Pentecost. The Holy Spirit is God within us, the sense of the presence and the power of God abiding within our personal lives. This means that Jesus did not see as sufficient for Christian mission the concrete proof of his resurrection in terms of this one dimension of the space-time world. He pointed them to what more was needed—the indwelling of the Holy Spirit.

The significant thing for us is this: the Holy Spirit is available to us today. We do not need to envy those early Christians because they had a proof of the resurrection in Jesus' physical presence. They were not ready to go forth until they had the same confirmation that is offered to us today—the presence of the Holy Spirit in our lives.

In John 20 there is a story that closely parallels the Gospel for today. The disciple Thomas has heard from others that Jesus has risen from the dead, but he refuses to believe in their testimony. He says that he cannot believe until he has seen and touched Jesus for himself. When Jesus appears to Thomas, Thomas is allowed to touch him. Thomas then believes and hails the risen Jesus as his Lord and God. Jesus, however says to him, "Have you believed because you have seen me? Blessed are those who have not seen and yet believe." As in our Gospel reading Jesus warns the group to wait until the Holy Spirit comes, so Jesus tells Thomas that those who come to believe without the concrete evidence given to Thomas are to be blessed.

The Holy Spirit calls us to lift our eyes beyond this one-dimensional world in which we live. The Holy Spirit brings us into the presence of that which transcends the space-time reality. Why believe the resurrection of Jesus? Is it enough that once, far away, some men actually saw and touched the risen Jesus? Or do you believe because Jesus, through the Holy Spirit, lives in your heart today? Surely, Christian faith rests on the presence of the risen Lord in our lives.

When the Holy Spirit lifts our eyes beyond this one-dimensional world, we no longer seek the proof of Christianity in concrete and material

131

terms that can be offered by it. We know that the apostle Paul had some "thorn in the flesh" from which he prayed to be freed. If the miracle had occurred, it would have been the kind of proof that the one-dimensional world could understand. It would be material evidence of God's presence. But, Paul tells us, no miracle occurred. Nonetheless Paul could affirm his faith in the beautiful passage from Romans 8, where he affirms that no tribulation, distress, persecution, nor death itself can separate us from the love of Christ. Paul had the inner assurance of the Holy Spirit, and that gave him the power to continue to follow Christ faithfully even when everything in the space-time world seemed to say that he was abandoned. When we live in the Holy Spirit and the Holy Spirit lives in us, we shall no longer seek proof of our faith in material success or physical health, or other such things.

The Desire to Control

One-dimensional thinking leads us not simply to look for proofs of our faith in this space-time world and its gifts, but it also has conditioned us to think that we need always to so manipulate and control things that we bring about the desired results. Human beings have made great progress in controlling and using this space-time world. We engage in research to control disease; we put in hard work and lots of money to get a craft into space; we seek inventions to build computers and to harness the power of electronics. All of this is as it should be, although we sinful human beings do not always put our physical triumphs to the best use. The trouble arises when, as one-dimensional people, we assume that the same principles apply to our relationship to all of reality. In that case our faith itself becomes a matter of our putting forth the proper effort, using the right ideas with diligence. If we are to have faith, then we must manipulate ourselves into faith with the right actions.

Waiting for God

The Gospel of the morning gives us a radically different picture. After the crucifixion the followers of Jesus were not rushing about looking for the risen Jesus. They were crushed and defeated, and they huddled together to try to get some comfort from sharing their sorrow and dismay. It was then that Jesus appeared in their midst. And when Jesus left them, he did not tell them to search for and find the Holy Spirit before beginning their ministry. On the contrary, he told them to stay in the city and *wait* until the gift of the Spirit came. I am sure that, as the disciples waited in the city, they told and retold the incidents of Jesus' life and resurrection. And that is what we can do. We can listen again and again to the Word that comes from the Scriptures. Today, as in the times of the first Christians, the risen Christ appears as the Holy Spirit where the story is told and retold.

In this Easter season the minds of Christians are called back to the report that Jesus arose from the dead. Our doubting age has trouble with such a story. In our one-dimensional world we are certain that dead people don't return. How can we commit our lives on the basis of such reports? Perhaps, if only we had been there to see and touch Jesus we would believe. But would we? Even those who saw and touched him needed more. They were not ready for the mission to which Jesus called them until the Holy Spirit clothed them with power from on high. The same Spirit can do the same for us as was done for the first witnesses of the resurrection. And then we shall be able to sing in the words of the hymn:

> All the doubting and dejection
> Of our trembling hearts have ceased;
> Hail the day of resurrection!
> Let us rise and keep the feast (*LBW* 131).

WILLIAM E. HORDERN, PRESIDENT
Lutheran Theological Seminary
Saskatoon, Saskatchewan

FOURTH SUNDAY OF EASTER

Shepherds We Want to Trust
John 10:11-18

"The trouble with political jokes," goes a one-liner making the rounds these days, "is that some of them get elected." We like to joke about our caretakers, politicians, and other leaders, but in truth we trust them. At least we want to trust them. Indeed, we desperately need to trust them, for they are our hedge against chaos in a disorderly world seemingly full of capricious, dangerous forces. Because we so much want and need to trust our leaders, mostly we do, and despite our jokes we choose to see them as wise, trustworthy, and faithful to those of us who are the

133

led and the protected. Machiavelli was right when he advised princes, "Everyone sees what you seem to be, few experience what you really are."

So it is that we are stunned with fright when startled with the revelation that a president engaged in a cover-up, a police force was on the take, a medical scientist was faking the data of experiments, a professor was taking advantage of a student, a parent was numbing a crying infant with alcohol so as to buy a few moments of quiet. When such things happen, the fabric of society's defenses are rent, the public trust is violated, and we try to salve our wounds with a dose of cynicism. We'll not be fooled again! But we will, sooner or later—and probably sooner. We will again be surprised, though we should not be.

The figures on Mount Rushmore are now solid and sturdy as rocks, but the original editions of those leaders were quivering flesh and blood like ourselves, knowing fear and confusion and loneliness and hatred and jealousy and pettiness and ecstacy and nightmares and a deep, deep need to be loved. Only because those particular leaders never let slip the stuff that would have soiled our image of them, we have now set them up like gods upon a mountain. Others less fortunate fell from grace, the myths of their character and competence exploded. And we fell with them. They proved to be human like ourselves, quivering flesh and blood, needing deeply to be loved and willing to do most anything so as to know such love. The trust that is really shattered is the trust we have in ourselves, a trust to which we barely cling, knowing as we do our own weaknesses. When our leaders prove themselves human, we can only respond with fear of and for ourselves.

When anybody in the Bible talks about shepherds, the speech is really about leaders, and the same is true of Jesus' "Good Shepherd" discourse. When a Jew in Jesus' day heard "shepherd," he or she thought "king" or "queen" at least as quickly as "sheep herder." And the Jews had had their fill of monarchs. There had been some fabled good ones, all right, but even the best of them had their foibles: David his lust, Hezekiah his doubt, Josiah his fanaticism. But there had been some tragic reigns, too, and in the end there was the pronouncement of Ezekiel upon them all: "Ho, shepherds of Israel who have been feeding yourselves! . . . The weak you have not strengthened, the sick you have not healed, the crippled you have not bound up, the strayed you have not brought back, the lost you have not sought, and with force and harshness you have ruled them" (Ezek. 34:2-4). The same words could have applied to Jesus' day, as the Herods had sold the Jewish people to the Romans. What could it mean to speak of a good shepherd? Such a figure could only be the stuff of a bad joke or a wild dream, hardly anything resembling reality.

Yet, no king, no leader, not even the Herods of the world, sets out to lose the flock or feed it to predators. Rare indeed is the public official, the board member, or the pastor who decides to do what is surely reckless and evil. But the best of intentions, when mixed with the complex formulas of the juices that flow inside each of us, produce poisons that weaken, incapacitate, and kill the spirit of a community, a congregation, a people. Worse, each of us is a monarch, a leader, a ruler of a kingdom, however tiny. We affect the lives of others, usually many more than we stop to consider, and sometimes, inevitably, we shepherd badly. With the best of intentions we try to lead, to parent, to husband, to wife, to pastor, to teach, to judge, to administer. But the quivering flesh and blood is uncertain, afraid, addicted, too alone, too weak, too tired. We are lost leaders who wander astray and thus take others along with us deeper and deeper into thickets of a delusion or despair. And leaders, of course, are not allowed to cry out for help. The followers might overhear and the panic be unimaginable. So in the thicket we pretend to know the way. On we go, whistling in the dark (The tune? "Who's Afraid of the Big Bad Wolf"), onward and downward—lost.

Jesus, the Good Shepherd

What we need is a truly trustworthy shepherd, a good shepherd, a rescuing shepherd, one who will seek us out even when we remain unaware of our lostness, one to catch hold of us when we choose deliberately to ignore the fact that we have gone past this same sign three times now and are obviously going in circles. We need a shepherd for the shepherds. The Christian gospel proclaims that such a shepherd has come among us and is hard at work. Who is this good shepherd and what makes him good? Is it one made of teflon and alloys and silicon chips? Not exactly. Though he is one set apart from eternity, we confess, he is quivering flesh and blood, prone to pain and vulnerable like any mother's son.

In one way it is fair to say that it is precisely this which made Jesus the Good Shepherd. He came as one of us with flesh and blood that was his to save or his to give. He chose to give, and that gift, which he willingly made of himself for those he came to seek and to find in their lostness, is what sets him apart from others. For that the Father loved him, says Jesus, and for that we call him good.

That he was one flesh and one blood with those he came to rescue made him different from the hireling; he knew his own, knew them intimately, they were his own flesh and blood. He gave his flesh and

135

blood for his friends—like friend Lazarus, lost in the awful isolation of the tomb for three stinking days, for whom Jesus wept the bitter, wrenching tears of true grief that set his flesh to quivering. He gave his flesh and blood for the crowds upon whom he had compassion, for whom his insides were set to stirring as he watched them lost and hungry like sheep without a shepherd. And he gave his flesh and blood, pierced and wracked with the pangs of death, for his mother and for his beloved disciple as they sat beneath his cross. He knew they would need something, someone, lest they become lost from one another, his good Jewish mother and his faithful Christian disciple. How the threat of that lostness, the lostness of fracture and division, set his flesh and blood to quivering! He gave his dying breath that such terrible lostness be avoided, or if it happened, that it might be undone.

The Good Shepherd was good because he gave his life willingly. He was not robbed of it, not taken advantage of and used. "No one takes my life from me," he proclaimed. "I lay it down of my own accord in order to take it up again." What he had to give he gave. He sacrificed; that is, he gave away for the sake of love what he had to give, and that was his flesh and blood. And the Good Shepherd is also good because he gave what he had for the entire flock, the whole community. His sacrifice was not complete until all of the lost were found, even if that meant leaving the 99 in the wilderness to go and find a single lost one. The Good Shepherd was good because he gave all he had, without reservation. He gave to the death, and that "for the joy that was set before him" (Heb. 12:2). He did not seek suffering, nor glory in it, but suffering stood between himself and his flock, and he chose to give his quivering flesh into that gap that he might have the flock and the flock have him.

The Good Flock

The Good Shepherd who gave his life did indeed take it again. He was raised—in quivering flesh and blood. What he had given away for the sake of love was returned to him. Still it quivered. Still it was pierced. Thomas could stick his finger into the wounds if he wished. But the Shepherd was whole. Still today he gives away for the sake of love his flesh and blood. That he does every time he gives you to me and me to you, taking your fears and anguish and your bitter tears and transforming them into compassion so that you might lay your fleshy hand on mine. And despite its trembling, your hand will assure me I am not lost, not alone. You are there, his flesh and blood for me. I need not fear. Every time he makes your blood boil to watch the injustice that infests and

136

perverts the world and makes even the strong to stray from the ways of wholeness and integrity, he is giving you, sacrificing you, for the sake of love so that others might not be lost.

You are his flesh and blood—quivering, but his. And because you are his he gives you as generously as he gives himself. He gives you his Spirit, and by that Spirit you are led to the places where the giving of your flesh and blood is needed. You, too, give willingly, so that your giving is a true gift, not something taken from you in helpless regret. You need not find places where you will be used, taken advantage of, wasted. But even should there be such misuses of you and the gift that is you as his flesh and blood, there is no giving of your flesh or spilling of your blood that will ever leave you drained forever, discarded, or lost. The promise of the Father is that whatever life is sacrificed, given away willingly for the sake of love, is never lost but is always found—found for eternity and redeemed to the life which knows no bounds.

Still he gives his flesh and blood, also in the meal that we share as the body of Christ. At this table we find our place of belonging, our truest home, our source of strength, our deepest joy, our gladdest songs. We shall never be lost so long as we find our way back to this table, so long as the others of this community hold us close to them and to this fellowship of Christ with the strength of their quivering flesh and blood. Trust this community. It is the good flock of the Good Shepherd. So, let us eat heartily. Let us drink deeply. Let his strength be ours. And let us be on our way.

FREDERICK A. NIEDNER JR.
Valparaiso University
Valparaiso, Indiana

The Vital Vine
John 15:1-8

I remember the day the bulldozers and graders came to our farm. They came to make funny little dirt ribs along the contours of the hills in one of our fields. It was sometime after that before I understood what they were trying to accomplish.

I was riding on the fender of the tractor as my father planted corn in that same field. He was following along one of these strange ribs, making winding rows around the hill until the field was planted from top to bottom. I told him that I thought this seemed quite a bother, a lot of extra work to plant this way. But he said that it was worth it.

He explained to me that these ribs were called "terraces," and they would help to keep the soil from washing into the creek below. It was a way to take care of the land that was taking care of us. Maybe it wasn't the most efficient way to do things. But I remember realizing at the time that there was something very important about this land my family farmed. It demanded our love, our thankfulness, and our tender care.

The Promise of Life in Christ

Over the years, that farm has been not only a means to make a living, to bear fruit as such, but a metaphor of our dependence on our creator God for life itself. In the Gospel for today Christ uses a similar metaphor as he reminds his disciples of the promise of life given to them. He says: "I am the vine, you are the branches. He who abides in me, and I in him, he it is that bears much fruit, for apart from me you can do nothing."

That promise, made to the disciples, is ours today as well. Because Christ abides in us, we are given life and the means to bear fruit. It is a promise that finds its source and strength in the vine—not in the branches nor the fruit, but in the vine, the vital vine. Still it is a promise we find hard to hear.

Branching Out on Our Own

To hear that we are dependent on Christ for life and productivity is not always good news. We all have a tendency to want to be independent and in control of our own lives. No one is immune. A child on the playground demands, "I'll play only if I can be captain!" A construction worker bemoans the ineptitude of his coworker, and cries out "I'd rather do it myself!" It's a process that began the day the doctor severed the umbilical cord that connected us to our mothers. From that moment on, in even the smallest of children, we find ourselves trying to conquer life on our own.

Even the terraces on our family farm are now gone, worn down by age and not replaced. Rows of corn now run by fence lines instead of contours. Production is geater, yes, but at what expense? We who would like to sit in judgment on the farmer, find ourselves demanding low prices for our groceries, and thus increasing pressure on the farmer to produce at all costs. The result is that many of us no longer respect the land, nor live thankfully in its presence, nor seek to care for it. We seek instead to be independent of it and thus able to dominate. We have severed the life-giving line that connected us to the land that cares for us. The result is eroded soil, polluted waters, and an uncertain future.

Because of our desire to be independent and in control, our relationship to Christ suffers the same consequence. We don't want to be dependent on another. We want to dominate, to be like God ourselves. We think we can bear fruit away from the vine, so we sever our ties to Christ, and branch out on our own.

But the text is clear. There is no life apart from Christ. In John 21 Jesus revealed himself to the disciples by the Sea of Tiberias shortly after his resurrection. The disciples had been fishing all night, but had caught nothing. When morning came, Jesus was standing on the beach nearby. He told the frustrated disciples to throw in their nets on the right side of the boat. Suddenly there were so many fish that they were unable to haul them all in. The meaning here is clear. As long as the disciples acted on their own initiative, they caught nothing. But under the Lord's direction and in his presence, they took many fish.

We have no life, and can produce no fruits apart from Christ. If we seek to branch out on our own, we will be lost. The vinedresser will take us away, if only because we have already cut ourselves off.

Fretting over Fruits

There can be a still deeper tragedy in today's lesson. What if we believe that Christ abides in us, yet life still isn't so great? What if the fruits we expected to bear have gone sour?

We know the prevailing thought: one gets what one deserves, or one reaps what one sows. But for many of us, the evidence just isn't there. We have a very real sense of the tragedy of life. Sin, death, and evil still exist. Their power is yet evident in the rampages of cancer, the unpredictability of a deadly accident, the terror of crime and injustice. None of these seem to be just fruits for the labors of God's people. But God's people do suffer. They suffer, and ask why.

The lesson for today responds in two ways. First, we are told that it is the vinedresser's business not only to take away dead branches, but to prune, or to cleanse, living branches. God has taken it upon himself, through the cleansing act of the cross, to finally and completely overcome sin, death, and evil. Through that cross, the vinedresser forgives our sin. Through that cross, the vinedresser conquers death and evil. Only by

139

the vinedresser's careful pruning, careful cleansing, can we continue and even increase the fruits he gives us to bear.

Second, we are reminded that the fruit does not give life. We love to fret over fruits. They usually get all of our attention. Who has ever heard of someone walking into a grove of fruit trees at harvest time and exclaiming, "Why, look at those beautiful trunks!"? We look instead at the fruits. The glory and attention are theirs.

We are always looking to results, to fruits, for proof of our worth. We like to count coup upon the enemies we overcome, and tally up our daily accomplishments. Often it is only when tragedy enters our lives that we realize that our fruits are a poor measure of our value as human beings. Only then do we realize that the fruit does not give life. It is not what is vital.

The Vital Vine

What then is vital? The vine. We are saved, not by the fruit, but by the vine. Because the vine lives, so too we are given life.

When we moved into our home, there was a small tree that had just been planted in our front yard. It was tall and thin, but had several healthy branches at the top. One day it met head-on with a little girl on a bicycle. The little girl was OK. The bicycle was OK. The tree was not. It had been broken off about two feet above the ground. Throughout the rest of that fall and winter, it sat there, like a dead twig marking a make-believe grave.

We made plans to remove the twig that spring and to plant another. It was such a wet spring that we didn't get at it until late in May. Finally one day, armed with spade and shovel, we set out about the task. But to our surprise and delight, there on the tip of that twig were two little buds, just beginning to leaf out. Somehow through all of that winter, it had survived, and with the warm rains of spring, it had come back to life. That summer, it gave life to two new branches, and many more in the years hence.

Because the vine lives, we are also given new life. It is the message of the resurrection we echo each Sunday throughout the year. It is the good news of our Gospel today. Because Christ abides in us, we have life and the means to bear fruit.

The vine, branches, and fruit—all are held together by the one life-giving blood, that of the crucified Christ. That life flows to you and to me through the Word and the sacraments. It is life that flows in you today, even as this Word begins to abide in you. You are given life, not by branching out on your own, or by fretting over fruits, but by the vine, by the grace of Jesus Christ.

BARBARA LUNSTAD-VOGT
First Lutheran Church
Mitchell, South Dakota

SIXTH SUNDAY OF EASTER

You've Got a Friend
John 15:9-17

Many a heart-warming story has been told about friendship, though in these sophisticated days we tend to sneer a bit at sentiment. We keep such careful guard of our emotions that we likely don't allow ourselves to think through what having a real friend might mean to us, and we keep such careful guard of our lives that we never allow ourselves the luxury of having a real friend.

Perhaps it's the mobility of American society that does it. Our family has moved five times, and each time we've had to wrench ourselves away from folks we've grown to love and then find new people in our new place, which isn't easy. In between we've had friends move away from us, just as we would move away from them. Maybe, after a while, we grow wary of starting new friendships that will wind up as nothing more than names on the Christmas card list.

Then, too, human nature being what it is, we might feel as if we've been burned a few times by our friends, and the memory of those experiences makes us hesitant. Friends are as human as anyone else, of course, so they don't always come through for us. They aren't always as sympathetic to our needs as we need them to be, and they are capable of taking us for granted or undervaluing our sensitivities or betraying our confidences. When those kinds of things begin to happen, we find ourselves choosing to do without close friends—not happily, of course, but we don't like to be hurt.

Even so, once in a while, maybe once in a lifetime for most people, we find a friend, a real friend. Another dimension to our existence is thereby defined that cannot be understood in those relationships constructed only of affection or blood or law. Charles Kingsley, when asked

141

the hidden secret of his life, answered, "I had a friend." Many others would say the same, or regret their inability to say it.

This kind of a friendship is of such unique value because it is a relationship without constraint. You need not care about a friend, but you choose to do so. You are under no obligation to tell a friend how you feel, what you hope, what you've done, where you're going, but you want to share your life with that person, even as your friend will share in equal measure with you. A friend could walk out the door of your life at any moment, but will not. Neither will you leave that friend. You would do anything for that person and that friend would do anything for you.

Jesus and His Friends

In the hours before his crucifixion, Jesus talked to his friends about the extent and nature of his friendship. As only he could, he described without embarrassment his love for them, for that motley group of simple men he'd called from their fishing nets and garden patches to go traipsing the dusty roads of Palestine with him. He also commanded them to love one another. And then, feeling the ominous pressure of those insidious forces gathering themselves for the inevitable, Jesus said that the greatest love a person could have for his or her friends would be to die for them.

We've read stories about the nobility of courageous people under extreme circumstances. Fortunately hardly any of us are called on to set such ultimate priorities, but realize what Jesus is saying about friendship. If you would willingly die for a friend, that would be so remarkable an action that it would define a "greater" love.

Parents, for example, have been known to plunge into burning buildings to rescue their children, and to do so without regard for their own safety. Most of us, if pressed, could come up with a list of people in our lives for whom we would willingly lay down our own lives—children, parents, grandsons and granddaughters, brothers, sisters, spouses. But we could be excused for not feeling quite so committed if the life in question is only that of a friend.

A friend holds us under no obligations. There is no defined responsibility between us. So if indeed we would die for the sake of such a relatively casual relationship, could there be a greater love?

Loving without Obligation

It's clear that Jesus understood what was about to happen to him in such terms. For the moment forget all the doctrine with which we properly define his mission and his nature, and see him simply as a visionary—like hundreds of others who have appeared on the world's scene across the years—who had attracted to himself a small band of followers. Not a one of them was worth his trouble and pain in any tangible sense. Nor was he under any obligation to honor the idealism with which they'd been infected because of his teachings. Without a word he could have deserted them, could have disassociated himself from all he'd said to anger the authorities, and slipped back to Nazareth to live out his days in obscurity and safety.

But this he would not do. There he was in the upper room with Peter and Andrew and James and John and all the rest, and if he gave it up now, all that he'd said and done for them would go down the tube. "I am . . ." Jesus had said to them. "I am living water, the bread of life, the good shepherd, the resurrection and the life, the light of the world." "Before Abraham was, I am." And the incredible promise also recorded by John in his gospel: "I am the way, the truth, and the life. No one comes to the Father but by me." Then in those last hours: "You are my friends."

So there was no turning back, not if he loved them. They had invested too much of themselves in him and his gospel, and he was a man of honor. And somehow—he always knew it—somehow it would even be by his death that they would live. He would die because of his love for them.

A Changed Relationship

That Jesus called them his friends as the minutes of his life ticked away demonstrates a new understanding of their relationship to him, a dramatic but necessary change in anticipation of the tragedy that was about to occur. While he lived, Jesus was the authority figure for his disciples, their rabbi, their visible, audible lord and master. He set the direction of their travels, determined what they would do, said what would be said, and decided the audience for the message. The disciples only followed, watched, listened, and obeyed.

But the time came for the disciples to become the apostles. The new pilot must fly solo; the new surgeon must hold another's life in hand without the reassuring presence of an instructor; the new executive must make the lonely decisions appropriate to the office. Jesus told his friends, "I do not call you servants any longer, because a servant does not know what his master is doing. Instead, I call you friends, because I have told you everything I heard from my Father."

143

That good news—everything Jesus heard from his Father—became theirs now to share with the world. And they spread the news with power and perseverance and sacrifice, until new disciples became their friends and the gospel became known to new generations, new tribes and nations, even to the present.

Friends of Christ Today

We today are testimony to that process as it has continued through the centuries. We are also the friends of Christ, and in our time we have been chosen to tell what we have heard, to minister to others even as others have ministered to us.

Friends, we remember, impose no constraints on each other. Our friendship with Jesus Christ is not jeopardized by our reluctance to do his will. His love for us continues regardless. We need not earn his favor any more than he must earn ours.

Nor do friends give each other orders. That had happened with Christ and his disciples, for he was the master and they were the followers, the servants, even the slaves, in a sense. But all that had to change. He gave them one last, all-encompassing commandment: that they love one another as he had loved them. Then he declared that they were no longer his servants, but his friends.

How were they to go about loving each other? What might that have meant in the matter of the Roman occupation of their country or in dealing with the problem of divorce or in defining a code of ethics for rival fishermen along the Sea of Galilee?

That, of course, was up to them, even as similar issues are up to us. We who follow his way are not programmed like computers to spit out canned answers to difficult questions. We are not robots mechanically going through the motions of the Christian faith. We have heads, and we are to use them. We have many convictions colored by our heritage and our associates and even our genes, and there are no two of us alike. The first disciples, legend has it, went in different directions with the gospel—north, south, east, west. In different places, the church took different shapes, had different emphases. There is one body, as Paul declared, but we are many members.

What matters is that there be results. You should go and bear fruit, Jesus told his friends, and your fruit should remain. Otherwise the words are empty, the preaching so much oratorical fluff, the singing and the praying only sentimental pablum. That love with which we have been loved must reveal itself in daily life, in the setting of priorities, in the attitudes we bear toward one another, in the commitment we have to

144

the meeting of human need. The how of it might take as many forms as there are believers, but without results, without fruit, the Lord Jesus is not loved and served.

And as he is our friend, we would love and serve him with all of our being. He gave his life for us. This we declare and believe, and as his friends, now, we give our lives for his people.

CARL T. UEHLING
St. Matthew Lutheran Church
Moorestown, New Jersey

THE ASCENSION OF OUR LORD

Blessed Assurance
Luke 24:44-53

Do you remember the "space race"? It all began in the late 1950s, as the United States and the Soviet Union competed to be first in exploring the various reaches of outer space. Perhaps you recall the names of some of our early astronauts, persons such as Alan Shepard, John Glenn, and Neil Armstrong. They possessed the "right stuff" for being launched into the unknown and doing things never attempted by any other human being. But how about the name of Yuri Gagarin? Do you remember him? On April 12, 1961, this Russian cosmonaut became the first person to travel in space. His spacecraft, *Vostok I*, orbited the earth at a speed of better than 17,000 miles per hour for a total of 89.1 minutes. At the highest point, Gagarin was about 203 miles above the earth's surface. By today's standards, this feat seems small indeed. At the time, however, it clearly threatened our nation's hope of leadership in space.

Yuri Gagarin also said something that compounded America's consternation. Upon his return to earth, this cosmonaut declared that while in orbit, he found no trace of God in outer space. Some of us back then may have wondered, "Is this man attempting to call the ascension of our Lord a hoax?" Perhaps we would still consider it scandalous for anyone to say something similar.

Actually, Yuri Gagarin's statement is irrelevant to the ascension of our Lord. In the Gospel for this day, Luke does inform us that when Jesus parted from his disciples, he "was carried up into heaven." However, this does not mean that he simply drifted up, up, and away like a

145

balloon into space, there to remain through the centuries of time, until his return in glory. Nor does it imply that the Son of God went to a place where the human eye might see him one day through the window of a space capsule. On the contrary, the realm of God transcends the dimensions of human existence. His earthly mission completed, Jesus was in fact cutting the cord that confined him to a moment in time and limited him to a single plot of Palestinian ground. His ascension was his way of freeing himself to be everywhere at once and to reign supreme in all the coming ages. This is the "blessed assurance" that we are here to proclaim and celebrate again today.

Assurance Promised in Christ's Blessing

Let's begin with the biblical record. The risen Christ, we are told by Luke, gave the disciples final words of instruction and promise. He then "led them out as far as Bethany, and lifting up his hands he blessed them." Jesus was doing for them what the Old Testament priests had done over the people of Israel and what Christian pastors still do at the conclusion of every worship service. His hands raised in blessing were promise of God's continuing favor and support. According to Matthew, Jesus verbalized this assurance: "Lo, I am with you always," he said, "to the close of the age" (Matt. 28:20). Henceforth, those disciples would never find themselves alone. As they fanned out from Jerusalem after Pentecost to turn the world upside down with the gospel, their Lord went with each one of them. He walked with Peter along the hot and dusty paths of Judea. At the same time, he accompanied Thomas perhaps as far as India, and with John, he went into exile on the island of Patmos.

As the Ascended One, Jesus was promising to be with his apostles in every age. His presence also inspired those monks who helped preserve the Christian legacy of faith during the Dark Ages. From him Martin Luther drew strength each day for the awesome task of reformation. To him scores of Christians who sought to build a new life in America looked as they struggled to adjust to their environment, to build their homes, and to raise their children. The return of those first disciples to Jerusalem "with great joy" immediately after Jesus ascended from them indicates that they understood this. Do we?

Mission Objectives for the Church

Interestingly, Luke connects such assurance with the church's mission. In fact, the ascension appears both at the end of his gospel and at the opening of Acts, the book in which he sets forth the first chapters in the

146

story of the Christian church. Compare our text with the First Lesson for this day (Acts 1: 1-11). In addition, the nature of its mission was clearly the subject of Jesus' final conversation with his disciples. In Acts 1, we find signs that they were still groping for direction from him. "Lord, will you at this time restore the kingdom of Israel?" they asked. At least some of those disciples still believed that their master might go "political" and become powerful enough to put Caesar in the shade. Jesus moved quickly to dispel all such thinking. For them and for the church in every age thereafter, he defined the mission as one of bearing witness to the gospel. According to Luke 24, he "opened their minds" to understand the central truth of Scripture, "that the Christ should suffer and on the third day rise from the dead, and that repentance and forgiveness of sins should be preached in his name to all nations." To "these things," he also said, "you are witnesses."

Pentecost and the outpouring of the Holy Spirit set this same mission into motion. Together with the other disciples, Peter stood up and directed the crowds whom the Spirit had drawn together to the meaning of Jesus' death and resurrection. He called attention to familiar Scriptures from the Old Testament and proclaimed that the great "plan" that God had chosen to work out through him was for their redemption. "Repent," Peter declared, "and be baptized every one of you in the name of Jesus Christ for the forgiveness of your sins; and you shall receive the gift of the Holy Spirit" (Acts 2:38).

This witness still defines our mission as the Christian church of today. Pope John Paul II dramatized it at Christmas in 1983. He went to Rome's Rebibbia prison and in a bare, white-walled cell, tenderly held the hand that had held a gun aimed to kill him. For 21 minutes, this Christian sat, talked softly to his would-be assassin, Mehmet Ali Agca, and personally forgave the trespass. In a world filled with nuclear arsenals, hostility between nations great and small, terrorism, and unforgiving hatreds, John Paul embraced his enemy and pardoned him. For a moment at least, humankind felt the power of the gospel of Jesus Christ. As it echoed round the world, we were convinced that this is the only real hope for us all.

Tests of Our Faith

We must admit, however, that there are moments that leave us less certain of Jesus' ascension promise. I will always remember my first ascension sermon. The year was 1968, and the place was Washington, D.C. The preaching assignment came during my internship year at a

147

congregation located there. Interns like me customarily drew the less-attended festivals of the church year. Hence, I got the Ascension of our Lord. But back then as much as now, I knew that there could not have been a better moment to proclaim the gospel to which this day points both you and me. That particular spring, Martin Luther King Jr. was gunned down in Memphis; Looting and burning scarred the major cities of our land. The threat of violence hung over the seat of America's federal government every day. On the heels of these events there came the assassination of Robert Kennedy, the Poor People's March on Washington, and rioting in the streets of Chicago while the Democratic Party tried to nominate its presidential candidate. It was enough to shake the confidence of just about everybody. In one way or another, many were asking, "Where is God in all of this?"

The ascension of our Lord provided an assuring answer for me. It announced that Jesus Christ has not left this world to its own devices. Rather, he is its reigning Lord. The context of Luke's account is Christ's triumphant resurrection. Its purpose is to reinforce our assurance of his complete victory over death and all the hosts of evil. Paul, writing to the Philippians, declared that God has also "bestowed on him the name which is above every name, that at the name of Jesus every knee should bow, in heaven and on earth and under the earth, and every tongue confess that Jesus Christ is Lord, to the glory of God the Father" (Phil. 2:9-11). Today and every day, Jesus Christ stands, as it says in our Second Lesson from Ephesians 1, "far above all rule and authority and power and dominion." God our Father "has put all things under his feet and has made him the head over all things for the church, which is his body, the fulness of him who fills all in all." Despite the evidence to the contrary, the Ascended One remains in charge. Even when the world is coming apart at the seams, he holds the loose ends together in his hands. He is, as we confess in the Apostles' Creed, "seated at the right hand of the Father."

Assurance Renewed As We Bless God

The ascension of our Lord still conveys such assurance. Our faith in Christ's promise to stand with us always gets bolstered as we continue to join the Christian community at worship. Perhaps it is more than a coincidence that Luke's gospel begins as it ends. The opening chapter gives us Zechariah's *Benedictus* (Luke 1:68-79). Like him, we are also here to say, "Blessed be the Lord God of Israel, for he has visited and redeemed his people." For with such praises of our God comes the assurance that he will indeed "save" us from "our enemies" and "the

148

hand of all who hate us." The final scene in Luke's gospel, of course, depicts Jesus lifting up his hands, blessing his disciples, and thus assuring them of his continuing favor and support. He gives no less to us, as we, like those disciples, allow God's Spirit to open our minds to understand the Scriptures and to believe the promise that Jesus Christ declares, so that through us, "repentance" and "forgiveness of sins" might be "preached in his name to all nations." May this same "blessed assurance" of our ascended Lord become yours and mine again this day.

JON T. DIEFENTHALER
Bethany-Trinity Evangelical Lutheran Church
Waynesboro, Virginia

SEVENTH SUNDAY OF EASTER

The Name, the World, the Truth
John 17:11b-19

Jesus' work on earth is drawing to a close. After his last supper with his disciples before his crucifixion, he goes off by himself to pray. In a few moments Judas will arrive on the scene to betray Jesus to the soldiers, who will arrest him.

With events around him rising to a climax, what is uppermost on Jesus' mind as he pauses to speak to his Father? We listen as we hear him pray for his disciples, this small, frightened band of 11 men. Sometimes this prayer is called his "high-priestly" prayer, because as a priest stands before God on behalf of the people, so Jesus speaks to God on behalf of his followers.

It is important for us to listen to these words, because as his followers, the prayer is for us. As we listen, we discover that this prayer is a treasure house for us. Many of the great themes of the Bible are compressed into this one prayer—the *name of God; the world, joy, fullness; the Evil One;* and finally *the Word and truth*. There is a grand economy in this language, as we realize how much Jesus is saying in such a short time. As we listen, we learn as much about ourselves as we learn about him and his Father.

The Big Questions

What are the most urgent questions we human beings want answers for? Are there any more important than these?

149

1. Who am I?
2. What is my place in the world?
3. What can I believe?
4. By what standard can I live?

After asking these crucial questions, look again at Jesus' prayer, and three words leap to your eye: the *name* of God, the *world*, and the *truth*.

Who Am I?

Ask people that question, and they will immediately give you a name. Ask me who I am, and I will not say, "I am a man about 6 feet 2 inches tall." No, I will say, "My name is Michael Rogness." That's who I am. My name is who I am. My first name identifies me as an individual. My last name connects me with a family. Sometimes I use "Preus" as my middle name, which identifies me with my mother's side of the family. Whatever your own names are, they tell people who you are.

The giving of names is terribly important. Are you named after somebody? Then you will always feel a special relationship with that person. Are you named after somebody in the Bible? Then even though your knowledge of the Bible might be sketchy, you will most likely know who your namesake is among all those hundreds of people we meet in the Scriptures.

In many countries, when persons are baptized they will take a biblical name as their "Christian" name. Last weekend at our Northern Minnesota District Convention I sat across the table from a man who was visiting our churches from Tanzania. His name tag said "Michael Tomito." Since we had the same first name, I was curious and asked if he had been given that name at birth. No, he said, at birth he was given the Masai name *Kisaruni*. When he was baptized, he took the biblical name of Michael the Archangel. It became his "Christian" name.

In the Roman Catholic church it has been customary that people entering a convent or monastery to become a nun or monk would assume a new name. To change their name meant that in a very deep sense they were changing *who they were.*

When we listen to this prayer of Jesus, we add another name to our own. Jesus prays that we will be safe by the "power of God's name." Furthermore, Jesus says, it is the name which his Father gave him. He speaks, acts, and lives in the name of God.

Just as Jesus lived by his Father's name, so he gives us a new name when we become his followers, to show that we have changed who we are. The new name is "Christian." It comes, of course, from the name "Christ." The Bible tells us that early in the Christian church the people of Christ were called "Christian." That identified who they were. "Michael Rogness, Christian." That's who I am.

John Bunyan's great Christian classic, *Pilgrim's Progress*, is an allegory about a man's life journey. Bunyan gives him the name "Everyman" because he symbolizes every person in the pilgrimage through life. But in the course of his journeys his name is changed. He is no longer "Everyman." He becomes "Christian." His very identity has changed.

Who are you? Give your name, then add "Christian." That's who you are.

What Is My Place?

Jesus moves on to this next tremendously important question. His disciples, he says, "do not belong to the world, just as I do not belong to the world." On the other hand, he continues to pray, "I do not ask you to take them out of the world, but I do ask you to keep them safe from the Evil One."

When our family lived in France, we were very much part of French society. We had a *carte de sejour*, a resident's card; we paid taxes; we drove with French driver's licenses and car plates, went to French doctors and dentists, shopped in French stores, and so on. But we did not belong to France. We were spending time in France, but we belonged to the United States of America. When we were together with other Americans, we sensed that we were with "our" people. We might be very different from other Americans, but there was this powerful bond that transcended all those differences. We belonged together, because together we belonged to the same place.

So it is with this world. As Christians we are in this world, but we are here as pilgrims. We are passing through. While we are here, we participate fully, and in many, many ways we like it here a great deal. But in the long run we belong someplace else. While we are here, we live under the name "Christian," because that tells everybody where we really belong. To set our sights only on this world would mean to lose the whole point of who we really are and where we really belong.

What Can I Believe? By What Standards Can I Live?

The next important questions would clearly be: While I am in this world, what can I believe and by what standards can I live?

Jesus now comes to that. "Dedicate them to yourself by means of the truth," he prays, for *your Word is truth*." There is a hunger in the world for truth. There are so many conflicting ideas in the air that we could

151

very easily live in a state of vague confusion all the time. We sense that values once taken for granted by society are now disregarded and even ridiculed. It is an uneasy time to live, if you want something to hang on to and do not know quite where to grab.

But Jesus says he brings the truth. His Word is truth, he says. His Word about God is truth; his Word about himself is truth; his Word about human life is truth; and his Word about us is truth.

That is a plenty solid base upon which to build! In an uncertain world, that is a sure foundation.

Who am I? My name is Christian, and every time I pray our Lord's Prayer, I ask that his name be hallowed in my life and in this world.

What is my place in this world? I am in this world, but I belong to a greater place than this.

What can I believe in? By what standards can I live? I hold to his Word and his truth as a guide in this anxious and uncertain world.

MICHAEL ROGNESS
First Lutheran Church
Duluth, Minnesota

THE DAY OF PENTECOST

Playing Your Part in God's Mission
John 7:37-39a

While waiting for a bus early last week, I found myself standing before a large advertisement of Laurence Olivier's production, *King Lear*. Olivier's finely honed features were framed with a majestic mane of white hair down to his shoulders, his noble head supporting a jewel-adorned royal crown. Suddenly a youngster came up next to me and asked, "Mr. Priest, is that God?" Not knowing quite what to say, I stammered, "No, he's only an Englishman who acts divinely." That probably only confused the child, but at least I didn't have to lie.

While viewing the actual TV show some three days later, I couldn't help but hope that the impressionable youngster wasn't also watching. While Olivier's *Lear* was certainly one of the towering performances of his illustrious career, Shakespeare's *Lear* was anything but God-like. In fact, the difference between the tragedy of Lear and the gospel of God constitutes the very heart of our message this morning.

152

Lear: From Cursing to Madness

Lear is a vain, frightened, and lonely old man. Engaging in some emotional, parental blackmail, he brings his three daughters before him to have them perform:

Tell me, my daughters,
Since now we will divest us both of rule, interest of territory, cares of state,
Which of you shall we say doth love us most?
That we our largest bounty may extend
Where nature doth with merit challenge.

Goneril and Regan and Cordelia are then supposed to upstage each other in order to placate the old man's vanity and be duly rewarded. The first two go through the hypocritical charade with acquisitive zest, but Cordelia loves her father too much to play such selfish games. She will not open her mouth. She refuses to recite empty words in order to gain paternal compensation.

Therefore, Cordelia elicits the wrath of her father who tragically responds to her seeming ingratitude with what he considers to be a well-deserved curse:

Hear, Nature, hear! Dear goddess, hear!
Suspend thy purpose, if thou didst intend
to make this creature fruitful!
Into her womb, convey sterility!
Dry up in her organs of increase,
And from her derogate body, never spring
A babe to honour her! If she must teem,
Create her child of spleen, that it may live
And be a thwart disnatur'd torment to her!
Let is stamp wrinkles in her brow of youth,
With cadent tears fret channels in her cheeks.
Turn all her mother's pains and benefits
To laughter and contempt, that she may feel
How sharper than a serpent's tooth it is
To have a thankless child!

King Lear's wretchedness, in the wake of his daughters' duplicity and perceived insensitivity, drives him to the depths of madness. In one of the most awesome scenes of Shakespeare's tragedies, Lear courts self-destruction in defying all that nature can throw at him, as he taunts the heavens above:

Blow, winds, and crack your cheeks! Rage! blow!
You cataracts and hurricanoes; spout
Till you have drenched our steeples, and drowned the cocks!

153

You sulpherous and thought-executing fires,
Vaunt-couriers of oak-cleaving thunderbolts,
Singe my white head! And thou, all-shaking thunder
Strike flat the thick rotundity o' the world!
Crack nature's molds, all germens spill at once
That make ingrateful man!

Rumble thy bellyful! Spit, fire! spout, rain!
Nor rain, wind, thunder, fire, are my daughters:
I tax not you, you elements, with unkindness;
I never gave you kingdom, call'd you children.
You owe me no subscription; then, let fall
Your horrible pleasure; here I stand, your slave,
A poor, infirm, weak, and despis'd old man.
But yet I call you servile ministers,
That have with two pernicious daughters join'd
Your high-engender'd battles 'gainst a head
So old and white as this. O! O! 'tis foul.

Christ: From Blessing to Gladness

The self-serving challenge, "Who loves us most?" results tragically in
both the cursing of Cordelia and the madness of Lear. How very different
from the heavenly king, Jesus Christ, whom you and I worship as Lord.
He, too, asked virtually the same question of his would-be disciples, but
then gave an entirely different and selfless response. We read in John
21:

> When they had finished breakfast, Jesus said to Simon Peter, "Simon, son
> of John, do you love me more than these?" He said to him, "Yes, Lord;
> You know that I love you." He said to him, "Feed my lambs." A second
> time he said to him, "Simon, son of John, do you love me?" He said to
> him, "Yes, Lord, you know that I love you." He said to him, "Tend my
> sheep." He said to him the third time, "Simon, son of John, do you love
> me?" Peter was grieved because he said to him the third time, "Do you
> love me?" And he said to him, "Lord you know everything; you know
> that I love you." Jesus said to him, "Feed my sheep" (vv. 15-17).

Not feed my vanity, not feed my insecurity, not feed my loneliness,
but "feed my sheep" is what New Testament Christianity is all about.
It's not satisfying some pouting old man in heaven whom we call God,
who's likely going to deal out favors and rewards to those who faun and
grovel at his feet. That's Lear—leering.

I'm proclaiming the God who was in Christ and who commissioned his disciples by challenging, "If you're on my side, feed my sheep. Show me how much you love me by how you love them."

Unlike King Lear, Christ the King sends his faithful daughters and sons—the church—into mission. Authentic Christian mission is not preoccupied with doling out "godly goodies" to those who disregard the least of his—the poor, the sick, the needy. We are saved in order to serve. Therefore, knowing that you and I "cannot by our own reason or strength believe in Jesus Christ, [our] Lord, or come to him," God graciously provides the power with which that kind of sacrificial service might be performed. That's what Pentecost is all about.

Christ's promise of the mission-empowering Spirit of God was made repeatedly during his earthly ministry. Consequently, we read in today's Gospel:

> On the last day of the feast, the great day, Jesus stood up and proclaimed, "If any one thirst, let him come to me and drink. He who believes in me, as the scripture has said, 'Out of his heart shall flow rivers of living water.'"

To which the author of the Fourth Gospel adds:

> Now this he said about the Spirit, which those who believed in him were to receive; for as yet the Spirit had not been given, because Jesus was not yet glorified (John 7:37-39).

What was the setting for these words of promise? Our Lord was in the midst of the Jews. They were celebrating the Feast of the Tabernacles, near the pool of Siloam. It was an autumn festival—a kind of Thanksgiving service, in which they commemorated the wilderness wanderings and the blessings of the Promised Land. In gratitude for a good harvest, water was used in praising God, for without that water the parched ground of the desert would never have come forward with the bountiful harvest. And Jesus, seeing the people so "harvest-minded," so "water-conscious," proclaimed to them: "If you want a real drink, come to me. Trust in me and what will pour out of your heart will be living water to irrigate a heavenly harvest that's a pure gift of God's grace."

Christ was promising that his disciples would receive the Holy Spirit in order that they might be empowered to go forth in mission. And to encourage them along the way, he elsewhere outlined in simple form a table of those kinds of characteristics—those kind of qualities—that describe the kind of life-style appropriate for baptized Christians, church missionaries. Again unlike King Lear, Christ the King conveys to his beloved not curses but blessings.

155

We call them the Beatitudes, and I address them this morning to you as God in Christ intended. Christ is talking about *you*, filled with the Holy Spirit in Baptism, when he promises,

> Blessed are the poor in spirit, for theirs is the kingdom of heaven. Blessed are those who mourn, for they shall be comforted. Blessed are the meek, for they shall inherit the earth. Blessed are those who hunger and thirst for righteousness, for they shall be satisfied. Blessed are the merciful, for they shall obtain mercy. Blessed are the pure in heart, for they shall see God. Blessed are the peacemakers, for they shall be called sons of God. Blessed are those who are persecuted for righteousness' sake, for theirs is the kingdom of heaven. Blessed are you, when men revile you and persecute you and utter all kinds of evil against you falsely on my account. Rejoice and be glad, for your reward is great in heaven, for so men persecuted the prophets who were before you (Matt. 5:3-12).

Christ-like gladness is offered as God's answer to Lear-like madness. Heavenly reward is promised as the consequence of our discipleship, but it dare never constitute its motivation. We do not serve madly in order to be saved; we serve gladly because we have been saved. The church is then here for the sake of those who do not yet belong to it. So the church lives by mission, as a fire lives by burning. It is not a kingly church that has missions to the world; it is a servant church that views itself as God's mission in and for the world.

Mission: Triumph beyond Tragedy

The Spirit promised by the incarnate Christ is then received by the disciples through the risen Christ. The author of the Fourth Gospel provides his own version of Pentecost in his account of the heavenly inspiration of the apostolic community.

> On the evening of that day, the first day of the week, the doors being shut where the disciples were, for fear of the Jews, Jesus came and stood among them and said to them, "Peace be with you." When he had said this, he showed them his hands and his side. Then the disciples were glad when they saw the Lord. Jesus said to them again, "Peace be with you. As the Father has sent me, even so I send you." And when he had said this, he breathed on them, and said to them, "Receive the Holy Spirit. If you forgive the sins of any, they are forgiven; if you retain the sins of any, they are retained" (John 20:19-23).

Just as promised, human fear is transformed into divine gladness. You have no moral right to be unhappy. You have been blessed beyond measure. You are the fortunate recipient of the undeserved gifts of God.

156

Christ loves you enough to be willing to enlist you into his company— the company of the committed—to share his cross, that one day you might also share his crown. I'm asking whether you believe that about Christ; I'm also asking whether you believe that about yourself.

Few of us have Olivier's artistic gifts. None of us will likely ever perform *King Lear*. But God doesn't expect the same thing from all of us, because God hasn't given the same thing to all of us. What God does expect is 100% of what's been given. You're not to compare yourself at your worst to Olivier at his best. You're to compare yourself at your worst to yourself at your best. And then it might just be that you are performing far more creditably on that awesome stage of life on which we're all actors and actresses, than Sir Laurence himself.

My friends, Lear-like self-love is sinful. But we are called to love our neighbors as ourselves. This is possible only by confessing that as Christ has died for us, he means to live in us and to work through us.

There is no such thing as Christian tragedy. That doesn't mean you have to go through life as if it were some *Midsummer Night's Dream*. In the real world, there's a lot of pain, a lot of suffering, a lot of anguish. Nor do I mean for you simply to "grin and bear it." However, I do mean that any of you who look upon this world or yourself as tragic are denying the God who has created you in his holy and loving image, and who means to bless the church's mission with the inbreaking kingdom of God. Therefore, no Christian dare utter the pitiful words with which Cordelia ends:

We are not the first
Who, with the best meaning, have incurr'd the worst.
For thee, oppressed king, am I cast down;
Myself could else out-frown false Fortune's frown.

It is not "false Fortune's frown." it is Christ's cross and crown, that gives your life meaning and this world hope. Even if you can't out-Olivier Olivier, you certainly can out-Lear Lear on the stage of life as a child of God, baptized into the mission of God, to the glory of God.

WILLIAM H. LAZARETH
Holy Trinity Lutheran Church
New York, New York

We Are Members of a Strange Family
John 3:1-17

This is the Sunday to preach about God. Children here in the congregation may wish to draw the picture that they have of God. Two
news items come to mind. In California a resourceful young man began
a business in which he helped people who suddenly came into large
amounts of money to accept their situation. He found that people who
suddenly win the lottery or a contest sometimes have great difficulty
adjusting. He claimed to be able to help them. The other is the local
report of a couple, both former professors, who showed up at every
reception and every event at the university and enjoyed the refreshments
and the air-conditioning. It was helpful to them because they were living
in their car in the parking lot. Both situations sound strange because
they are so different, unusual, and opposed to normal activity. And now
to God!

So much time in the lives of people is spent trying to fit different
things, different events into their scheme of life. Their goals demand
that adjustments be made. Their aims call for accommodation. Their
purposes don't always fit into the purposes of the rest of society. We
work for things that seem to bring us closer to our dreams. We may
even just fall into things that we didn't expect that seem to make our
dreams much more of a possibility. Life revolves at a furious pace around
this struggle to get or to use or to reject or to adopt and mold the future.
This is probably the reason that a person may have great difficulty
suddenly dealing with a windfall of money. Just what do you do with
a situation that you didn't expect to have to deal with?

At the very same time there is another scramble in our lives. It is the
scramble to be accepted by others and by society. We try hard to fit our
lives into the pattern of life around us so that we will be considered
successful. Now the catch! We do this very same thing with God, and
it won't work. You can hear Nicodemus operating this way. Faithful he
was, but working with a pattern that wouldn't work with God. Christians
are members of a strange family.

Trying to Fit God into Our Molds

We should make no pretense about it, and confront the truth that
there are quite a number of people who make no pretense about believing

158

in God. They may make some feeble effort when it is helpful, but there is no struggle, no commitment, no real relationship. There is another category of people who need to call attention to the fact that they deny God. It is a part of their image, and they want to preserve that image. There is still another category of people who are very sincere in their belief. They want to believe, and they do, that they have life with God. The basis of their faith however, is simply that like all human beings they have life and were given life, and by virtue of this creation they are in full relationship with God. Faith for them is not unlike the other talents they have been given or have managed to acquire. They are very religious and often take satisfaction in their religion. They insist that like automobiles human beings come equipped with what is necessary, and all that is necessary is to bring out the proper use of this equipment.

It is rebirth that they overlook. This is not unusual. Every generation invents its own gods and we still do it today. "All who are led by the Spirit of God are sons of God" (Rom. 8:14). It is not just natural birth that makes us a member of this strange family. As Jesus told Nicodemus, you don't pick up this kind of family membership merely by trying hard enough.

We continually try to squeeze God into our molds. When you go hiking, there is that time each day when tent, sleeping bag, and other equipment has to be packed into those small bags. You push. You shove. You pound. And now and then it just seems as if there is no way to get those things back into the sacks. At some time in our lives we do this with God.

Nicodemus has this problem. Look at the account once more. Nicodemus is trying to understand. This is no half-hearted effort. He is to be commended for his interest. We want to make God what is comfortable and understandable to us. God's grace and love are *strange* to the world. In fact, the world just doesn't understand. Even when we so confidently affirm the Father, the Son, and the Holy Spirit, and even when we try to explain what we mean by this, and even when we speak glowingly of God as divine or as God in human form in Jesus Christ—all of this can be a very brave way of trying to squeeze God into our mold so that he is more understandable and we are more comfortable.

A Longing for Something Better

In the musical *Sweet Charity* a group of girls stand around the room and watch the door. They are ready to dance with anyone who enters and hope that the person will choose them. They will accept the invitation and the money of anyone, but they are always talking about just that

159

one person who will come through the door and take them away to the happiness for which they so desperately long. One of their songs is "There's Got to Be Something Better Than This." It may be inaccurate to say that everyone "thirsts for God," but there does seem to be an incompleteness in the life of everyone that stirs at least some of the time. A person may experience this differently at different times and periods of life. The Spirit of God can become the agitation our life needs. The Spirit blows. The Spirit stirs. The Spirit invites. The Spirit troubles. The Spirit can and does meet this need of our emptiness.

We can be bold enough to confess that we don't always meet this need in people as a community. When we are accused of missing the power of the Holy Spirit and depending on our own resources, it's true. As people of the church we should not be too defensive about this. This does not mean that the organized church is impotent. While it may misread the signs and while it may be misled into other sources of power that don't really work, God still moves and creates and recreates through the use of Word and sacrament and through a group of people that is not perfect by its own merit and work. The human need is being met and will continue to be met by the blowing of the Holy Spirit. The Spirit still calls. The Spirit still gathers us into this strange family. The Spirit still nourishes and cherishes the family so that the kingdom comes.

The Strange Family

Nicodemus had high praise for Jesus. He knew that somehow God was with him. He couldn't do the things that he did unless it were so. Then Jesus comes along with the conversation about being "born again." This is strange to Nicodemus. It must have sounded like nonsense. At least Nicodemus shows how silly it is, "How can a man be born when he is old? Can he enter a second time into his mother's womb and be born?" (John 3:4).

Jesus takes it a step farther. It is the birth by water and the Spirit that is necessary. It is not just natural birth but something beyond this that is necessary. While Nicodemus sits puzzled, Jesus uses the example of the wind. The wind blows and you don't see the wind. You hear it and yet the wind does its own thing, and you know that it is there. The Spirit unfurls our sails in exactly the same way. Nicodemus is still caught with a puzzled look. How can this be? (John 3:9). Jesus then invites Nicodemus to leave his effort to "make it on his own." He clearly describes how God breaks into human history to do what human beings could not do. It is the indescribable love and mercy of God that causes him to come to earth in the form and way that human beings can see

160

and understand. He asks not that we go to such great efforts and pull together all of our wisdom, but rather that we depend upon him.

The conversation of Nicodemus and Jesus is a little like standing off and looking at a picture or listening to a radio drama. The spotlight comes to rest on us. The gospel comes to us in the same way. We too have this kind of confrontation with Jesus Christ. Beware that you don't quickly claim immunity from the kind of problems that Nicodemus had. We have them too. Jesus is urging us to consider our family membership. This is really a very intimate scene and a very intimate invitation. One thing is sure: it is an invitation that is not to be lived with in fear. It carries with it all of the promise of inheritance, the inheritance of eternal life. We know from Romans 8 that it brings with it suffering and struggle, but we live in this family in the assurance that we can always and under all circumstances call to God with that loving address, "Abba, Father." This is a name of intimacy. It is a name of love.

The gospel invitation is not just something that was talked about. God demonstrated it. God carried it through to the finish. This is what we see in Jesus Christ. It is so drastically different from anything else that we know.

This family to which all belong who have been claimed by the power of God's Spirit is concerned with forgiveness and patience and love and goodness and self-control. Why is this so strange? Because human beings know best about the use of power. Human beings triumph by out-smarting, outperforming others. Human beings who have become wise to the world know that you need to think of yourself first and always if you are to maintain any kind of position. God created the world in wholeness. God's intention is for this wholeness to be restored to every-thing. We are included in this, as is the whole family of the human race. When God has placed this claim on us, there is no way that our life-style will not seem strange, as we live out our family heritage. Despite the fact that the song says that "love makes the world go around," most people know that in the cold hard corners of life it is not so.

This family of ours does not claim perfection in all things. This family of ours is ready to confess failures. This family of ours fights against the slavery of fear. This family of ours is ready to do battle with selfishness and greed and oppression and brutality. This family of ours is not content to live in the sleepy warmth of materialism, despite the fact that it is so easy to get caught up in it. Ours is a strange family.

In some notes written in the margin of an instruction book I found these comments on the Creed. I do not know where the notes came from, but they are appropriate. "The doctrine of the Holy Trinity and the Creed are not just things that you meditate about with your feet on

161

the desk and a pipe in your mouth." Certainly we do need to formulate what we believe about God, but at the same time we have to learn how to use the wealth of God's grace calling us to freedom in the power of his Spirit. We need to encourage each other to live our lives by the urging of the Spirit, especially when this seems strange. This is the miracle and the mystery of our God—Father, Son, and Holy Spirit.

Like Nicodemus, right now is the time for us. Each one of us is urged to take advantage of it. Come to the Supper. Take up the involvement in this risky kind of life that dares you to be strange and at the same time inheritors of God's grace.

ALFRED M. BULS
Bethel Lutheran Church
University City, Missouri

SECOND SUNDAY AFTER PENTECOST

That's the Thing I Don't Like about Jesus!
Mark 2:23-28

Years ago I heard a song by John Ylvisaker that has stayed in my mind ever since. The first verse tells the story of a woman who complains to her pastor about serving wine at Communion. She doesn't think that the church should be in the business of serving alcohol. The pastor replies by saying that Jesus drank wine, in fact, once he even turned water into wine. "But," says the woman, "that's the thing I don't like about Jesus."

Next a man complains to the pastor about seeing some black people in church. "They're just not our kind. Why don't they go where they'll be more comfortable." The pastor reminds him that Jesus associated with all people, including the outcasts of society, eating with tax collectors and sinners, running around with fishermen and prostitutes. "Yes," says the man, "but that's the thing I don't like about Jesus."

Too bad the Pharisees didn't know the song. They would have loved it! You can hear them complaining, "Look at the disgraceful behavior of your disciples, Jesus, picking grain on the Sabbath. Haven't you taught them that's against the law?" And Jesus replied, "Don't you remember the example of David? Anyway, the Sabbath was made for human beings, not the other way around, so the Son of man is lord even of the Sabbath."

162

Can't you just hear the Pharisees going down the road mumbling to each other, "What nerve! He acts as though he knows what's more important than God's law. Now that's just the thing I don't like about Jesus."

I know that most of us don't like to admit it, but there are things that we don't like about Jesus. You see, every time we think we have things figured out, every time we've got faith under control, Jesus comes along and shakes us up. The Gospel for today is a perfect case study.

That Was Then

The Pharisees weren't entirely wrong. They had started from the right place—the law as God's gracious gift. In Deuteronomy the observance of the Sabbath is commanded. It is an observance based on what God has done for Israel in the Exodus. On the Sabbath, Israel is to remember the time when it was a people who were no people, slaves in the land of Egypt, who were rescued by God with a mighty hand and an out-stretched arm.

Israel is to remember, first of all, by setting aside the Sabbath as a day of rest. It's a fitting remembrance, for slaves to celebrate their freedom by being freed from work. At the same time there is to be the same concern for others. Freedom is to be extended to all—one's children, one's servants, strangers, even cattle and beasts of burden. The command to observe the Sabbath is seen as a response to God's gracious act and is oriented to human need.

Unfortunately, the Pharisees couldn't let well enough alone. They fell victim to the natural human tendency to spell everything out in excruciating detail so that there would be no doubt as to what was proper observance of the Sabbath and what was not. Without going into that elaborate detail, this little scene from Mark's gospel makes it clear that the Sabbath observance had been distorted and loaded down with countless restrictions, making it a burden rather than a gift. Thus attention was shifted away from remembrance as a celebration of the gift of freedom, to having to remember what is forbidden activity. The focus on God's act was lost, and human actions became the priority.

It was threatening to the Pharisees to have Jesus come along and point out just how they had lost sight of the meaning of the Sabbath observance. First of all, he pointed out that there was a great precedent for setting aside the regulations. David himself violated the rules in the face of human need. Jesus went on to remind them of what they already knew, that human beings were created by God before God instituted the Sabbath rest. Thus, priority lay with human need. The Sabbath was

163

created *for* humanity, not humanity for the observance of the Sabbath. Finally, Jesus asserted his own authority. As Son of man he wielded the very authority of God and so had the final determination of what is and is not permissible on the Sabbath. No wonder the Pharisees didn't like Jesus!

The Pharisees had lost their perspective. They insisted on strict observance, but the reason for the observance had been largely lost. No longer was the Sabbath a gift, but a burden. Jesus, as Lord of the Sabbath, rediscovered it for humanity. He removed the burden and gave the Sabbath back as a gracious gift. Jesus freed humanity to see laws and regulations in their proper perspective, as aids for life, designed for human beings by a loving God whose purpose was to free them from bondage.

This Is Now

Jesus sure told the Pharisees off. But what does that have to do with us? We're not Pharisees. Why get all worked up about plucking heads of grain? And anyway, if we, as Christians, have been freed in Christ, rules and regulations aren't our problem. Are they?

"Pastor, can I talk with you? I've got this problem with my roommate. She says she's a Christian, but I know she's not. She comes in late every night—and I just know she's been to the pub. I hardly ever see her reading her Bible. Once I looked in it and it's not even a red-letter edition! Hardly anything is underlined. I'll bet my Bible is at least a pound heavier because of all the ink in the underlining! I asked her once when she came to know Jesus as her Savior and you know what she said? When she was baptized! What kind of answer is that? I happen to know she was only six weeks old at the time. How can a baby know Jesus? Anyway, I've confronted her with the truth, and all she does is get mad at me. I'm just doing it out of love."

"Pastor, can I talk with you? I've got this problem with my roommate. Ever since she's found Jesus, she's been a real pain in the neck. She spends all her time in those fellowship groups talking about what Jesus has done for her. Doesn't she know that Christians are supposed to reach out to the hurting people in the world? She goes to some church downtown; she says that liturgy isn't worship for her. She even got baptized by total immersion. Once in the room she started talking real weird. I guess she was speaking in tongues, but I thought it was creepy. Anyway, I've told her that I'm not interested in her kind of Christianity.

Like the Pharisees, both these students lost their perspective. They insisted on strict observance, but had forgotten the reason. The discipline of the Christian life was no longer a gift, but a burden—especially a burden imposed on someone else. Each had come up with her own checklist of what kind of behavior identifies a Christian. And each used her list to tabulate how closely one does what God requires. Each knows she's not perfect, but as long as there are more checks in the "do" column than in the "don't" column, each can feel pretty self-righteous.

That's a convenient way to live the life of faith. You don't have to *think*; all you have to do is memorize a list of do's and don't's and then check them off one by one. And the really neat thing is that you apply exactly the same list to everyone. You can deal with everybody the same way—much less time-consuming than relating to individuals. Like the incident in the Gospel, it doesn't make any difference that the disciples were hungry. What they did was wrong, and that's that. The law says no harvesting on the Sabbath, period.

That's the Thing I Like about Jesus

Jesus' answer to the Pharisees and to us is to set us free from the burden of the law, but it is a freedom that demands great responsibility. God doesn't take away the checklists, but frees us to see them in their proper perspective, as aids for our lives, gifts from a loving God. And in giant letters God adds a preface to each checklist: *Remember that these are designed for my beloved children. My love for them comes first.*

It is Jesus, not the law, that comes to bring life and bring it abundantly. We are always going to be jolted out of our security, out of our slavery, by Jesus. That's the thing I don't like about Jesus.

But Jesus had his priorities straight. He broke the Sabbath law again and again to heal the sick. He shocked the self-righteous by associating with the outcasts. He was accused of blasphemy for daring to forgive sins. For Jesus, people were always more important than the law—even people like me. And that's the thing I like about Jesus!

KAREN G. BOCKELMAN
Luther College
Decorah, Iowa

165

A Family Picture

Mark 3:20-35

A Crazy Situation

It was a zoo! There hadn't even been time to catch their breath, much less grab some food. Jesus had been going like a house afire, and the disciples were running to keep up with him. Immediately after his baptism came the 40-day fast in the wilderness. That ended when John the Baptist was thrown in prison, and Jesus instead of being drained was energized to collect disciples. He taught, cast out demons, healed a host of people, including Simon's mother-in-law. And that was only the first day.

The next started with Jesus climbing a mountain "a great while before day" in order to pray. The peace and quiet lasted until Peter found him with the news, "Everyone is searching for you." It was another day of casting out demons, healing lepers, and preaching. This was interrupted by some people who opened the roof where Jesus was to let in a lame friend. Instead of doing the obvious, Jesus forgave his sins. The Pharisees took a dim view of that, but then they didn't seem to like the physical miracle either. Ever interested in people's wholeness, Jesus healed someone else's withered hand. When it became apparent that there was more than any one could do, Jesus multiplied his ministry by appointing the Twelve to "preach and have authority to cast out demons." It was at that point that he went home, and the word caught up with him that his family thought he was mad.

That's actually a little more blunt than what they would have said. They had heard the stories and thought he was beside himself and just needed a little rest and relaxation. The Pharisees however weren't so charitable. They made no bones about what they thought. "Why does this man speak thus? It is blasphemy!" Their growing dissatisfaction was enough to encourage them to seek out counsel with their rivals the Herodians on how to destroy Jesus. They were not about to have their religion tampered with, because it was hopelessly tied to the finely balanced and fragile truce with Rome. You'd have to be crazy to rock the boat in the middle of such a lake.

Mad, but Not Like You Think

Somewhere along the line we tend to agree. The wisdom of the Pharisees and people is irrefutable. We, too, are likely to say with them "What is this? A new teaching!" At least that's the word of the crowd today, and it is not usually said with much respect. Ultimately in this world to be loving is to be mad. The line we hear from the highest echelons of government down to the street corner is that you have to be tough. Unless you can match everyone else in sheer power and cunning shrewdness, you have no place playing in the game. Instruments of death and destruction get dubbed "Peacemakers," as if peace was brought about by bringing others to their knees. We speak of a "peace-keeping force," without any awareness of the apparent contradiction in terms.

Jesus didn't spend much time training his followers in methods for controlling the crowd or enforcing God's peace. Rather he led the way in being loving. And his love has a distinctly different quality of strength to it. In his own life that meant not the shedding of other's blood in order to make peace, but the shedding of his own. That's why people questioned his sanity. For Jesus love meant challenging all that was disrespectful to human dignity and wholeness. That's how he got more enemies than friends. For Jesus, love meant questioning the assumed holiness of profits over human welfare. That's why he got strung up on the cross. For Jesus, love meant being sensitive to the poor and the downtrodden and those who didn't count—like women—and calling them sister and mother. To associate with those of low degree even today is still madness.

Jesus' family unwittingly played into the Pharisees' hands when they said he was beside himself. Fractured relationships that turn family member against family member and make them more ready to judge than to listen form a microcosm of our world. It can trace its heritage back to the garden when the man said "She did it," and the woman said "It did it," and the serpent just smiled. Broken relationships pave the way for protecting myself against all others. They make it expedient to take advantage of another's vulnerability—it's either me or you. They make it easy to be suspicious of those around—can you really blame me? They remind me that if only the strongest survive, then I must be stronger than my neighbor—that's just the way it is. These are the facts of life based on fears known well to every age, including the first century. And listening to fears instead of listening to that which is stronger than fear is death.

Yes, Jesus was mad, but not in the way you might think. The Pharisees charged that Jesus cast out devils by the authority of the chief devil. That

167

was tantamount to saying that he was himself possessed. The answer Jesus gave cleverly caught the teachers of the law in their own classroom with their homework undone. He pointed out that even if what they said was true, they were only arguing for the strength and power of Satan, and who wants to be caught doing that? It is like robbing a house, said Jesus. It just cannot be done unless one first ties up the homeowner. Then the burglars may proceed to do as they please. The question simmering below the surface, directed to the Pharisees, and not without irony was, "Are you really saying that I am capable of tying up Satan?"

That's not all. Jesus spoke of God's folly in the forgiveness of sins. Jesus' ministry demonstrated the length to which God is willing to go in order to forgive. God prizes human worth more than the law. That wouldn't have been news to Adam and Eve—or Moses, for that matter. God even cherishes human choice, and that to the extent of granting the freedom and the privilege saying no to God. Jesus verbalizes this on behalf of his hearers, who were already plotting to bring about his death. The unforgivable sin, says Jesus, is denying God the power to forgive sins. The context in which Jesus issues this most terrifying warning of any in the Bible is precisely where Jesus stresses the fullness and completeness of God's forgiveness. This is the craziness of our God, which ultimately offered the flesh and blood of Jesus, God's very life, on our behalf. This is the craziness at the heart of our faith, as continually we are the people who return to take God up on the offer. We eat the body and drink the blood of Christ so that we live. Only the true followers of our Lord can penetrate the mystery. In the person of Jesus of Nazareth God is at work to liberate all from bondage to sin, death, and the devil.

Meanwhile the family was still trying to get through the crowd to pull Jesus away. Maybe they felt their family name was at stake. Maybe they were getting pressure from the religious right. Maybe they were genuinely worried that Jesus had gone off the deep end. They just wanted to take him home. When that word reached Jesus, he spoke what on the surface must have sounded like sheer nonsense. "Here are my mother and my brothers!" His words are not unconnected to the previous dialog with the Pharisees but form yet another link in the gospel message of God's grace. Whoever prizes human worth more than the law is my family. Whoever cherishes with respect human struggle and sadness is my family. Whoever seeks to forgive as they have been forgiven is my family. Whoever risks with grace instead of playing it safe with the rules and regulations is my family. "Whoever does the will of God is my brother, and sister and mother."

168

Who's Crazy?

We don't have to sugarcoat it. There's nothing easy about doing the will of God. Those who follow our Lord, his example and his teaching, see clearly the path they are on and its cost. One might even understand the sanity which would say "No, thanks," to the journey of faith. "The cost is too great." But we, however, through Baptism into Jesus are already inextricably linked with his life and ministry, his death and grave. We are being prepared for the eternal weight of glory—the Easter resurrection, the ascension, and enthronement of Jesus into the presence of the God and Father of all. There is no way for us to get out of this world alive playing by the rules of this age. Generations upon generations have died with hands empty and hopes bankrupt. Yet we are the ones with an insight into the center of the universe. We know our place in the heart of God. And that makes it possible to be alive now. It is through choosing to live this way that the world will not be without comments regarding our sanity.

All of God's favorites throughout the ages have carried the label of mad. Think of Noah building the ark long miles away from any water. Think of Jeremiah up to his armpits in the mire of the cistern where he had been dumped by the king for preaching about the downfall of Jerusalem. Think of Elijah running for his life because Queen Jezebel had sworn she would kill him for killing her priests of Baal. Think of Paul when being interrogated by the governor gave as his defense the story of Christianity only to be told "You are mad!" Think of Francis of Assisi, who through listening to the grace of God in creation about him took our Gospel text to heart, called all nature his brother and sister, and even went as far as preaching the good news to them. Think of Martin Luther King Jr., who dreamed of a world devoid of hatred and prejudice where people of every color could sit down at table together. Think of the vice-president of the Evangelical Lutheran Church of Southwest Africa, the Reverend Zaphaniah Kameeta, who against great personal odds has said publically of the apartheid system that it is "not only sin, but a form of violence regarding people as God's mistakes in creation. It is not only an ideology, but a reality that is killing people daily."

And think of us. Are we called to live sanely and placidly, not challenging the way of the world, or are we called to something different? Are you really crazy enough to follow the Christ? Maybe that is asking the wrong question. Is God's love great enough to embrace even the likes of you and me—our apathy, our reluctance, our fears, our flaws?

169

And if you are crazy enough to believe that, then it is with joy Jesus says of you, "My brother and sister and mother."

JOHN C. MANZ
Gloria Dei Lutheran Church
St. Paul, Minnesota

FOURTH SUNDAY AFTER PENTECOST

Lord of the Big Surprise
Mark 4:26-34

A Surprise in the Field

In today's Gospel text, Jesus compares the growth of his kingdom to the surprise that comes as insignificant seeds grow to produce a mighty harvest.

In the first parable seed is planted in a field. At the beginning the conditions for growth may not appear to be ideal. But the seed is planted nevertheless. After that the planter must simply wait. Surprise! The seed grows. First there is the tender blade; then the ear, carrying its promise of fruit to come; then the full grain upon the ear. The great potential mysteriously stored in a little seed has been realized once again. The planter is pleasantly surprised.

In the second parable Jesus speaks of the mustard seed. Perhaps he even held one of these almost invisible seeds in his hand, for the mustard tree grew in abundance in the region where Jesus taught. In any event, everyone knew that from the looks of it you couldn't expect much to come from a mustard seed—a tiny shrub, at best. But it doesn't work out that way. The mustard seed grows into a good-sized shrub, and then keeps on growing some more, finally reaching a height of 12 to 15 feet, extending branches so large that they become the shelter and refuge of nesting birds. Surprise! There's a lot more power in that tiny seed than ever met the eye.

God's Surprise for the Church

Jesus' point is that the coming and growing of the kingdom of God is like those seeds. God has some big surprises in store for us. In a field where everything appears to be dead and lying in a grave, God is alive and working still.

We need this promise of the kingdom's surprise. As we look at the state of the Christian church in today's world, the situation looks grim. This is due in part to the fact that we are accustomed to thinking of the Western world as the wellspring of the Christian faith, and it appears that faith is drying up.

But already the reports of God's surprises are beginning to roll in. Projections show that in about 15 years the continent with the most followers of Christ will be the continent of Africa. There is a vibrant Christian church growing there, not because this is the easy way to go, but in the face of many forms of persecution. Furthermore, by far the fastest growing church group in all of Lutheranism is the Lutheran church in Kenya, Africa. Again, through the mysterious, relentless power of God, there is a growing kingdom movement among the young people of Eastern Europe. Finally, where total communist suppression had appeared to have taken place, we are hearing reports of a strong, purified, and unquenchable Christian movement in the Republic of China. Surprise! The "branches" of the kingdom are reaching out into new space all the time.

Perhaps such reports make us all the more discouraged as we consider the many apparently insignificant congregations that dot the landscape of our own country. The vast majority of congregations number less than 200 members, and most of them seem to be struggling merely to survive. Even in those congregations that are larger and give the impression of affluence, not much seems to be happening. The churches of today seem to have little voice in daily affairs.

Even in this dismal scene God is working out his surprises. Out of such institutionally insignificant gatherings God still raises up people who are mighty witnesses in their daily life. In these small gatherings there is still being woven the moral fabric that gives strength to our people. Through the small congregation, so easily criticized and dismissed, the miracle of the seed of the Word of God is still taking root, bringing about new growth, and bearing witness to the power of God is still taking place.

God's Surprise in You

But perhaps the biggest surprise of the kingdom of God is the surprise that is going to take place through you. I say this because in more than 33 years of preaching in several congregations I have found that by far most of the people I talk to are far more disappointed in themselves than

171

they are with the condition of the church as a whole. Perhaps I am talking about you. Most certainly I am talking about *someone* who is very close to you. You are discouraged because you don't see the growth and the development in yourself that you would like to see.

Well, surprise again! God is alive and working in you. Furthermore, he will keep on working in you until that day of Jesus Christ, when you will be exactly and fully all that he has desired you to be. For this is the promise Paul once made, not only to the Philippians, who received his letter, but to you and me who hear that word today: "I am sure that he who began a good work will bring it to completion in the day of Jesus Christ" (1:6). And then Paul goes on to say: "It is right for me to feel thus about you. . . . for you are partakers with me of grace" (1:7).

Those last words of Paul contain the key as to why I can say that God is at work in us. Together we are partakers of God's grace. We must emphasize again and again the real nature of God's kingdom. The kingdom of God is not a force way out in space somewhere. The kingdom of God is not a place we will visit when we die. The kingdom of God is not the church. The kingdom of God is God's gracious rulership. Jesus spoke of this rulership when he told people: "If it is by the finger of God that I cast out demons, then has the kingdom of God come upon you" (Luke 11:20). He promised them: "The kingdom of God is within you" (Luke 17:21). And we have the words of Paul: "For the kingdom of God [or the rulership of God] is not food and drink but righteousness and peace and joy in the Holy Spirit" (Rom. 14:17).

Surprise! He who has begun a good work in you will bring it to completion. Of course, we all get tired of waiting at times. We get impatient with ourselves and with one another, especially those we love the most. We tend to forget both for ourselves and for them the basic rule of the kingdom: first the blade, then the ear, then the full head of grain. Halford Luccock once wrote of our impatience as we wait out that passage from childhood to mature adulthood by quoting an exhausted father who exclaimed, "I have always admired a manly man and a womanly woman, but I sure can't stand a boyly boy." Luccock then went on to say that if we can only sentimentally enjoy the charm of childhood or respectfully admire full Christian maturity, but have no patience for what is in between, then we still have much to learn about being a farmer in God's field, understanding how his kingdom works.

So sit back for a change. Be like the farmer who day by day gets up and goes to rest, knowing that God is giving the growth. Let God get at the church and at you. Believe that he is the God of the big surprise. The early Christians had to believe that. The people of Rome to whom Mark wrote his gospel were then facing a bloody Nero who had ascended the throne. It looked like the kingdom, after a good beginning, was going to be wiped out then and there. Well, it looked like that when Jesus was murdered, too. But God had other plans. He always does. And so he invites you to say to him right now:

Lord, I am going to leave the surprises up to you, including the surprise you can work in me. I shall confess my sins, ask for the pardon Christ Jesus won for me on the cross, pray humbly for the coming of the Holy Spirit, and believe that your kingdom—also at work in me—is like seed in a field. It doesn't just lie there. It's alive!

Vernon R. Schreiber
Resurrection Lutheran Church
Yardley, Pennsylvania

To a Sleeping God
Mark 4:35-41

"You better not never tell nobody but God. It'd kill your mammy." That is the premise of the novel by the gifted storyteller Alice Walker, *The Color Purple*. The novel is a collection of letters written by a young black woman named Celie about her life of suffering and poverty in the rural South. Because their content would break any mother's heart, the letters begin "Dear God." Celie's childlike faith is shaken by repeated indignities. Her father is lynched. Her mother goes mad. Celie is abused and raped. As her life is pulling apart into fragments, she writes a "Dear God" letter that concludes, "You must be asleep."

An Absentee God?

God, you must be sleeping. I wonder if in the midst of some crisis anyone here has ever felt like saying that to God? We who are so at home with God, talking with God as though he were a cosmic pal, sometimes find ourselves in situations of anxiety and even panic when our true status is brought home to us with fearful realism. We are not God, nor God's pals, but God's creatures. Most of us live a few hundred or a few thousand dollars away from bankruptcy and financial chaos. We live one drunk driver away from physical ruin or a few microbes

173

away from bodily disintegration. We are a people living always 40 minutes away from nuclear extinction. We are creatures. But creatures of God! In crisis situations we creatures don't approach our God with reasoned calm but as a child with a bloody knee cries to its mother to make the hurting stop. When God does not respond in the way we wish, we say, "God, you must be asleep." When God doesn't snap to attention or leap to our defense, we feel alone and vulnerable, as though in an automobile in a snowbank or in an open boat in the midst of a storm.

The idea of a sleeping God is not novel. Many have agonized over the seeming absence of God. Luther spoke of the "hidden God." In the 19th century the philosopher Nietzsche proclaimed the death of God. In the 1960s even theologians wrote studies in honor of the dead God. In the 1970s the flower children sang to their "dancing God." And today, in the turmoil of the 1980s, we may expect an ode (or a complaint) to a sleeping God.

Chaos Versus Peace

We have in our Gospel from Mark a story about the sleeping God, told with Mark's uncanny eye for detail. This is Mark's picture: Jesus has been teaching beside the Sea of Galilee, which is really a medium-sized lake. The crowds have been so urgent that the teacher has moved into a small fishing boat, while the people, no doubt some of them standing calf-deep in the water, press around the boat. Mark adds that there were other boats, perhaps anchored around Jesus', giving the appearance of a flotilla of fishing boats. From his boat the teacher has been instructing the crowd by means of parables, mysterious stories of the kingdom of God. Then at dusk, when most boats would be coming to shore, Jesus abruptly suggests they they weigh anchor and head across the lake.

Normally the atmosphere over the lake is hot and still and heavy. But often the cold air surrounding the peak of a mountain to the west of the lake whips down the mountain and crashes into that stillness, producing instant and fierce storms. They weigh anchor and head across, when suddenly out of nowhere one of these "nor'westers" attacks the boat. The wind is shrieking. The little boat is thrashing like a drowning man, heaving at desperate angles to the horizon. One of the crew cries, "We're taking on water!" Anyone who's ever been to sea knows that this is the time for panic.

Every hurricane has an eye where all is calm, and all is still. The eye of this one was in the stern of the boat. Have you seen those little cushions that double as a life preserver? Jesus had found one in the stern and was curled up on it fast asleep. Mark wants to freeze this frame of the narrative for us, so that we can see the contrast between panic and serenity.

Then comes the appeal to the sleeping God. Moffatt translates it, "Teacher, are we to drown, for all you care?" Nothing irritates us more than someone who can sleep through a crisis. The verb is present tense, "We are dying!"

Jesus awakes, rebukes the wind, and says to the sea, "Peace! Be still!" The lake calms, the wind disappears, the stars have begun to twinkle, and it's a beautiful night to go sailing. But now the disciples are filled with an even greater fear: who is this, that even wind and sea obey him?

There is something fishy about this sea story. The old fishermen are scared to death in a storm. The landlubber carpenter-rabbi is a picture of calm. What's going on here? Mark loves to paint portraits of chaos with Jesus at the edge of it and in complete control over it. Jesus and his friends are, in fact, journeying toward another chaotic situation. When they arrive in Gerasa, they will meet the madman of Gerasa, so filled with demons that he has the entire village in a state. Once again, Jesus will master the situation, create peace, and the crowd will be filled with fear.

Hearing the Word in the Wind

The first church that heard this Gospel from Mark read was probably First Church, Rome. It too was facing a chaotic situation. Nero was feeding good Christians to the lions and illuminating his garden parties with the burning flesh of the faithful. Peter had been crucified, Paul beheaded. When the Roman Christians read this story of chaos on the lake and the sleeping God, who do you imagine they thought of? Of course, they thought of themselves.

Now, 20 centuries later when we read the same story, if we don't think of *ourselves* and our peculiarly 20th-century brand of chaos, we are not letting the Scripture work on us the way the Spirit wants it to. The American church is not undergoing persecution, but we are in no less a state of disorganization. Let's focus for a moment on our own region. In our part of the country there are as many Christians who believe our state's 38 residents of Death Row ought to be executed as there are Christians who believe they ought to be spared. In our part of the country there are as many Christians who accept abortion as a fact of life as there are Christians who are appalled by it. In our part of the lake there are as many Christians who have joined the so-called sexual revolution as there are Christians who are seeking a better way. In our

175

part of the lake there are roughly as many Christians who consider it their *Christian* duty to vote for the conservative candidate, as there are Christians who consider it their *Christian* duty to vote for the liberal. What appears to be lacking is a fixed point of reference or a still center that will hold. Perhaps it is an exaggeration to say that today's church is like a dinghy taking on water, but many of us are acting like nervous ex-fishermen scanning the horizon for a point of reference and finding none. Once on a ship 1200 miles out of New York City I overheard a young woman ask a fellow, "You from around here?" How is that for being at sea without a compass!

Our first instinct in any chaotic situation is to try to look outside it for help. Look outside the boat, away from the water. Look to money or power or pills or any quick fix to stop the pain or end the anguish. At least the disciples had the good sense—Jesus wouldn't grant them "faith"—to look to the one who, though sound asleep on a little cushion, was in the boat with them.

Christ is not *out there* but in here. He is in the midst of our difficulties and the scary moments of our life, but not susceptible to them. He is with us in those decisions for which there does not seem to be a "right" or typically Christian answer. He offers not principles but his own presence. He says, "You must make decisions on moral, economic, and political issues on the basis of the kind of God you have. God is the creator, the God of life. Your God is the redeemer, the God of mercy. I have not gone away or asleep. I am with you."

I am haunted by the book by the Jewish writer Elie Wiesel, *Night*, in which he tells of his experiences in a Nazi concentration camp. He tells of one day when the guards hanged a small boy in the presence of all the inmates. Because the boy's body was so light, his death throes were cruelly extended. Wiesel remembers that while they stood there and watched him die, he heard from behind him in the crowd an outraged voice, "Where is God? Where is he?" Later Wiesel says he heard a voice deep from within himself answer, "Where is he? Here he is—he is hanging here on this gallows."

This is the message of the incarnation and crucifixion of Jesus. God has come into the midst of us in Jesus Christ, not only to let us know who he is, but to give us his peace. Christ has assumed our chaos in order to redeem it. Humanity's perennial question is some variation on "Where are you, God?" or "God, are you sleeping?" God's eternal answer in the crucified Christ is, "Here am I in the midst of you." He is in the midst of whatever chaos you are experiencing, and in the midst of our church, guiding us on to whatever mission lies before us. Look for the still center. Is it not possible today to experience it in the Eucharist we are about to share?

God's word to us is virtually the same word addressed to the raging sea: "Peace! Be still!"

RICHARD A. LISCHER
Duke University Divinity School
Durham, North Carolina

SIXTH SUNDAY AFTER PENTECOST

Go in Peace and Be Healed
Mark 5:24b-34

Mark's story today is about a woman, a powerless woman with a 12-year flow of blood. This woman reminds me of another powerless woman I once met. Let's call her Lydia. Or, as many of her friends referred to her, "Silent Lydia." She was silent, that is, until the choir sang. In the choir and in her solo work, Lydia shone. But outside of her music, Lydia didn't say much.

We talked about her silence one day, Lydia and I. She told me a sad story. Lydia had been a bright student in grade school—bright and gifted. She excelled in music. Her teachers encouraged her, and she looked forward to developing her musical skills one day. But that day never came for Lydia. When she finished eighth grade, her father informed her that her public school days were over. "But the boys got to stay in school," she had pleaded with her father. "They even got to go to college."

"College is a man's world," her father replied. So Lydia took a two-year business course and went to work in a number of offices throughout her life. I first met Lydia after she had retired. "I hated every minute of my life as an office worker," she told me. "My retirement day was the happiest day of my life."

"It must have been difficult for you all those years," I said to her. "How did you manage it?"

"Well, you cry a lot," she said.

The system, in this case a male-dominated view of life, had beaten Lydia. Her vision of herself had died. Her dream of herself had vanished. Her personal goals for her life had been crushed out. And she became a silent person, a powerless person. She didn't feel good enough or smart

177

enough or educated enough to join most adult conversations. So she sat silently feeling powerless. She was a victim of life's circumstances.

A Word to the Powerless

I would like to invite Lydia and all persons who share her sense of powerlessness, for whatever reasons, to join this woman in Mark's story of the powerless woman. Her sense of powerlessness came from her body. She had a flow of blood that would not stop. For 12 years she had suffered. Mark goes to great lengths in telling this story to underscore her plight. She had suffered much under many physicians, he tells us. The system, the medical establishment, had only made things worse for her. She had spent all her money on doctoring and still she was no better. In fact, her condition had worsened.

It isn't hard to feel the sense of powerlessness in this woman's life. There was nothing she could do about her condition. There was no place to turn. She was one of life's victims. Circumstances had laid her low.

So what did she have to lose? Jesus, the healer, was passing by. Maybe if she could reach through the crowd and touch him she would be all right. It was risky, but what did she have to lose? *If I touch even his garments, I shall be made well,* she thought to herself. So she reached out. She touched him. The powerless woman touched the powerful Savior. The power flowed into her instantly. The hemorrhage ceased. "Who touched me?" Jesus said. In fear and trembling she confessed her deed. Can't you see her cringing in fear at Jesus' feet? *Now what? What is he going to do to me?* she thought.

And Jesus said: "Daughter, your faith has made you well; go in peace, and be healed of your disease."

The powerless person came to the power-filled man. He sent her away—he will send you away—with a simple benediction: "Go in peace, you are healed."

Invisible Henry

Mark's story today is about a woman, an unclean woman with a 12-year flow of blood. This woman reminds me of a conversation I had some years ago with a black friend. Let's call him Henry. Henry was a good friend, a pleasant person, but he carried a lot of resentment deep inside himself. I suppose you could best describe those feelings as feelings of alienation.

I'll never forget him telling me about growing up in the South and about a high-school basketball game he played in. It was to be something

178

new in the community. His all-black team from his all-black school was going to play the all-white team from the all-white school. The day came. He and his teammates came to the all-white school gym for the game. "My eyes just about popped out of my head," he told me. "I had never seen a gym like that in my whole life. I didn't know such gyms existed."

He kind of laughed when he told me the story, but the laughter couldn't hide the pain. It was the pain of being defined out of a large part of life because of the color of his skin. "I was defined out of schools, I was defined out of restaurants. I was defined out of the front seats on the bus. And on and on the list goes. And it hurts. Have you ever read Ralph Ellison's book about blacks in America?" he asked me. "It's called *Invisible Man*. That's a good title. That's about how it feels. There is a whole world of life going on, and that world doesn't even acknowledge that you exist. You're just invisible—black and invisible."

Henry had a lifetime of alienation bottled up inside of him. Every now and then parts of it would spill out. Many of us know what Henry is feeling. Alienation, being defined out of life, can happen to any one of us. Maybe we were the invisible one in our family. Maybe we were the invisible one at school. Maybe we feel like an invisible person in our community or even in our congregation. Do you know what that is like? It's like having people look at you as if you weren't even there. People see right past you. It's as if you don't exist, as if you are invisible.

A Word to the Alienated

I would like to invite my friend Henry and anyone who has felt the sting of alienation to join this woman of Mark's story of the alienated woman. Her alienation was harsh and severe. It was caused by the fact that she was unclean. The law in this matter was very clear:

> If a woman has a discharge of blood for many days, not at the time of her impurity, or if she has a discharge beyond the time of her impurity, all the days of the discharge she shall continue in uncleanness (Lev. 15:25).

A person's uncleanness was determined by the priests. Such determination was deemed very important in Israel. The Israelites were to separate themselves from all that was unclean. God and uncleanness could not come in contact with each other. That idea was still strong in Jesus' day. The woman in our story was clearly an unclean woman. That meant that she was defined out of normal human existence. She was defined out of normal human existence because anyone who touched her would become unclean. Any place she sat would become unclean. Any place she laid or anything she touched would become unclean. So

179

she was cut off from life. She was defined out of life because of her uncleanness.

One wonders what she was doing in this crowd of people. If anyone had recognized her, they would surely have sent her on her way. Maybe she had been invisible to them so long that they didn't see her any more even if she was there.

Think of the inner struggle this woman must have gone through. "If I touch even his garments, I shall be made well," she thought to herself. "But, if I touch his garments, he will become unclean too." That must have been a tremendous barrier for her to overcome. Somehow she did overcome it. She reached out. She touched him, and the hemorrhage stopped. Jesus took her uncleanness unto himself and made her clean again. Now she could be restored to life in the community. Now she could rejoin the human race. Now she could become visible again.

"Who touched my garments?" Jesus asked. Jesus would make this matter of healing between the two of them a matter for the whole crowd to experience. The woman came forward. Jesus heard her story. He said to her: "Daughter, your faith has made you well; go in peace, and be healed of your disease." Jesus said that in front of the whole crowd. The woman had been unclean to the public world. Now the public world would receive her back in their midst from the hand of Jesus. They would see that she was clean. They would see her. She was no longer invisible to them. The days of her uncleanness and alienation were past.

An alienated and unclean person came to one who was filled with God's cleanness. He sent her away—he will send you away—with a simple benediction: "Go in peace, and be healed."

Touch the Bread; Taste the Wine

I have invited Lydia and all her companions in feelings of powerlessness to join the woman in this story. I have invited Henry and all his companions in feelings of alienation to join the woman in the story. Come, you powerless ones. Come, you invisible ones. Come along and touch Jesus. This woman's courage and trust, this woman's faith, was made manifest for all to see in her touch. Faith reaches out to touch Jesus.

But where shall we find this Jesus that we might touch him? We touch him in the meal set before us this day. "This is my body, given for you. This is my blood, shed for you." Faith touches Jesus at this table. Faith tastes the presence of God's life given for us at this table.

This morning we have sent out a special invitation to those who feel powerless about their lives. Powerless people are invited to encounter a powerful Savior in this meal. Come forward and touch the bread. Come forward and in and through the words of institution hear Jesus bless you as he blessed the woman in today's story: "Go in peace, and be healed."

We have also sent out a special invitation to those who feel alienated, cut off and invisible. Invisible people are invited to touch the Savior here. Come forward and touch the bread. Come forward and be part of this community of people. You are certainly not invisible to God. God sees you at this table. You are visible to God here as a person who belongs to this community. Come forward, and in and through the words of institution hear Jesus bless you as he blessed the woman in today's story: "Go in peace, and be healed."

It may well be that as you sit in your pew this morning you don't feel those things we have been talking about. Powerlessness and invisibleness don't describe your personal reality. Whoever you are and whatever you feel, rest assured that you, too, are welcome at this table. Jesus Christ came as the Savior of every person. Bring your need to this table this morning. That is what faith is all about. Faith brings its needs to Jesus. Faith reaches out to touch Jesus. Come forward and touch the bread. Come forward, and in and through the words of institution, hear Jesus bless you as he blessed the woman in today's story: "Go in peace, and be healed."

RICHARD A. JENSEN
Lutheran Vespers Media Ministry
Minneapolis, Minnesota

Jesus—Offensive?

Mark 6:1-6

Most of us probably harbor notions of Jesus as a kind and pleasant chap, eager to help people and care for them tenderly. After all, he is pictured as a good shepherd, one who knows his flock and cares for each lamb with untiring concern and devotion. Meek and mild, pleasant and attractive—these are some of the characteristics we usually ascribe to Jesus. Certainly he was the kind of person you would bring home and introduce to your parents, right?

181

One day Jesus did come home to his family and neighbors, and he didn't receive a cordial reception. News of his teaching and healings had spread through the country, and one might have expected that he would have received a hero's welcome. But there was no celebration for Jesus that day when he came home to Nazareth. He went into the synagogue with his disciples and began to teach. While the people were astonished at his teaching, they were even more offended at him—not exactly the response we might have expected.

What Was Offensive?

Why were his own townspeople offended at Jesus? The text suggests that the people had trouble squaring the wise words and marvelous works of Jesus with his identity as a person in the town. After all, he was known by all to be no more than a carpenter, a handyman. He wasn't a successful businessman or an elected official. He wasn't even an ordained pastor or a professor of theology. He was only a carpenter, and a carpenter wasn't much in those days. He was a nobody, and he probably spoke with a heavy accent.

In addition to his occupation, there was his family: no one spectacular among them either. They might even have lived on "the other side of the tracks," where the outcasts and trash live. Certainly Jesus' family was known by the townspeople, and they didn't think of the family as being all that terrific.

The nub of the problem with Jesus was this: he seemed to be speaking the Word of God with authority, and he was doing the works of God in healing and teaching, but God certainly wouldn't work through a common man like Jesus in his common circumstances, would he? Perhaps that explains why Jesus' family and friends thought he was insane. The problem was Jesus' common and lowly identity.

Luke suggests that the people were offended at the message Jesus preached. Mark simply records that they were offended at the person of Jesus—who he was and what he did—and at his family.

The Offense Continues

That happened one day when Jesus came home to Nazareth, and times have changed, circumstances are different with you and me. We aren't likely to be offended at Jesus, are we?

I wonder about that. Most of us enjoy reading stories of persons who move from rags to riches, Horatio Alger stories. Recently I read of a woman who was born and reared in unbelievable poverty, and now she has become owner and manager of a leading advertising firm in a major urban center. I enjoy reading stories of persons who manage to surmount the grim circumstances of their birth and youth and become somebodies. Maybe you enjoy reading those stories too, stories of people moving from rags to riches. That's the movement that tickles our fancies.

But what about a reverse kind of story—a movement from riches to rags, which seems to depict the movement of God among us in Jesus. Aren't we still somewhat offended at this activity of God in identifying himself with us in the common and ordinary aspects of our life? We'd like something more spectacular, more successful, more extravagant than what God gives us in Jesus. Regarded by some to be insane, having no-where to lay his head, rejected by the people, and then finally pushed out of the city and strung up on a cross for all to gawk at, Jesus moved from riches to rags.

We would probably prefer a divine Messiah to a human one. Robert Capon notes that "the true paradigm of the ordinary American view of Jesus is Superman." Offended at the humanity of Jesus, people try to jazz it up. They try to transform the carpenter into a Superman who relentlessly battles for truth, justice, and the American way—and, of course, he always prevails. This Superman-Jesus looks like a man, but inside he is more than human.

Capon concludes, "Don't laugh. The human race is, was and probably always will be deeply unwilling to accept a human messiah. We don't want to be saved in our humanity; we want to be fished out of it. We crucified Jesus, not because he was God, but because he blasphemed: He claimed to be God and he failed to come up to our standards for assessing the claim. It's not that we weren't looking for the Messiah; it's just that he wasn't what we were looking for. Our kind of Messiah would come down from a cross . . . . He wouldn't do a stupid thing like rising from the dead. He would do a smart thing like never dying."

Yes, the offensiveness of Jesus persists even today. And that attitude towards him impedes the works he can do among his people. Mark reports that Jesus could do no mighty works in Nazareth, except that he healed a few sick people. Mark's point seems unmistakably clear— that people's attitude toward Jesus can help or hinder his work.

The importance of one's attitude toward and relationship to Jesus is highlighted in Mark's gospel by the way in which Jesus is depicted as having power and authority over nature but not over people. Jesus heals diseases, casts out demons, controls the winds—but he does not control people and dictate their response to him. He commands people to be silent, and they go and blurt out everything he told them. He commands the women at the tomb to go and tell his disciples the news of his resurrection, and they go and say nothing to no one because they are afraid.

Since Jesus does not control human beings, their attitude toward him is a crucial factor in determining the works he can or cannot do among them. He cannot heal people who have no desire to be healed. He cannot forgive people who have no desire to be forgiven. He cannot teach people whose minds are closed. He cannot bring new life to people who have no desire for it. He cannot create peace in people and among people whose desires are expressed in hate and revenge.

Our Offense Transformed

Your attitude and my attitude toward Jesus affect the works he can do among us. And while we may harbor some offense at Jesus, that probably isn't our chief attitude toward him. Otherwise we wouldn't be here worshiping and praying, even our half-baked prayers. Maybe we are present here in church because we want to live out the blessing Jesus gives on another occasion: "Blessed are they who are not offended at me."

And the source of his blessing is the same as the cause for offense, namely, his complete and total identification with you and me in the common and ordinary circumstances of our life. Precisely because God so totally identifies himself with us in Jesus—identifies himself with us in our failures and in our successes, in our sorrows and in our joys, in our doubts and in our faith, in our fears and in our courage—we can be freely open to Christ's works among us, and we can expect them, too.

Chief among those works is finding ourselves little by little changed into the likeness of Jesus. For he comes among us not to change the circumstances in the world around us to suit ourselves, but to change us for the circumstances in the world.

That's what one man discovered at a church council meeting. He had met with a group of the council before the scheduled meeting in order to firm up opposition to a program that had been proposed to advance the mission of the congregation in the broader community. The council meeting was a stormy session; tempers flared; more heat was generated than light. Finally the man who had been at the earlier caucus spoke up and said, "This isn't Jesus' way among us, and we are Jesus' people." The meeting was adjourned shortly thereafter. No decisions were made. But one man discovered himself being changed into the likeness of Jesus.

And as that change occurs in us, we will find ourselves, sometimes surprisedly, carrying on the work of Jesus—carrying on his works of healing, visiting, teaching, laboring, sharing, and loving among the brothers and sisters around us. Our offense at Jesus becomes the glory of Jesus among us.

Then we will understand the meaning of the blessing Jesus intends for each one of us: "Blessed are you who are not offended at me."

MORRIS J. NIEDENTHAL
Lutheran School of Theology at Chicago
Chicago, Illinois

Our Turn for the Better
Mark 6:7-13

According to the New English Bible, "Jesus summoned the Twelve and sent them out in pairs on a mission." There seems to be no escape clause in the Lord's call to mission. Remember the words from the TV serial *Mission Impossible?* "Your mission, should you decide to accept it . . . ." We would prefer that kind of phrasing, that kind of option, not only on the general contract but on the day-to-day schedule.

Amos said, "I am no prophet, nor a prophet's son; but I am a herdsman, and a dresser of sycamore trees, and the Lord took me from following the flock, and the Lord said to me, 'Go prophesy' " (Amos 7:14-15). No escape clause there and none asked for.

The disciples heard Jesus' simple words, "Follow me." And they did. At the formal choosing of the Twelve, Jesus "went up into the hills, and called to him those whom he desired; and they came to him. And he appointed twelve, to be with him and to be sent out to preach and have authority to cast out demons" (Mark 3:13-15). No escape clause there, and none asked for.

And now the mission of this Gospel. No question that the assignment would be accepted. It seems as if it was not possible for them to think of Christ's mission as impossible. Ought we not then think of it as possible? It is our turn now. We have been taking our turn, true, but think of the levels of the assignment. We have been doing some things right. Perhaps we can improve. Now, perhaps, it is our turn to do it better, our turn for the better.

185

To Be with Him

Think of our Lord's first choosing of the Twelve: "He appointed twelve to be with him" Being with him—that is the first part of mission. That is really all those disciples are described as doing up to this chapter in Mark. The two things they are credited with saying didn't reflect much credit upon them. In the storm they cried out, "Teacher, do you not care if we perish?" When the woman was healed by touching his garment and Jesus wanted to know, "Who touched me?" they said, "You see the crowd pressing around you, and yet you say, 'Who touched me?' " Still, that seems to be all that the Lord expected, that they should be with him.

They were there to learn. *Being* with him is necessary before *going* for him. Others, from demons to lepers, were not permitted to talk about him. Evidently not only the disciples but those others too had to learn before they should witness. In their enthusiasm and euphoria they were apt to say the wrong things about him. Meanwhile by being with him the disciples were being prepared for the mission. They heard him "preaching the gospel of God and saying, 'The time is fulfilled, and the kingdom of God is at hand; repent, and believe in the gospel' " (Mark 1:14-15). And while he spoke to the crowds in parables, "privately to his own disciples he explained everything" (Mark 4:33).

At no time during those first days of discipleship did Jesus say anything like, "Why don't *you* say something?"

Of course, simply in their being with him, they were already saying a great deal. They were certainly saying that being a disciple of Jesus beat catching fish or collecting taxes or doing any of the other things the Twelve had been doing.

That ought to make us all feel better. Of course, it does make us sound like beginners, and most of us have been with Jesus for a good long time. Has it been a good time—these years you have been with him? How do you feel about him? That should tell you what being with him has done for you and whether you are ready for a turn for the better.

We don't speak about it much, don't put it into words—except in prayer. And then only to him—or when singing hymns like "Lord, Thee I Love with All My Heart." We had a venerable upright piano in a fourth-floor apartment when Seminex was young. Often seminary students would gather around the piano and fold in the edges of the evening's last moments with hymns. That was always a favorite, "Lord, Thee I Love." Years later standing in the oldest level of Chartres Cathedral down below the chancel in an ancient chapel we heard a German choir in the chancel above singing that chorale. Do you have a hymn that brings tears to your eyes? Is that a way to sense your faith, your joy in just being with our Lord Jesus Christ? Are you not on this first level of mission—being with him?

To Go for Him

To go for him! That's the second part of mission.

Go for him—not very far, just around the villages here, just to ordinary people. Don't get dressed up, just wear your ordinary clothes. You don't have to pack a lunch or take any money; this won't take long. In fact, your first stop may be upstairs in the bedroom, where someone is crying or lonesome or irritatingly demanding. It may be just down the street, where someone is ill or where some demonic spirit is raising havoc in a household. You've made these trips before. You've stopped to say hello every now and then. This time just go for him.

"When you are admitted to a house...." You don't have to force your way in. When God sends you, God opens doors. Just go for him. He knows his way around. He knows where he is wanted. And he knows he is wanted even where people don't know they want him.

What can you say? One would think that would be the first thing the disciples would have asked Jesus as he told them to go out—"What shall we say?" Here the Lord doesn't say.

In that time, in those villages conditions of hospitality were different. Strangers, pilgrims would be invited in, food would be shared, a place to sleep offered. But the conversation would have been much like our usual banal beginnings. "It's been hot. Where are you traveling that you would be passing through our village? Strangers seldom show up here." This gave the disciples the opportunity to make clear that they had been sent by Jesus. "We've been with Jesus. He suggested we travel through here and stop and call on you." Where does the conversation go from there? I don't know. No wonder the Lord told the disciples not to be concerned about what they were to say when they would be called up in front of judges. The Holy Spirit will guide the conversation. But we need to make it clear that we go for Jesus. Can you imagine these disciples leaving a home, congratulating themselves that the subject of why they came, from whom they came, never came up: "Well, managed that one. No embarrassing questions. Didn't even have to mention the Lord."

When we go out to talk to people we need to find something to say that makes it clear we are involved with God, who is involved with Jesus, who sent us to be involved with you. Perhaps it is no more than to say, "Last Sunday at church one of the lessons..." or "One of the

187

things that struck me in the sermon . . . ." But if it is his mission, it begins by letting people know you are *for* him.

A Turn for the Better

The issue, however, is still finally, "What shall we say?" And that is the third part of mission—to recommend a turn for the better.

The disciples evidently were expected to say something that would arouse a rather violent reaction. They were told to shake off the dust from their sandals at those who refused to receive them or to listen to them. What did they say? They preached repentance.

What does that mean in terms of actual conversation? Accusation? "You'd better shape up around here. If things are going wrong, it's clear you must be doing something wrong"? No, not accusation—invitation!

What is repentance? It is a new orientation, a turning to a new center. Preaching repentance is saying that life is not just going around in circles, hanging on for dear life to all the dizzying circumferences of life. It is getting beyond the busy-ness of our lives to the center, where God loves and reigns, where Jesus Christ who gave himself for us is highly exalted and given the name at which every knee should bow.

It can't all be said at once, perhaps not at all in the first villages we visit. But when the right time comes to speak of the hope that is in us, we can recommend a turn to the better, a turn for the best.

The Second Lesson gives one of Paul's attempts:

Praise be to the God and Father of our Lord Jesus Christ for giving us through Christ every possible spiritual benefit as citizens of Heaven! For consider what he has done—before the foundation of the world he chose us to become, in Christ, his holy and blameless children living within his constant care. He planned, in his purpose of love, that we should be adopted as his own children through Jesus Christ—that we might learn to praise that glorious generosity of his which has made us welcome in the everlasting love he bears towards the Beloved. It is through him, at the cost of his own blood, that we are redeemed, freely forgiven through that full and generous grace which has overflowed into our lives and opened our eyes to the truth. For God has allowed us to know the secret of his plan, and it is this: he purposes in his sovereign will that all human history shall be consummated in Christ, that everything that exists in Heaven or earth shall find its perfection and fulfillment in him. And here is the staggering thing—that in all which will one day belong to him we have been promised a share (since we were long ago destined for this by the one who achieves his purposes by his sovereign will), so that we, as the first to put our confidence in Christ, may bring praise to his glory! And you too trusted him, when you had heard the message of truth, the gospel of your salvation.

And after you gave your confidence to him you were, so to speak, stamped with the promised Holy Spirit as a guarantee of purchase, until the day when God completes the redemption of what he has paid for as his own; and that will again be to the praise of his glory (Eph. 1:3-14 Phillips).

We come now for that other guarantee, that food for the journey, the body and blood of our Lord. It's a long haul, this mission, But it's really living. And at its ending, when our Lord calls us back, we will report "all that we have done and taught." And then we will discern, too, what dying really is—our turn for the better.

GEORGE W. HOYER
Pacific Lutheran Theological Seminary
Alameda, California

NINTH SUNDAY AFTER PENTECOST

Which Shepherd?

Mark 6:30-34

It is not flattering to be compared with sheep. Yet we and everyone we know seem to do a lot of just milling around. Nothing seems to work properly. Nothing seems to be ever completed. Nothing seems to be fully resolved. Even we who live in small-town and rural areas find ourselves overscheduled, overorganized, and overtired. We can understand the desire of Jesus to escape "the madding crowds" and take his disciples to a place of peace and quiet. Perhaps there the true leader will be found.

Too Many Shepherds?

We do not, however, lack would-be shepherds. We have more than we can ever hear, let alone follow. We who call ourselves Christians have made a major contribution to the confusion. It has been estimated that there are more than 1200 Christian denominations in our land. Then add the veritable riot of "new religions" that have swept across our land in the last few years to further complicate our situation. It is no better in any of the other important areas of our lives: government, science, media, education. All are filled with would-be leaders and qualified experts beyond our counting.

189

There is one further, more subtle, problem for us today. Those who would be our leaders know a great deal more about the methods which can be used to persuade us to follow them. I am reminded of a conversation with my good friend Dennis. He is a third-generation sheep rancher in southwestern North Dakota. I was helping him move some sheep in the pens and noted the way he handled the animals. So I asked him what was the most important thing to know about working with sheep. He thought for a moment and then replied, "You have to know what a sheep is going to do before it even thinks about doing it." Much time and effort is being expended these days in trying to determine what we will do even before we know what we want to do. These efforts are dignified with titles such as "opinion polls" and "market research." The intention is to lead us in a particular direction in voting, purchasing, or thinking.

The Best Defense

Since we do have higher mental abilities than sheep, we know some tricks too. We organize. We educate. We protest. We join organizations beyond counting. Like you, I go to many meetings during the course of a year. A common theme is present in many of the meetings. Whatever problem the group is attempting to solve, someone will take the floor and say "What we have to do is educate people." So we devise a plan, simple or complex, to educate the public. We carry out our plan with intense effort. We wake up the next day and find that the problem is still there. We discover that our friends and neighbors are on the other side of the issue. We find ourselves confronted with a new and more serious problem.

This is why I have been fascinated by the reaction of Jesus to the situation he faced in our text for today. His first reaction is one that we know well. It is compassion. But this is not your average "I sure feel kinda sorry for..." compassion. This is the kind that you feel right down in your midsection. It's the feeling I get when the phone rings and I am informed of the death of someone in the parish. It is the feeling I get when I visit someone who is seriously ill. You know what kind of compassion I mean. It is part of what it means to be human.

The strange action on Jesus' part is the second one. "He began to teach them many things." At first glance, this seems positively silly. Is Jesus no more than an early version of the classic old liberal notion that the solution to all human problems is just more education? Hardly! All you need to do is just read the gospel of Mark. Skim through the gospel.

Ignore the travels. Pass by the miracles. Pay no attention to the arguments with the Pharisees. Just read what Jesus teaches.

His opening line is this: "The time is fulfilled, and the kingdom of God is at hand; repent, and believe in the gospel" (Mark 1:15). There you have it, it is the kingdom of God that Jesus would teach us about— the kingdom that is like the treasure hid in the field and the pearl of great price, the kingdom that is here now, the kingdom that calls to us to lose our lives so that we may save them.

Now It's in Focus!

The message of the kingdom is a clear call to us to look at ourselves and the world around us with different eyes. It is no longer a matter of observing everything around us, examining the evidence, learning all of the details, and then proceeding onward and upward with some marvelous plan. Instead, we are called to focus on something distinct but not distant. The bright beacon of the kingdom of God gives us the point of reference by which we can orient our lives as surely as the sailor uses a lighthouse. The kingdom of God is the most important thing that there is to know about being human. The kingdom of God is a vision of freedom. We will be able to distinguish between that which is ultimate and that which is only second place for our lives.

The Final Question

But we still really want to know if all of this kingdom talk is truth. We have been deceived too many times in our lives. Those would-be shepherds keep on fooling us with their shrewd and clever schemes. We get tricked, or worse, trick ourselves into believing that something— anything—is better than what we have now. If we could just see it, weigh it, touch it, count it, compute it, then we would be happy. Then we would know which leader to follow.

There is one more teaching of Jesus that applies: "He was teaching his disciples, saying to them, 'The Son of man will be delivered into the hands of men, and they will kill him; and when he is killed, after three days he will rise' " (Mark 9:31). Here is the point by which the true and the false leaders are separated. Just ask them this one question, "Will you go to Jerusalem for me?"

He who answers yes is the one who has true compassion, the compassion of God himself for a disordered creation and a fallen humanity. He who answers yes is the one who is willing to lead us to the Father's home, even at the cost of his life. He who answers yes is the one who

191

truly loves us, lost, confused, and thick-headed as we are. He who answers yes is the only one worth hearing and following.

CHARLES J. TAFT
Grace and West Scandia Lutheran Churches
McClusky, North Dakota

Christ's Sufficiency and Ours
John 6:1-15

The miracle stories are the headlines of John's gospel. They signal dramatically and vividly the key messages that the evangelist is sending out for all to hear. The feeding of the 5000 is a boldface, front-page headline in this gospel, announcing the all-important fact that the Word of God and the Bread of Life are inseparably bound together in Jesus Christ.

The carefully crafted story of this miracle—told in each of the four Gospels—pictures Jesus at the center of a huge hungry and tired crowd. They have followed Jesus for miles; they have sought him out. They have heard him or they have heard about him, and now they need him. They need him to have faith in, and they need him to give hope and meaning and direction to their confused and uncertain lives. In the process of their search for him, they have ignored everything—even food to eat. So now they surround him and press in on him, needing food for their bodies as well as nourishment for their spirits. And the point of the story is that Jesus more than satisfies both their needs. The headline reads, "Word of God and Bread of Life Inseparably Bound Together in Him."

An All-Sufficient Savior

Sufficiency is the word that captures the message of this passage. Jesus stands in the center of the crowd as God's all-sufficient representative, who feeds every human hunger and meets every human need. There is no choosing here between bread for the stomach and food for the soul, no artificial separation between a spiritual Jesus and a material Jesus. Physical needs and spiritual needs are combined together or collapsed

192

in Jesus. Filling empty growling stomachs to capacity becomes one of the ways he conveys his great love for humanity and shows forth his sovereignty over all the earth.

Jesus is in full charge. In the Gospel for today it is almost as if the miracle of the feeding of the 5000 is a part of a carefully laid plan in his unfolding ministry. John says that Jesus knew all the time what he would do, but just to test his disciples, perhaps to stretch their minds with the magnitude of what he was about to do, he confronted them with the problem. "Where are we to buy bread to feed all these people," he asked. Obviously distraught over the question and without a clue as to what to do, Phillip answered, "Five hundred dollars would not be enough money to buy bread so everyone could have a little." See the scene: a throng of people, weary from a long walk, yet far off in the country and now hungry. The stage is set for a chaotic climax. But then Jesus stopped his testing and his teaching and took charge. "Make the people sit down," he commanded. Then he took the scant provisions at hand, lifted the loaves and gave thanks and distributed them to the people. He did the same with the two small fishes, and the crowd feasted, eating all they want. And then, just to make the point crystal clear, Jesus ordered that the leftovers be picked up, and 12 full baskets were gathered.

The Word of God and the Bread of Life are inseparably bound together in Jesus the Christ. That's the headline. All we need to give hope and meaning and direction to our uncertain lives we have in our all-sufficient Savior.

The Eucharistic Feast

The miracle of the feeding of the 5000 can't be explained, but it can be experienced. John relates this miracle to the Eucharist feast of the church. Here we and millions in the world experience the all-sufficiency of Jesus. Think of all the ways this holy feast speaks the powerful word of faith to us and satisfies our cravings. When we eat and drink the body and blood of Christ, the pain and sorrow of our sin is overcome and our fear is transformed into hope. We are bound again to the maker and meaning of our lives. We are "in Christ" as St. Paul puts it—one with Christ and part of his future in God.

We feast in celebration at births; we break this bread at funerals; we spread the table at bedsides and at the marriage feast; and we eat together when we gather in the name of the Lord. And in this eating and drinking we too experience the miracle of our all-sufficient Savior. Hearts are healed; strangers are drawn together; the body of Christ with all its diverse members, interdependent and global in scope, takes form and

193

grows whenever we eat this bread and drink this cup. So we experience also, in our miraculous feeding, the all-sufficiency of Jesus, who combines for us the Word of God and the Bread of Life.

Our Sufficiency

But the word *sufficiency* not only captures the message of this story as it applies to Christ; it also describes the message of the story about us.

It is an affirmation of our sufficiency to do and to be what is required of us in God's mission in the world. It is Andrew, the disciple who is always in the background, the one a great preacher labeled, "the saint of rank and file," who breaks in on Philip and Jesus with the report that there is a boy in the crowd with five barley loaves and two small fish. And then, as if he is embarrassed for mentioning it, Andrew adds, "But what are they among so many?" Yet, in the hands of Jesus, these humble resources, blessed and distributed to many, became all-sufficient for the purposes of God.

Not many of us feel sufficient in all the commitments and requirements that press on us from our family relationships, our work, our community—to say nothing of our responsibility as Christians in the modern world. We find easy identity with reluctant leaders in the Bible like Moses, Jeremiah, and Peter—each of whom suggested good reasons why they were less than adequate to serve the cause of the kingdom. Yet the Word of God to each of them is the word that emanates from this lesson. "In spite of all you are not, in spite of your inadequate resources, what you are and what you have is sufficient for God's work in the world." For God promises to gather up our meager resources, ourselves, our loaves and fishes, and through the power of the Holy Spirit to miraculously multiply them too.

A Hungry World

This confidence in our own sufficiency to play a role in God's mission in the world is especially important when we remember that the message of this miracle is about physical hunger of the body as well as spiritual hunger of the soul. Jesus cares about both. In fact, in a strange way they go together in the mind and ministry of Jesus and in the message of the gospel. The Word of God and the Bread of Life are inseparably bound in Jesus the Christ. The Bible leaves no doubt that hungry people are the special focus of God's concern and must be the urgent priority for God's people in mission.

The fact of world hunger and its expanding global dimensions is one of the most distressing and depressing realities of our modern world. Biblically speaking, hunger cannot be regarded solely as an international issue or a political issue or an economic issue. It must be regarded fundamentally as a religious issue. "I was hungry and you fed me, thirsty and you gave me drink." These are the startling words of Jesus by which he proclaims his solidarity with the hungry of the world and calls his people to focus on this priority. "Since you have done it unto the least of these, you have done it unto me."

It has always been difficult for most Americans to imagine hunger. The cornucopia has been more than legend in the United States. Food, plenty of it for most of us, has been a virtual right of every citizen.

Yet, the times are changing, and most of us are slowly becoming aware and concerned that we live on a very hungry planet. How hungry? Statistics vary, but one food-science professor at Michigan State University says bluntly, "There are 1.2 billion well-nourished people on the globe and the rest, 2.5 billion, who are underfed and malnourished." Robert McNamara, the former head of the World Bank, claims that 500 million of our global companions live in absolute poverty. And what is most distressing and constitutes an urgent call to Christian action is that these figures are all being revised upwards.

"One of his disciples, Andrew, ... said to him, 'There is a lad here with five barley loaves and two fish; but what are they among so many?' " We can easily share the frustration, the embarrassment, and even the anger of Andrew as he comes forward with his ridiculous pittance in the presence of 5000 empty bellies. But Jesus didn't laugh. He took the offering. Its significance was not that it was small, but that it was all that was available, and it was given freely. And with prayer and power, Jesus multiplied these scant provisions and made them sufficient.

Let us not withhold our loaves and fishes because they are few. We can all make our contribution.

Ripples of Hope

We can make a point to consciously remember every time we pray the Lord's Prayer, especially the petition, "Give us this day our daily bread," that this is a global prayer, all in the plural, all prayed by us on behalf of all humanity, especially the hungry.

We can inform ourselves about this most urgent human need. The causes are complex and multiple. They include the breakdown of ancient agricultural customs, misguided political policies, the concentration of

195

land and wealth in the hands of a few, the conversion of national farm-lands by commercial interests to grow cash crops for faraway markets, wars, inadequate and inappropriate technology, tribal conflict, ignorance, neglect, and hunger itself, which like a vicious downward spiral begets more hunger. Loving our global neighbors begins by knowing their needs.

We can give to the World Hunger Appeal. Lutheran World Relief is one of the great arms of mercy stretched around the world. It is your arm in a very direct way. You are feeding the hungry, many more than 5000 every day in troubled spots around the world. You are also digging wells and building dams and starting herds and teaching new agricultural techniques and doing many other things to change the horrible picture of hunger.

And we can become advocates for the hungry people of the world in our own country. A special burden we bear as U.S. Christians is the fact that although our country is one of the nations rich enough to help others, our per-capita assistance to the hungry ranks toward the bottom of the list of affluent countries. Our Christian brothers and sisters in hungry lands plead with our missionaries to be their advocates to increase our national aid to the destitute nations of the world and to help change the structures of injustice that keep two-thirds of the world in poverty and hunger.

Loaves and fishes all, but who knows if they might not be sufficient?

Nearly two decades ago, Robert Kennedy made these moving comments as he addressed beleaguered workers for justice in South Africa:

> We must dispel the notion that there is nothing one person can do against the enormous array of the world's ills, against misery and ignorance, injustice and violence. Few will have the greatness to bend history itself, but each of us can work to change a small portion of events and in the total of these acts will be written into the history of this generation.
>
> It is from numberless diverse acts of courage and belief that human history is shaped. Each time a person stands up for an ideal or acts to improve the lot of others or strikes out against injustice, that person sends a tiny ripple of hope, and crossing each other from a million different centers of energy and daring, those ripples build a current which can sweep down the mightiest walls of oppression and resistance.

Loaves and fishes. Don't dispise them. Let us offer them up together and pray earnestly for a miracle.

WILLIAM E. LESHER, PRESIDENT
Lutheran School of Theology
Chicago, Illinois

The Deepest Hunger Satisfied
John 6:24-35

One good way to enter into the life situation to which our Lord Jesus speaks in today's text is to call to mind our pre-Christmas frame of mind. The holidays are approaching. Preparations for gift exchanges, Christmas meals, holiday travel, and a flurry of other things that go along with December 25 fill up the days to the fullest. Underneath the customarily hectic pace, however, there is a hunger. It is the inner longing that somehow and in some way all the exertion and preparation will not leave us exhausted on the inside, but satisfied and at peace in our souls, because the Lord whose birth we celebrate gets through to us in spite of all the hoopla. Without that inner nurturing of the spirit the Christmas holidays wear us out. But with the keeping of what one ancient Advent prayer calls the "wide, sweet spaces of the heart" for the Christ to make his dwelling, all is changed. The deepest hunger of life is satisfied.

The Clue Given by the Evangelist

As the sixth chapter of John's gospel begins, there is a phrase we must notice. "Now the Passover, the feast of the Jews, was at hand." That's a clue to meaning, not just a chronological detail without significance for the entire chapter. It was a preholiday moment there among the Jews of Galilee, where Jesus had just performed the signs of the feeding of the 5000 and the walking on the sea. Families were assembling to eat unleavened bread and the flesh of an unblemished lamb. Like our mid-December days, the hours were extra full. For well over a thousand years the faithful of Israel had kept on remembering the great event that lay at the foundation of their faith and life, the mighty work of God in bringing them out of bondage in Egypt to the land of promise. The remembrance of that past event was bound up with food and dress and custom and gatherings, all of which required effort. But beneath the external accoutrements of unleavened bread, the ceremonial cup of wine passed, the unblemished lamb prepared, the liturgical prayers of the elders, and the questions of the chidlren about the meaning of it all, there was the inner hope for a present deliverance and for the coming of the messianic deliverer himself. Would the keeping of the outward forms of Passover ever lead to the meeting of the deepest inner needs of life? Would the time ever come when memory of divine deliverance

197

in ages past and the hopes for the coming deliverer would be fulfilled? Jesus spoke to that question that would appear to be unanswerable.

The Bread That Endures

His answer is himself: "I am the bread of life; he who comes to me shall not hunger, and he who believes in me shall never thirst" (John 6:35).

In this great "I am" passage which concludes today's Gospel reading, Jesus proclaims the truth of towering preeminence. He himself is the food that endures to eternal life, the bread that never perishes. The forms of Passover observance, which carried the hopes of the faithful down through the centuries, received their fulfillment at last. The manna by which God sustained his people in the desert wanderings did not satisfy them perpetually. Moses, their leader, called to show them the way through the wilderness, came to the end of his own life's journey. The Passover ritual was the link of continuity to the great things of old. But in the person and ministry of Jesus the old gave way to the new work of God.

What makes Jesus Christ the bread who endures is the offering he made of his life blood for the world. He came among us from the bosom of the Father to make atonement for our sins. By his sacrifice alone the way is opened for our return to the family of God. Even when we do not fully recognize it, our deepest hunger of life is to return to that fellowship with God that our transgressions have broken. Religious ceremonies alone will not fill that inmost void. The Son of God has been raised from the dead. He sends to us again today the Holy Spirit, both in the gospel of Christ's cross that is proclaimed and in the supper of the Lord to which we are invited. On Christ Jesus, God has "set his seal." The empty cross is the mark of that seal. Look to it again today and receive God's forgiveness and acceptance. We have it by hearing and believing that all that Jesus did he did *for us*. It is our gift as we claim it with a penitent heart, trusting that this Lord loves us as we are.

The Heart Has Its Hunger

Each day in our part of the world the television industry produces words and images on the screen that bear promises: this product, that investment, yet another attractively packaged creation promise instant gratification. But we all know the advertising lines are overblown in their promises. Houses filled only with consumer products are houses filled with people who are discontented. More and more gadgetry won't

198

fill the void either. We can't fill that inner hunger of the heart by plunging ourselves into our work or meet it by straining ourselves to the limit for the best education our schools can offer. Meeting and satisfying that hunger does not come with retirement, nor even in the experience of seeing our children grow to productive adulthood.

I suppose the highest form our society can find to express its answer to the ultimate hunger of life is the lottery. The million-dollar winners are touted extensively, and the media time it perfectly to give us their shrieks of delight and excited tears of ecstacy in being handed the seven-digit check. "Now our worries are over. Now we can really live!" they seem to say.

Have you ever been treated to life stories of past winners? I have not heard about the winners of five years ago or even last year. That isn't the story the public wants to hear, for the relentless truth of that part of the story is that people have counted on the food that does not endure—the size of the lottery check notwithstanding. The heart hungers on; our spirit will find no peace until the bread that lasts is placed within it.

How much the human spirit longs for something that is lasting came home to me recently in a story told me by a doctor. He is one of those exemplary physicians who goes out of his way to attend to the deeper needs of those who suffer. Among his patients was a 24-year-old man who had burned out his body on drugs, alcohol, and venereal disease. No family paid him any attention, having long since given up on him. Whatever circle of friends he once enjoyed had disappeared as well. He was soon to die, and he knew it. In his bitterness about his life he had built up a thick wall against any spiritual penetration. With what little strength he had left, he fought vociferously against any talk of God or prayer or sin or hope. His attending physician did not force the Bread of Life on him. Instead he simply went to this hapless fellow's bedside each afternoon at 4:00 and spoke quietly to him, touching his hand to tell him he was there (the patient had lost his eyesight).

One afternoon the man asked a startling question of the doctor. "Could you take sperm from my body and impregnate some woman who wants to become a mother, so that there might be some kind of future in connection with my name? I've really blown it. But if you doctors can bring it off, I'd like to be a part of another life—one that could last a lot longer than mine and add up to something I never became."

The doctor had to tell him it couldn't be done. But something better came as the result of that sudden opening in the granite wall of one desolate soul. The doctor spoke of him who said, "Work for the food that endures to eternal life."

"What does that mean?" the young man asked.

199

"This is what it's all about—that you believe that in spite of everything, Christ the Lord is for you and not against you. Let him have his way."

In that hospital room the truth of this text came alive with a transforming power. The doctor who told me of it will not forget it; neither will any of us who heard his testimony.

What Does Our Experience Teach Us?

Living in the light of our faith, we learn by experience what satisfies and what still leaves an inward hunger. The true bread for our souls is not found in things. Even the most impressive stockpile of consumer goods does not nourish that spiritual center of our lives which marks us out as beings made in God's image. Augustine's classic sentence that our hearts are restless until they rest in God is a truth that holds for every human.

In this era of the human story it is particularly true for us First World citizens of the Western world. Throughout so much of western Europe one sees churches empty and superhighways crowded with Mercedes Benz's latest models. In Scandinavia, where the state is looked to for all the needs of life, the tiny percentage of worshiping Christians stand out against the background of masses of people somehow unsatisfied with the good life that has no vital spiritual center anymore.

To the east of the Iron Curtain, where the banners and slogans of the socialist utopia are everywhere, trying to impress citizens with the glories of the classless society, there is the undertow of restless people who not only yearn for freedom but for that bread which endures beyond all the fatuous promises of society builders.

In Japan, where the economic miracle of the 1960s and 1970s has catapulted that nation into unprecedented material prosperity, there are new problems the Japanese never anticipated; juvenile delinquency in alarming proportions and increasing numbers of children who simply refuse to go to school at all.

In our own land we have about 10 million latch-key children, who come home daily from school to nothing but a TV set, since mother and father are both working outside the home in order to maintain the life-style of affluence. But what is the harvest of that inordinate investment of time and effort away from children in the lives of these children? The horizon is shadowed, and question marks grow in proportion to the increased pace of frenetic "laboring for the food that perishes."

The Gift and Blessing of Sabbath

In an increasingly secular culture we are not called either to capitulate or to despair. The momentum of the Holy Spirit in our hearts is toward firmer and deeper grounding in a spiritual life that does not wither in the face of these forces. Amid all the pressures and distractions of our surroundings, cherish the Sabbath. For us Christians it is Sunday, the day of Jesus' resurrection, the "mini-Easter," that is meant to be an oasis for our souls. Keeping the Sabbath is not burdensome; it is a joy and a gift. Christ our living bread is present in the gospel proclaimed and the sacraments offered. Our Lord dwells amidst the praises of his people. It is the first privilege of our lives to come together with other believers to pray and sing to God and open our souls to his truth. We need that nourishment regularly, and as our lives fall into the well-ordered rhythm of gathering for nurture and dispersing for our serving and witness in the world we find that the Sabbath is increasingly important. Thus does God meet us and reach us at our inmost self, where he alone can minister to our hungers of the heart.

There are people of the faith in other parts of the world who risk their lives and well-being for the privilege of coming together for Sabbath worship. Not many months ago I attended a Sunday morning service of Christians in Nanjing, China, which was full to the doors—and the faithful of the Lord had filled that sanctuary a full 45 minutes before the stated time of worship. For years their church building had been turned into a granary by the government. Now the doors were once again open for the praise of God as his people gathered with a deep sense of the wondrous privilege of keeping the Sabbath together. That gift is also given to us. We do well to cherish it, in the name of Jesus Christ our Lord. He grants us no temporary snack, but the food that endures to eternal life.

F. Dean Lueking
Grace Lutheran Church
River Forest, Illinois

Good News and Bad News
John 6:41-51

We've all heard good news and bad news stories. This week's Gospel is a little different: its first the bad news, and then the good news. The bad news is in verse 44. Jesus said, "No one can come to me unless the Father who sent me draws him." The good news is also in verse 44. Jesus said, "No one can come to me unless the Father who sent me draws him." Yes, the *same* news is bad news *and* good news, depending on how we hear it.

The good news and the bad news is that faith in Christ is itself a gift from the Father. Jesus says it again in verse 65: "No one can come to me unless it is granted him by the Father." But is that *bad* news? Some of the disciples apparently thought so. Verse 66 says, "After this, many of his disciples drew back and no longer went about with him." Only the Twelve remained. This is the first time in the gospel of John that the disciples are numbered as 12. Jesus then said to the Twelve, "Will you also go away?" Peter answered, "Lord, to whom shall we go? You have the words of eternal life. And we have believed and have come to know that you are the Holy One of God." Jesus answered them, "Did I not choose you?" (v. 70).

Bad News for Pride

There it is again, the bad news and good news: the choice is not ours, but his: not that we chose him, but that he chose us. Still, how is that bad news? It's bad news, because part of us starts to think, "Well, that's all very nice, grace alone, God chooses us, and all, but I have some say in this too. I have to accept it. I'm not a puppet on a string; I have free will." "Wait a minute," we say, "what does it mean, 'No one comes to Jesus unless the Father draws him'? *I'm* an intelligent, self-sufficient person, I have some *freedom*, you know. I have my independence. How could St. Paul say, 'No one says "Jesus is Lord" except by the Spirit'?"

Part of us hates it like poison; its *bad* news. Like that old commercial, "Mother, please, I'd rather do it myself." What do you *mean*, God chose us for himself before we could even make any kind of decision? We have our pride, you know.

Ah, pride: that's the sad truth. We will not let God be God. We will not let God be all-powerful, for we want some of that power for ourselves, and a little freedom, a little free choice, and then perhaps a little credit for making the right choice. That pride is the old Adam in us, our sinful nature, our self-centered pride, arrogantly bound to our self-interest. But our will is *not* free; it is in bondage to sin and cannot free itself. Our will is in bondage to *itself* and cannot free itself. God's Word, that his leading us to Christ is by his will and graciousness alone, is *bad* news to our pride, and we don't want to hear it. We don't want to hear that God has simply decided for us, and so we hide behind two smokescreens.

First, we object, "Well, what about all the people in the world who have never heard of Jesus?" We can't hide there. This is not a general message about others, but digs into your heart, and mine. Can *you* honestly take credit for your faith as some free-will decision? Looking back, can we not see God leading us, giving us faith?

Secondly, we complain, "Can that mean that everything in life is predestined, prearranged, predetermined? That nothing is free?" That won't work either. We're not talking about everything, about whether you like ketchup or mustard, about the things on our level. We're talking about our relationship with the Creator of heaven and earth. Is God in charge or not? Do we proudly hold out for a little corner where we are lords or do we praise God as Lord and thank God for choosing us by living lives of service?

Good News for Faith

The word of God's choice, that no one comes to Jesus unless the Father grants it, can be good news too. Part of us hates it as *bad* news, for we want to keep our pride and precious free will. That's the old Adam in us. But part of us welcomes it as good news, as a relief, and that's the new you, the faith God gave in Baptism, that is now starting to grow. It can be great and comforting news that being safe in his loving arms does not depend on our fickle choice, which goes up and down like the weather, but on his choice and his love, which shall never be moved. He chose us, he baptized us, and he will keep us in his hand. Jesus said later in John, "My sheep hear my voice. . . . My Father, who has given them to me, is greater than all, and no one is able to snatch them out of the Father's hand." Now, is that bad news or good news? Jesus said, "No one can come to me unless it is granted him by the Father." It's bad news, for the proud old Adam, *and* good news, for the new you and me that God is forming.

203

Thief and Homeowner

For example: Suppose a thief breaks into a house, ties up the home-owner, and begins looting. Then a police siren is heard, coming closer, and then just outside the door. The same siren is good news to the homeowner, and bad news to the thief, at the same time. The siren is like God's Word, and we are *both* the thief and the homeowner. There is a thief in each of us, a proud rebel, who robs God of his role as Lord, who seeks only his or her own power. God in his Word, his hard Word about the divine choice, is closing in on the thief, turning the loot into guilt, cutting off any escape, crushing the thief's pride. The siren is bad news, indeed, to the thief in each of us. But we are also the homeowner, held captive and bound up by thieving, looting pride and self-concern. For the new you and the new me, given in Baptism, the siren of God's word is beautiful music, for it means freedom and rescue. It means certainty, based on God's act, not our own weak will. The same siren, bad news to the pride of the thief, is good news of grace alone, of life and salvation to those who have ears to hear. Then are we free from anxious self-concern and free to meet the needs of others.

At the moment, we are both the thief and also the homeowner, and the siren of God's Word is both bad news and good news. But not for long, for God is at work in us to put to death the old Adam, the proud thief, and to raise up a new creation for whom this news is all good.

So batter down the door, Lord. Crush the thief. Rescue us from our bondage and set us free, free for service to others.

PAUL E. ROREM
Our Savior's Lutheran Church
Edison, New Jersey

THIRTEENTH SUNDAY AFTER PENTECOST

A Foretaste of the Feast to Come
John 6:51-58

What is the most consistent image of heaven given in the Bible? No, it isn't golden streets and pearly gates. It isn't harps and eternal singing. It is feasting with the family.

That doesn't mean that when we go to heaven we are going to eat forever and ever. Even if we could be guaranteed that no calories are

204

present in the food of heaven, that would grow old after a time. I believe that Jesus often started his parables, "The kingdom of heaven is like a feast ..." because he wanted us to know that heaven is for family to-getherness.

Fellowship through Faith in Christ

What is so good about the annual Thanksgiving and Christmas dinners and other family dinners? The food? Yes, but more. It is the coming together of family, the sharing, the laughter, the tears, and all that the years bring. Recently our family got together when our middle daughter came home from Iowa for a week and our daughter and her husband who had spent a year in Germany had returned. Our youngest daughter was home from college. The girls kept saying to one another, "Do you remember when ...."

Family festivity and community celebration—that's what heaven is about and that is what Christianity is about, this side of heaven: festivity in the life to come, yes; but festivity in the here and now as well. In the here and now we can have a foretaste of the feast to come. How? By faith in Christ and by feasting with Christ at the Eucharist.

Jesus said, "I am the bread of life" (John 6:35); "I am the bread which came down from heaven" (John 6:41) and "I am the living bread" (John 6:51). These "I am" sayings all have a focus on the here and now as well as the hereafter.

In the here and now, we have eternal life. "He who believes *has* eternal life," the gospel of John says. In theology this is called "realized escha-tology." Eschatology is the study of things that are yet to come in the hereafter. "Realized eschatology" is the experience of the hereafter in the here and now. That's what faith does. It gives us a foretaste of the things to come. This experience of eternity is not so ethereal that we are totally lifted out of our sinful selves. In the here and now we still have our feet fixed in the dust. We remain less than perfect, until we die, when the foretaste becomes a feast.

The living Christ meets us and greets us and makes us family in this life. That's a surprise to many who think of religion in terms of dry theology. "I never knew that faith could be so exciting," a new member told me recently. "I thought that it was drab and dull—all rules and regulations, thinking and theology, until I got involved. Now Christ is alive to me."

One of Peter Marshall's famous sermons is entitled, "Mr. Jones, Meet the Master." Garbage collectors and senators, poor people and rich peo-ple—all can share this common experience of meeting the Master through

205

faith. In the biography of Peter Marshall, *A Man Called Peter* we read story after story of how plain, ordinary human beings found a new zest for living through faith in the living Christ.

Leslie Weatherhead's book *A Plain Man Looks at the Cross* makes the same point. Plain and common men and women are transformed by faith as they stand at the foot of the cross and center their lives through faith on our Lord and Savior.

There on the cross Jesus suffered to help us all; Jesus died to save us all; Jesus' body was broken for us all; Jesus' blood was spilled for us all. This supreme sacrifice can change us all. The common person is transformed; the ordinary person becomes extraordinary at the foot of the cross. There we are being prepared for heaven.

In his book, *Hereafter*, David Winter tells of a little girl playing in the mud who asks her mother, "What's mud for?"

"For making bricks," said the mother.

"What are bricks for?"

"Making houses, dear."

"What are houses for?"

"People."

"And what are people for?"

People are made for God, to live for God in the here and now and to live with God in the hereafter. Eternal life is what people are for.

Here and now, as well as in the hereafter, we have our lives eternalized. Eternal life is a quality of life, not just a quantity of life. Eternal life begins now. This eternal life in the here and now is nourished through the sacrament of Holy Communion.

Feasting with Christ

Jesus said, "He who eats my flesh and drinks my blood *has* eternal life" (John 6:54). This saying has implications for the here and now as well as the hereafter.

In the here and now the faithful reception of the sacrament of the body and blood of Jesus Christ is food for the journey. "Your ancestors ate manna in the wilderness," Jesus said, "but I give you bread which will cause you to live forever." This eternal "bread from heaven" nourishes our faith for the rough journey through the wilderness of life. It causes us to abide in Christ and Christ in us (John 6:56). It means that we are fed before we are sent forth to feed others. It means that we feast with Christ before we work for Christ.

Mother Teresa of Calcutta, India, says that before she can work with the poorest of the poor in India's worst slums, she must receive the Holy Sacrament. It is food for the journey of offering mercy to the needy.

In the hereafter, we will feast with Christ and the family of God. In the here and now we have "a foretaste of that feast to come." As the pastor says, "This is the body and blood of Christ given and shed for you," you are receiving Christ, abiding in Christ, tasting the coming kingdom.

What is heaven like? It is like a family banquet. There we find and enjoy our loved ones who have passed on in the faith. There we enjoy and delight in the heavenly Father who has prepared the festivities for us.

Here we have a foretaste. There we have fulfillment.

RONALD J. LAVIN
Our Savior's Lutheran Church
Tucson, Arizona

FOURTEENTH SUNDAY AFTER PENTECOST

Take No Offense!
John 6:60-69

The Holy Gospel for today is the confession of Peter in response to the query of Jesus, "Do you also wish to go away?" Peter answered, "Lord, to whom shall we go? You have the words of eternal life." We use that confession each week as the verse sung between the Epistle (Second Lesson) and the Holy Gospel. The verse is the reminder that we regard the Lessons as the very words of God which give life. You notice that other forms and parts of the liturgy are taken from the Scriptures or are scriptural in content to help us worship with the confidence that we are dealing with the Word of God. Our interest in the verse today goes very deep. It reminds us that what we do in the liturgy has eternal consequences.

The incident which gave rise to the question of Jesus, "Do you also wish to go away?" occurred when certain of the people who had believed on Jesus were turned off by him. They decided to leave the ranks of his followers. They grumbled about what Jesus had taught them. They said, "This is a hard saying; who can listen to it?" What Jesus had been

207

talking about was himself. In that dialog, which has been the heart of the Gospels the past few weeks, Jesus had referred to himself as the Bread of Life come down from heaven. The Gospel last week reported how the people balked when Jesus said they should eat of his flesh and drink of his blood.

People Are Offended

Now, it appears that Jesus detects from their protest that they are offended that he said that he was come down from heaven. This is too much, as far as the people are concerned. Apparently these people who had been numbered among his disciples or adherents had been attracted to him for a variety of reasons. Or, they may have been enthralled by his teaching, his preaching, and the signs that he worked among them. All of that may have appeared miraculous, stellar, authoritative, and glamorous. Now he apparently stretched it too far. He claimed too much. He said he was from above and that people could eat his flesh and drink his blood.

Standing where we do, we are surprised that the people should take offense because of this. How in all the world can people take offense at Jesus when he has done so many beautiful things for the people and he had spoken so beautifully? This occasion, too, was one more marvelous demonstration of Jesus' love for the people. He had fed them. That was good enough. However, when they wanted to make him a bread king and begged him to feed them daily, he refused. He said he had something better to offer them. He is the Bread of Life, and if they receive him, they will gain eternal life.

More Offense

That is what offended the people. They were willing to settle for some materialistic miracle. They wanted free bread. If Jesus could supply that, they would believe. But when he talked about being the Bread of Life and offering heaven to them, they walked away. Jesus himself expressed amazement at this. He says, "Do you take offense at this? Then what if you were to see the Son of man ascending where he was before?"

How would the people be able to accept the fact that Jesus would suffer on a cross, die, be placed in a tomb, rise from the dead, and ascend to the Father in heaven? If the people were offended that Jesus said that he had come from the Father, how would they be able to handle the fact that he would return to the Father? The truth of the matter was that the people had seen nothing yet. Jesus said that his hour of glory was to be his death, resurrection, and return to the Father. If people could not accept this, they did not understand Jesus. Nor did they understand themselves and the reality of their predicament. Yet Jesus knew this all along. Painfully he reckoned with the fact that more and more he had become a stumbling block for the people.

People Are Offensive

It is strange that people are unwilling to accept this gracious offer of God in Christ Jesus. They are offended at the idea that God would come down from heaven and crawl into our skin, die for us, and rise again so that he could offer us the gift of eternal life. They are offended at the free offer of salvation. But who in the world is offended at the idea that we are rapidly preparing the world for its self-destruction? Who in the world is offended at the idea that we believe our safety and preservation is dependent on a nuclear arsenal that can blow the creation to kingdom come?

People are offended at the idea that God would come down from heaven to save the world. At the same time we permit the world to get itself poised for this hellish nightmare of a nuclear holocaust. Curiously, the Soviets have literally taken bread off the tables of their people in order to maintain their growth in nuclear arms. Their economy suffers, because they want to expand their arms. We are moving in the same direction. We take food stamps from the poor in our battle of the budget, and then we still have to worry whether there will be enough money around for the government to borrow to build its nuclear defenses. We get offended at Jesus' claim to be the Bread of Life. In the meantime we give up our daily bread to make nuclear power our savior.

The Human Condition

This gross contradiction should be so apparent, that one would think the whole world would fall to its knees in a confession of faith in this noble and majestic Jesus. Yet that is not the way it works. The fact that it does not happen that way is an indication of how trapped we are in the human condition. We read, hear, and watch the decadence grow in the society. We have all too few solutions to the enormous social problems that make life miserable for so many. We despair of what the future might bring. Yet this growing frustration in the world does not appear to force people to face up to the reality of the situation. We get only so far with the recognition of the causes. We do not want to recognize that all our difficulties begin with the lack of trust and faith in a gracious

209

and loving Father. That is what the problem was from the very beginning.

It was no different when Jesus confronted people with the offer of the Bread of Life. And it is no different now. We fail to create solutions to our problems, because we do not recognize the real causes. Our diagnosis is way off. The drug culture we live with is a good symptom of how we deal with the problems that haunt us. Drugs remain so attractive, because they provide the escape. They apparently offer very brief relief from what troubles people. Yet the misery and the trouble grow with the slavery to the drugs. That is exactly how it works with most of the temporary solutions that people offer for the problems that plague us. Yet we know that these solutions only create more slavery and ultimate disaster.

The Divine Solution

Jesus understood all that. He remonstrated with the people for their failure to believe. He informed them of their real difficulty. "It is the spirit that gives life, the flesh is of no avail; the words that I have spoken to you are spirit and life. But there are some of you that do not believe." There it is, pure and simple. People do not want to believe the Spirit of God, but they fall back on the answers of the flesh. That is, people look to themselves for the answers, rather than to believe that it is a gracious Father who stands ready to save them.

The evangelist adds that Jesus knew right along what this problem was. He knew that there were those who did not believe him. They would be the ones who would betray him and give him up to be crucified. They would not only refuse to believe him, but they would make the moves to destroy him. In doing that they destroyed the very best that God had to offer them. Jesus explained, "This is why I told you that no one can come to me unless it is granted him by the Father." God gave it his best shot. Here he permitted his Son to stand among these people, but they turned him down flatly. That was because they refused the Father. God had tried to make them willing. But they remained unwilling and preferred disaster.

The Spirit Gives Life

Jesus said, "It is the spirit that gives life ... the words that I have spoken are spirit and life." That is important. All of us would like to know how faith works. How does one make believers? Why do some believe and others do not? We can find some analogies in psychology, though they may be imperfect. When one college student finished his four-year football career at the university, he had to write a spring term

210

paper for a psychology class. He chose to interview coaches on the football staff to explore their attitudes toward preparing a team for the game. He discovered that some felt that the coach should not have to worry about "getting the team up." They assumed that the players should psych themselves up for the game. Others felt it was very important to prepare the team through words as well as preparing for the mechanics of the game. The student concluded that the fact that the head coach was one of those who felt he did not have to get the players up for the game was a major reason they had a poor season that year. He learned that words do have life. They furnish life.

We could find a thousand and one other illustrations of how words do have life in the manner in which they persuade and change people. However, all those illustrations point in the same direction. One has to make believers out of people. In order to do that there must be something behind those words. When the coach tells his players they can win, they must also have some ability to win. Thus the words that Jesus talks about do have spirit and life. They are the words of the Spirit. What is offered in these words is eternal life, which Christ has already won. They are not empty words. Behind them stands the gracious work and activity of God himself.

What Else?

Jesus noted that in spite of his gracious and urgent appeal to all of these folks, "Many of his disciples drew back and no longer went about with him." That is when Jesus asked that painful question of the Twelve, "Do you also wish to go away?" You can imagine the pained expression on Jesus' face. You can feel the lump in the throat. You can feel the butterflies in the tummy. Yet Peter responded with a beautiful and meaningful confession. "Lord, to whom shall we go? You have the words of eternal life; and we have believed, and have come to know that you are the Holy One of God." The disciples were just plain stupid about a lot of things. They appeared to know and understand far less than the enemies of Jesus did. They also seemed to have short memories. Yet, after all, they regarded Jesus as the Messiah. They believed him even when they made gross errors. They were sure that Jesus was right. They did follow him. They seemed oblivious of the way in which the enemies of Jesus regarded them as buffoons. They liked Jesus and they believed him. After all, when they got down to cases, what other options did they have? And when you think about it, there is none else for us either.

HARRY N. HUXHOLD
Our Redeemer Lutheran Church
Indianapolis, Indiana

211

Go Wash Your Hands

Mark 7:1-8, 14-15, 21-23

When I was growing up and could not tell time, there were no watches that had alarms or went "beep beep" every half hour. If I were having fun, I didn't care what time it was anyway. I was supposed to stay within hearing distance of home. When it was time to eat, if we were playing outside, my mother would call, "Come for supper." If we were playing inside the words were "Go wash your hands." I knew that "Come for supper" meant that I should go wash my hands, and that "Go wash your hands" meant that I should then come for supper.

Since Louis Pasteur and germs weren't a big thing for me, I couldn't see the point of it all. My hands didn't really seem dirty to me. I was supposed to eat with fork and spoon, not with my fingers. So if I wasn't supposed to eat with my fingers, why did they have to be clean? You either are or were a child, so you know that children don't win those arguments. But you also know that not winning didn't mean giving up the battle. Sometimes I would not use soap—and then of course the wet dirt came off on the towel, which made my mother lament, "It'll never get clean." Or I would wash only one side of my hands and then dutifully show them to her as I came into the kitchen for inspection. Mothers aren't fooled very easily, and she would ask to see the other side. Then I'd return to my argument, "I don't even touch the fork with that side, so why do I have to wash it?" But mothers carry on the traditions of the elders from their mother and their mother's mother before them. I eventually had to come to the table with clean hands. It was not a matter of religious purification, though I often heard that "cleanliness is next to godliness," which meant that I was a long way from both.

The Pharisees and Clean Hands

Mark records that Jesus' disciples were criticized by the Pharisees and some teachers of the law because they came to the table with dirty hands. They really weren't criticizing the disciples; they were attacking Jesus. If he were a real teacher, he would teach properly, and his disciples would listen to the tradition of the elders and come to eat with clean—that is, properly washed—hands. For his Gentile readers, Mark includes some matters of ritual cleansing that the Gentiles would find ridiculous.

212

However, they were carefully observed by the Pharisees and other religious Jews, who didn't think them silly at all. For example, when they came from the market, they would wash to purify themselves, because they might have bumped against a Gentile. The Pharisees and these experts on law from Jerusalem couldn't see how Jesus could ignore these teachings of the elders. The rules were not from the Law of Moses but were part of the oral tradition—a hedge which had grown up around the Law of God—and were often watched more closely than the actual Mosaic code.

Jesus' Response

Jesus responds with a quotation from Isaiah. "You hypocrites! Isaiah described you beautifully. You're so busy holding on to the traditions of men that you let go of the commandment of God. These people pay me lip service. Their worship of me is in vain because they teach as doctrine the commandments of men. You give up what God has commanded and you cling to what men hand down" (Mark 7:6-8 paraphrased).

Our text doesn't include verses 9-11 where Jesus cites an example of this. It is an isolated case but helps show how religious minds could ignore God's law by obeying man's. The example is called "Corban." If a person pledged money or property to God, he could not give it to anyone else. So if a person's parents were in need and he didn't want to give them his money, he could pledge it to the temple and it was "Corban." Then he could ignore his parents' needs. It was, after all, a vow to God and couldn't be broken, even if it meant ignoring God's commandment about honoring father and mother. And this was in an era without pensions and I.R.A.'s and Social Security! The only way parents expected to live in old age was through the care of their children.

Law and Piety

The laws men make are rules that the lawmakers are convinced they can keep—with some effort. Religious laws that are man-made are regulations that religious people can keep and that can be noticed when they are kept. Because man-made rules can be kept with real effort, and God's law cannot be kept perfectly, it's easy to see which would be used as a standard for moral cleanliness and piety.

In his commentary on Mark's gospel Eduard Schweizer says such legalism is "a pseudo holiness. Any piety which is striving for something measurable—whether the tribunal is one's own conscience, other men,

213

or God—remains nothing more than a piety based on appearances, because the externally visible is all that can be measured . . . the innermost person is inaccessible." But still claiming such obedience as holiness, Schweizer says "Instead of being humble before God, one might demand recognition from God on the basis of such a piety." And that is exactly what had happened. The Pharisees were expecting praise from God because they kept these laws and sought to humble those who did not.

Jesus' Response

But Jesus replied that obedience to the traditions does not make one clean before God. Washing the hands and the cups and the pots and the copper bowls and the beds wouldn't do it either. We can't scrub where the problem is. Lady Macbeth could wash and wash her hands but knew that even the great sea couldn't cleanse the spot, because the problem wasn't really with her hands. Pilate could wash his hands ceremonially but knew as he did it that it wasn't his hands that needed to be clean. Jesus said the uncleanness wasn't from the hands or from that which went into the person as food. It was from the heart and what came out of it. Writing to Gentiles who were bothered by Christians who were bothered by worries about food regulations, Mark said that Jesus declared that all foods were fit to be eaten. But Jesus didn't encourage the Jews to ignore the Mosaic Law and begin having pork chops and shrimp cocktail. It wasn't until after the resurrection and Peter's vision from the Holy Spirit as recorded in Acts 11 that food was declared acceptable even if the law had considered it unclean. Jesus would probably have argued with the Pharisees that the shrimp and pork wouldn't have defiled them as food—but if they ate it in rebellion against God's law, they would sin.

Having told the Pharisees, Jesus called the multitude and told them this revolutionary position on food and piety. Having told the multitude, he withdrew with his disciples to answer their questions, because they didn't understand. In verse 18, Jesus says bluntly: "Are you as dull as the rest?" They'd heard but they hadn't heard, which is not an uncommon experience.

Martin Luther was a monk. He had heard the Scriptures read at every meal, had studied them, had become a teacher of Scripture, and had taught them. But he still didn't understand how one was forgiven and made clean. It came as a joyous revelation to him that the righteousness God demands is the righteousness God gives. Or in words this text uses, the cleanliness expected is the cleanliness given. We may live half a lifetime or longer slaving to obey the rules in order to satisfy God and

214

have our neighbors notice our piety. But all the while, the uncleanness Jesus speaks of is still found in our hearts. It is not an exhaustive list but it is devastating as a catalogue: evil ideas which lead to immorality, robbing, killing, greediness, deceit, jealousy, slander, and pride. With that on the inside, our clean hands won't score many points.

Dirty Hands—a Symbol

I was always impressed by the raccoon who didn't have to be told to wash his food or his hands. I marveled that he would do this instinctively without being constantly reminded. I also believed that we ate about a pound of dirt a day (the exact weight is not important!). In those days, it was plain old clean dirt. Now it's no doubt contaminated with sprays and chemicals so that mud pies aren't safe.

Regardless of my maneuvering and rationalizing, the point was really clear: I didn't want to wash my hands because I didn't want to admit that I was dirty! That's a pretty good picture of grown-ups too. Scrubbing won't do it. We can't make ourselves clean. Only God can. We can wash away the dirt and shape up our lives to look good, but only God's water of cleansing can do the deep cleaning of the hidden sin. I don't want grace, because I want to do it myself. I don't want to be forgiven, because I don't want to admit my sins. I don't want to be saved, because I would rather save myself. To admit that I need salvation is to admit that I can't do what I need most of all.

The Pharisees kept the traditions and didn't want to admit that they needed to repent. They didn't take in anything unclean, so they were clean. Jesus thought they were only fooling themselves and possibly some gullible neighbors, but not God.

Mark says that Jesus came proclaiming the reign—the rule—of God. The disciples didn't really understand. But they followed, and they loved him. We may not understand how he can cleanse us inwardly and outwardly; we may always want to save ourselves, but like Peter in the upper room, we ask: "Lord, don't just wash my hands or my head . . . but all of me." Let me follow and be clean.

WAYNE T. TELLEKSON
Christ Lutheran Church
Palatine, Illinois

Bleeding Hearts, Do-Gooders, and Kingdom People
Mark 7:31-37

The great event all us young teenagers anticipated in my home of Greenville, Ohio, was to go to town on Saturday night. The car would be parked in front of Wagner's Bakery on Main Street, and parents would watch the people walk by. For junior-high boys like myself, coming to town on a Saturday night from a one-room school and a daily routine of chores morning and evening, it was considerable excitement.

We would gather together up by the benches at the courthouse and swap exaggerations of male prowess and wait for "Dummy Parker" to come down Fourth Street and then on to Main where we were located. That's what we called him: "Dummy Parker." He was a little fellow who was hearing-impaired and was probably 50 or 60 years old. He had learned that the only way he could get any attention in our community from the hearing world was to act a fool and be the town clown. How we boys taunted and made fun of him! He would pretend to get angry and chase after us up the courthouse steps and down the fire escape. But, oh, how he must have hurt when he went home all alone in his silent world and tiny apartment.

I guess I will regret the unfeeling, insensitive, cruel way I treated that man until I die. I hope he knows that with much more maturity and sensitivity, and thanks to a School for the Adult Deaf in my congregation, I am very sorry for the way I treated dear Mr. Parker.

Jesus came across a fellow like that. Mark tells the lovely story this way: "Some people brought him a man who was deaf and could hardly speak, and they begged Jesus to place his hands on him" (Mark 7:32 TEV).

A Call for Bleeding Hearts

I suppose everyone in the neighborhood knew this fellow. They probably watched him grow up, and he probably became a part of the "problem people"—the kind you just accept and know they will always be around.

However, a few "bleeding hearts" people, who today would be called "do-gooders," took some action to try to help this hearing-impaired man. They realized the isolation, the loneliness, the sense of always being on the outside. They sensed how it was to have thoughts to share and anger

216

and love to express. They must have known what it meant to want desperately to be included in the fun and companionship, but to have only silence. Perhaps there was indication of what it meant to be barely considered a human being and often treated more like a freak of nature and mutation of the race.

The TV show *60 Minutes* did a fascinating piece on Savant Syndrome. It told of people we would nickname "retarded," and yet they showed a sculptor who would see an animal once and then, from memory, sculpt it. They showed a person who would play whole concerts on the piano after hearing them just once on record or live. They showed a man who had the entire calendar memorized from day one. You wonder who is retarded in God's eyes: these who have been given, by the process of creation, such awesome capabilities and talents—or us, who in our little circle of what is sane and average, look down on them as slow and stupid?

I am so thankful that the Son of God, the most perfect example of how God wants us to treat each other, took time to help this man. This story certainly affirms how God is: that he notices our loneliness and he feels our hurts and isolation. It tells us that when the fickleness of genetic makeup and conception deals us a dirty blow, God cares and wants to help us make the most of it.

In fact, the scripture account of Jesus' life is quite clear that God has a very big place in his heart for those who are different around Galilee: the deaf and mute, the crippled and blind, the epileptic, those who were grieving, the mentally ill, the physically ill, and the beaten in life's ditches.

God took special notice of these people and helped them. God did something. Sympathy was not enough. In our day we can become thick-skinned and hard-nosed and fail to even notice the hurting. Jesus noticed and helped.

Our Lord's heart bled and he was definitely a "do-gooder." He would have us be the same. The opposite would be unthinkable: a "do-badder" or a "do nothing at all."

Listen: "So Jesus took him off alone, away from the crowd, put his fingers in the man's ears, spat, and touched the man's tongue. Then Jesus looked up to heaven, gave a deep groan, and said to the man, 'Ephphatha,' which means, 'Open up!' " (Mark 7:33-34 TEV).

Compassion Fatigue

Our Lord was using sign language for a man who could not hear. Notice he did not embarrass him by making a spectacle of him in front of the crowd. He took him off by himself and placed his fingers in his

217

ears to let him know that God was touching him. He spat to communicate the fact that healing was taking place, because humans have considered spittle as having a curative power. He touched his tongue to symbolize that it would be loosened so he could speak. He looked to heaven to let him know where the power for this healing was coming from.

No doubt the man could now speak, because he could for the first time hear how others spoke and hear himself speak. It was all done in a thoughtful and gentle way. That must be the way God treats us and wants us to treat each other.

Especially we men need to be liberated from the narrow restriction that has typed us as uncaring, selfish, nonfeeling individuals who must be aggressive, successful, and always self-confident. Our boys often grow up thinking that is what it is to be a real man. TV's Mike Hammer and James Bond reinforce this wrong impression.

As God's people gather today and hear this kind and gentle story read to us, we must be moved to look around us as well. We must bear the scorn and ridicule of others around us, notice and care about the blind, the deaf, the ill, the lonely, and those who hurt in any way.

There was a time when Americans were moved by pictures of the wretched conditions of the boat people from Vietnam and Laos, and we helped. But now Americans have "compassion fatigue." We have become worn out physically and emotionally, as needs are continually held before us. But the hurt is still there.

If we are to be the alive presence of Christ in our community now, we have no choice but to be "do-gooders" and "bleeding hearts."

A Promise Realized

This miracle was one of the things promised would happen when the Messiah came. Isaiah told the people that there would be one who would come and that this is the way it would be when he arrived: "The blind will be able to see, and the deaf will hear. The lame will leap and dance, and those who cannot speak will shout for joy" (Isa. 35:5).

Mike Pearson, a conservation officer in Michigan, was called to rescue two ducks frozen in ice in a pond. He took his life in his hands and walked out on the thin ice, holding to a rope; then he discovered the ducks were plastic decoys. Everyone watching laughed at him and he became the butt of many jokes in the community. It must have been embarrassing. Still, when interviewed by National Public Radio, he said if called, he would go again and try to help.

The world says, "Get all you can." "Don't be taken for a sucker." All who want to help are nicknamed "pinkos" and "liberals." It is so easy to allow the Chamber of Commerce to set our goals and priorities, rather than Scripture. The world will push us that way. The majority of voices will shout us down and make us embarrassed. However, we for whom the Messiah came and died on the cross and rose from the grave and remains with us in spirit see the community and people differently. We see them not as an opportunity to manipulate and from whom to extract the largest profit. We see them as a golden opportunity to be God's kingdom-citizens in the world, a chance to bring into being (if only for a brief time) God's kingdom. We see them experiencing for a little while a surprising serendipity of God breaking through into the hurting mass of humanity.

The Old Testament promised us over and over that things will be different when God's kingdom gets a beachhead. Radical changes are possible as that new kingdom gets established: enemies to friends, hate to love, greed to sharing, poor people cared about, hungry people fed, hearing restored.

I have witnessed it in my ministry, and you have seen it, too. God's kingdom begins to work miracles like drunk people finding sobriety, mentally ill people finding peace, criminals turning their lives around, ugly marriages becoming harmonious, sick people finding healing, and, yes, still as promised, people with hearing impairments gain their hearing and those who cannot speak start to speak.

Gisele Berninghaus, a seminarian and former instructor at our School for the Adult Deaf here at St. Johns, told me of a student she had who was more than 60 years old and who had lived her whole life as a deaf person. After careful examination Gisele discovered that the woman had the capability of hearing and then, because she could hear, she could speak. After the wax was cleaned out of her ears and she was assured that she could be a hearing person, she began to communicate verbally. It was not unlike the miracle described in the Gospel for today.

An Affirmation

Let's assure one another today that it is American and manly and certainly Godlike to be a "do-gooder" and "bleeding heart." Just as the man's friends brought him to Jesus and he was then able to hear and speak for the first time, so when we experience the presence of Christ in our lives we are enabled to hear the cries of pain from others. This loosens our tongue to speak the often-ridiculed words of compassion, sympathy, and love that have never before come from our mute mouths.

219

When I was a student at Wittenberg University, I worked Saturday mornings as a speech pathologist. Saturday morning after Saturday morning I worked with a woman who had suffered brain damage. The progress was painfully slow. After four months I wanted to give up. After five months it seemed impossible that we would ever know improvement and that she could ever speak. But after more than six months, the woman said out loud, "Our Father, who art in heaven." She and I both cried for joy, for one who could not speak had begun to shout for joy. It was as Isaiah had promised long ago.

To Take Home

Just in case you have closed your ears and become deaf to this message today because you thought it too liberal and "bleeding heart" for a red-blooded, competitive, macho Lutheran American, here is a summary for those who have ears to hear: Today's Gospel is the story of Jesus healing a hearing-and speech-impaired person. The story affirms that it is God-like to hurt for, and help, any person in need. It gives us an example of God's understanding concern for all who are different and struggle, and it certainly illustrates how we kingdom people ought to treat each other and reach out to comfort and help. It is Christlike. Perhaps there is a person like this you ought to visit on the way home from worship today.

We called him "Dummy Parker." It is my own shame I feel as I confess that to you. Even the nickname was degrading. As a kid, I joined other cruel and insensitive kids in taunting him because he was not like us. However, as Jesus opened the man's ears and loosed the man's tongue in our Bible story today, so he has opened my ears and loosed my tongue that I might speak with a new message this day and in this church.

When the Christ comes close to us—miracles never cease! "All who heard were completely amazed . . . 'He even causes the deaf to hear and the dumb to speak!' " (Mark 7:37 TEV).

JERRY L. SCHMALENBERGER
St. John Lutheran Church
Des Moines, Iowa

On the Side of God
Mark 8:27-35

"Whose side are you on?" we sometimes ask in irritation. When a player in baseball or football made a crucial error, my sons would sometimes designate him the Most Valuable Player—for the other team!" Whose side are you on, Peter?" Jesus would ask. "Certainly it is not God's thoughts you are thinking! Rather you are the Most Valuable Player for Satan. You are thinking the thoughts of men!"

Be a little sympathetic with Peter, though, and the rest of the disciples. Their natural ideas are formed, as yours are too, by what the old serpent, Satan, planted in us first in the Garden of Eden. There it is called "the knowledge of good and evil."

Peter and the Knowledge of the Good

First, there is the knowledge of the good—at least, what Peter and the disciples would naturally see and think of as good. By this time in the ministry of Jesus they shared a dream which had spread through all Galilee and even to Judea, that this Jesus of theirs was secretly the Christ. Their idea is something like what we today see in movies and cartoons as *Superman*. Outwardly, of course, Jesus looked like a kind of mild-mannered Clark Kent. But the signals were there, in his miracles and in his preaching of the kingdom. And the expectation was growing that one day, when the time would be ripe, Jesus would throw off his disguise and be revealed in his real glory, like Superman!

Ah, how exciting this dream was! How "good" it looked! It was exactly what the nation wanted, for they had long been waiting for a Christ who would defeat all their enemies and lift them up to glory! How exciting for the disciples to be in on it! All over Galilee people were talking about it secretly—the disciples too! But not openly. They did not tell Jesus! When he revealed it, they would act surprised. But they would be ready!

Jesus knew what was going on. In our text he was very troubled by it. This idea of glory the disciples had is a complete contradiction of the kingdom of grace, of gathering, and of healing which he had been proclaiming. The disciples wanted to see a holy war which sets people against people, as though the enemy were people! They did not even see the enemy within themselves—Satan, and his deceptive lies!

221

Therefore, on his withdrawal to the region of Caesarea Philippi, Jesus forced the hidden secret into the open. The disciples had served as his messengers all over Galilee. They must know what people are saying and thinking about him. "So tell me," he asked. "Who do they say I am?"

The first answers Jesus got were evasive. The disciples didn't really want to tell him. "Some say you are John the Baptist, risen from the dead," they said. "Others say you are Elijah, or one of the prophets." But Jesus was not satisfied. He pressed them further. "What are you yourselves thinking?" he asked. "Who do you say that I am?"

Finally Peter broke down and made the confession, sharing their secret. Jesus may as well know that they already knew who he is. It's kind of like telling Clark Kent that you knew he is Superman in disguise. "You are the Christ!" Peter said. Now their secret was out! It's probably good that Jesus should know, so long as the "enemies" don't know!

Later, of course, this confession of Peter became part of our Creed—but that was only after the whole meaning of the name "Christ" had been changed by his dying for our sins and rising again. Here it shows that the disciples were "not on the side of God, but on the side of men." They were ambitious for glory, just like all the nations. They wanted a God who would come through to fulfill all their desires and dreams of superiority.

Jesus responded, you notice, with stern reproof and warning. "You are not to be stirring up that kind of vision among the people to whom I send you!" he said. "When I send you out, tell them what I give you to tell them. Don't add to it! Tell no one that I am the Christ!"

Peter and the Knowledge of Evil

To see and want and grab for what is not given, this is the knowledge of the good. It belongs to the very definition of sin and disobedience. But our text reveals to us also how the other side of sin works, the knowledge of evil. That happens when God sets something difficult and fearful in our way, and instead of bearing it and willingly enduring the hurt or loss, we skirt around the trouble and save ourselves by avoiding it.

Jesus put Peter and his disciples to another test. He told them plainly what was going to happen to him—and it was not at all what they expected and dreamed of. He had to go to Jerusalem, and there "the Son of man must suffer many things, and be rejected by the elders and the chief priests and the scribes, and be killed, and after three days rise again." For Jesus would not live or be ruled by the wisdom of the serpent, grabbing for whatever looks "good" and running away from whatever looks like trouble or evil. He would press the Father's battle to the end, even if it killed him. And he would trust the Father's promise that he will not lose after all, but be raised from the dead. That's how the kingdom of God will come. That's what God's kingdom and life is all about.

Once again Peter became the spokesman for the wisdom of our flesh and sin. He rebuked Jesus! "No, Jesus, you must not talk like that! You are the Christ! And the Christ is a winner, like Superman, not a loser! Nobody is going to be able to hurt you, much less kill you! Come on, Jesus! Have a little faith in God! God will never let such a thing happen to you!"

"Great speech, Peter!" I can just see all the disciples ready to burst into applause! "That's telling him, Peter! That's what Jesus needs to hear!"

But Jesus saw the snake. He knew the twisting serpent whose name is Satan, and how he deceives and seduces us—first by arousing our lusts for glory, and then by preying on our fear of being hurt! When we fall into that trap, then we can no longer know God and serve him. Instead of walking in his straight way, we fall into the way of the crooked snake—darting this way to grab for whatever we see and want, twisting that way to escape being hurt. We don't hear God any more at all.

"Get behind me, Satan!" Jesus said. He knew how inviting Satan's crooked way is, but he would have none of it! And to Peter Jesus said, "You don't know what you are saying! Your mind and heart is not controlled by the wisdom of God, Peter. You have taken the side of Satan, and of the nations who don't even know God."

Your Choice: Whose Side Are You On?

God your Father has chosen you to be on his side, to be filled with his Spirit, and to think his kind of thoughts. In your Baptism he has brought you through the sea as he once brought Israel, his "first-born son" out of bondage in Egypt. In your case, of course, he has brought you through the baptism, death, and resurrection of Jesus Christ, his Son. For Jesus' sake he has named you too his "beloved son" or "beloved daughter." He has chosen you for an inheritance of eternal glory and called you to serve him. But God does not force you. The serpent is still there, eager to deceive and seduce you. He appeals to your lusts, to your knowledge of the good. "Here, this is 'good,' grab for it!" the snake says. Or again, "Look out! That is 'evil'! You will be hurt, and shamed! Run! Escape from it!"

There you stand, between those two voices—God's and the serpent's. Whose voice will you heed? What will you think and do? Whose side are you on?

That's a serious question, a life-and-death question. But don't be afraid of it. It is filled also with opportunity. That's why Jesus gathered the multitudes together with his disciples—you and me too among them— to share with us first a remarkable invitation, and with it a wisdom that penetrates to the heart of your faith and life.

Listen to his invitation! "If anyone would come after me, let him deny himself and take up his cross and follow me." Catch what Jesus is saying. He is calling on you to make a choice. To "come after" him does not mean to tour Palestine and take a walk up to Caesarea Philippi and then back to Galilee. You have to make a choice. It is no cheap business to be named a "Christian" with him, or to be called a child of God in your Baptism, as he was called in his.

"Deny yourself," Jesus says. Give up the notion that you own yourself, or that you rule yourself, for that is a devilish deception that will only destroy you. You belong to God your Father, and to Jesus your Savior. You do not belong to the snake, and you will not walk any longer in his crooked and twisting way.

"Take up your cross, and follow me. Don't run just because trouble lies in the way. Get over your fear of being hurt. Be willing to suffer, as I suffered hurt and cross and death for you. For if you are going to be so desperately self-protective, forever saving yourself and giving way to fear, you cannot possibly love people around as I loved you—or forgive as I forgave you. Hurts, and even death, are not the ultimate disaster. The deceptions of the serpent, living to satisfy your lusts, or to save yourself from what you fear—that is what will finally destroy you."

That's Jesus' word of invitation: "Follow me. Do it my way, even through the cross and death, into resurrection and life."

But this word of invitation is also wisdom—the heart-wisdom of your whole Christian faith, and life, and calling. Hear how Jesus says it in the Gospel of the day. "Whoever would save his life will lose it; and whoever loses his life for my sake and the gospel's will save it."

"Save your life!" the serpent urges you constantly. "Save yourself!" the mockers cried out to Jesus on the cross. But Jesus would not yield to that cry. Why not? Because saving himself was not his business, but his Father's. His Father would save him, even if it meant raising him from the dead on the third day, as he had promised.

As for Jesus, his business was to save these disciples of his, to save you and me, and the whole lost world. Therefore he would do his Father's will to the end, and love and forgive us to the end, and give us the body and blood of his very dying as the food for our life. If he had tried to save his life, and run out on the cross God had set before him, he would have lost everything. But by trusting his Father's promises and doing his Father's will to the end, he triumphed not only for his own sake, but for your sake too, and mine.

So now it comes down to you again. Whose side are you on?

PAUL G. BRETSCHER
Immanuel Lutheran Church
Valparaiso, Indiana

EIGHTEENTH SUNDAY AFTER PENTECOST

Afraid to Ask
Mark 9:30-37

Sometimes children are afraid to ask about something they don't understand. They may pretend what they heard is imaginary and will simply go away.

Today's Gospel is about children and about such a hide-and-don't-seek viewpoint. It is, however, the disciples who are doing the hiding, and it is the child who is the sign of seeking and receiving.

Jesus and the disciples were passing through Galilee. Jesus would not have anyone know it, not, however, because he had anything to hide. Nor was he protecting himself from the truth. He knew the reality of the situation only too well. He also knew it would be hard enough for the disciples to grasp, much more so for those who failed or feared to see him as the Christ. He was going through Galilee on his way to Jerusalem. After the transfiguration everything Jesus did was "on the way to Jerusalem," to his death and ultimately his resurrection. There was now an urgency to center on the essentials of his life and ministry with the disciples. He was speaking to them clearly now, as straightforwardly as he could. "The Son of man will be delivered into the hands of men, and they will kill him, and when he is killed, after three days he will rise."

The disciples did not want to believe what he had just told them, and so they were afraid to ask him to say more. Perhaps they, like we, thought that if they did not talk about it, it would simply go away. They did talk, however, to each other, about the things they always talked about,

225

about the things *we* always talk about. About who is better than whom. About their own ambitions. About who might be putting another person down. About their jealousies, their irritations, their hurt feelings.

We understand only too well how it was with the disciples that day as they were coming to Capernaum. That's the way it is every day, for us, and quite possibly, for the disciples as well. We know, that such preoccupying conversation would occur again, for later, in Chapter 10 of Mark, after Jesus tries to tell them what is urgently before them, the disciples are concerned with who is going to be honored by sitting at the right hand of Jesus. We Christians, living 2000 years later might be astonished that these disciples, who had Christ in their midst, could have missed the significance of that moment. Yet we, too, who have the Christ in our midst, in the poor and the poor in spirit, we to whom the world urgently cries, "Pay attention, you are on a death-producing course!" distract ourselves with conversations about prestige and power and position.

Christ Engages the Fearful, Distracted Disciples

Jesus will not be excluded, even by the foolishness of his own disciples. Our text says, "He sat down and called the twelve and said to them. . . ." He does not ignore their ignoring him. Jesus faced the distracted ones, the silent ones who could not turn themselves away from "who-was-the-greatest" discussion. He looked right at them, saying this is the way it is: "If any one would be first, that one must be last of all, and servant of all."

He marks his words with a sign, a beloved sign. He takes a child to set in the midst of these adults. Ironically this simple sign is a most profound one. The Christ who came as a child to dwell in the midst of us, the one who, in the words of our First Lesson, would all too soon be like a "gentle lamb led to the slaughter," says to the disciples, "Whoever receives one such child in my name receives me, and whoever receives me, receives not me but the one who sent me."

What could be more simple than a child? What could be more easy than servanthood? And yet, of course, servanthood is neither simple nor easy. The servanthood of which Christ speaks requires all the strength and courage of the most mature adult, even though it seems as powerless as a child. To be the kind of powerful servant of which Christ speaks to is receive people rather than stepping on them or pushing them out of the way. To receive people is to welcome them, love them, care for them, and to empower them to become the gifted people they were created and redeemed to be. That kind of servanthood discipleship is

226

strange to the world, even unwelcomed by the world, all the while so desperately needed. Even we disciples often misunderstand, believing that such a childlike religion may be all right for Sunday but would be weak and not respected in the weekday real world of fierce competition.

The Power of Servanthood

We assume that to be a servant is to allow ourselves to be stepped on (as though the only two alternatives were stepping on people or being stepped on). It seems as though servanthood is the antithesis of power. That may be a definition of subservience, but Christian servanthood is the heart of power. The only legitimate form of power in the church is servanthood. It is a completely different kind of power, because in receiving someone in Christ's name, in serving, one loves with Christ's unconditional love, a love that unlocks that person from bondage to self-seeking. Such receiving of another in Christ's name unleases love that can multiply beyond our imagination, creating partnerships where before only competition existed between, in the world's definition, the strong and the weak. Empowered by the Christ, and by the one who sent Christ, the mighty God, creator of the universe, who still holds this world in caring hands, we are secure enough to dare to change the course of human affairs.

Servanthood means to be open, to receive, and that means relinquishing control, control over our position in relationship to the Christ, or to each other, and control over the direction Christ is going. In Mark 8 Jesus first spelled out his calling: "The Son of man must suffer many things . . . and be killed, and after three days rise again." Then Peter said, "No way! That's not the way to do it, Jesus." Christ does not invite us to control his destiny, which was the cross, nor to fill our days with concerns about position. Christ invites us to receive his children—all of them—even the grown-up, recalcitrant ones. In so doing, we once again receive him.

There is so much to learn. Yet Christ continues to patiently speak to us—directly, again and again.

Let's Pretend It Won't Happen

In the strong, loving encounter with Christ, we gain the strength to listen to the hard words, for we who claim Christ's new life as our own, have no need to be afraid. Still we frequently play hide-and-don't-seek games. We don't intend to. Sometimes we hide the fact that we are

227

hiding, even from ourselves. In 1984, about this time, the country prepared to view the television program *The Day After*. This program about
the effects of nuclear war emerged as a national event, and was previewed
extensively, often with warnings that children should not see it. The
National Education Association said that no child should watch it alone.
That was sound advice.

Still, the abundance of "don't-let-the-children-see-this" warnings was
perplexing, particularly since parents are notoriously lax in supervision
when children watch violent programs every day. Perhaps the sudden
need to not let our children see was an attempt to hide the truth from
ourselves. Somehow this program would portray real possibilities, and
the adults knew it. Ellen Goodman, syndicated columnist for the *Boston
Globe*, pondered this, too. Her informal survey showed it was the parents
who were hiding, projecting their own reluctance to be confronted with
the reality of the danger of nuclear war on to the children, as they said
things like, "I'm not up to it." Goodman wrote, "A great part of the
fear of kids watching is a fear of questions they will ask. You can be
sure that they will ask, 'What are you doing to stop this?' And parents
will feel ashamed." Adults will be silent, and perhaps children will ask
no more. Perhaps no one will remember that year-old program. The
problem will go away!

Dr. John Mack, a psychiatrist quoted in Goodman's article, was indeed
concerned about children's reactions of fear, depression, hopelessness.
But, "The problem," said Dr. Mack, "isn't that we get upset. The point
is what we do with that upset."

It was hard for the disciples to hear Christ when he said he would
need to die. It is hard for us to face death, and extraordinarily difficult
to face the potential for global death. The answer lies not in hopelessness,
nor in helpless passivity. Christ did not redeem us for hopelessness or
for helplessness, but for servanthood, for powerful servanthood that receives people, even the strangers from the other side of the world, instead
of fearing or needing to conquer them.

War, of course, is not new, nor is the positioning for power. In today's
Epistle James asks "What causes wars and what causes fightings among
you? Is is not your passions that are at war in your members? You desire
and do not have; so you kill. And you covet and cannot obtain; so you
fight and wage war." Contrasting that is the grace of God, wisdom from
God which is peaceable and gentle, and open to reason, and full of mercy
and good fruits. "The harvest of righteousness is sown in peace by those
who make peace."

228

Possible Distracting Distortions

There are some distortions possible in considering these things seriously. The disciples were learning but were still off course. Some people today would say being peaceable means passively accepting what they consider inevitable, giving up on the world and waiting for the afterlife. The New Testament, certainly Mark's gospel, does not agree. In Chapter 10 of Mark, while the disciples are still arguing about who will be in the best position, Jesus says that they will be baptized into his baptism. His death and resurrection would be lived out in the world, through them. They would receive many blessings, brothers, sisters, children, land—and persecutions. The life of servanthood or discipleship would mean suffering, because it would mean they were fully engaged in the problems of this world, not merely hoping for heaven. Such a call to discipleship, to living out our Baptism, means we are called to be engaged in the world, facing deathly courses and becoming fully engaged with people, with politics, and with decision-making. One cannot hide and ignore the world and the world's people, for whom Christ died. And one does not need to, for the cross and the new life are ours. Now we can be in the midst of humanity, suffering humanity, receiving and caring and working for that harvest of righteousness that is sown in our peacemaking.

Christ's Children Are All in Our Midst

Another possible distortion from this text is the glorification of children, as though they are innocent (that's just the backside of our protecting them so that they don't know we adults are about to wage war). Children in Mark 9 are not innocent. Earlier in Chapter 9 Jesus encountered another child, and the child was demon-possessed. He needed Christ's healing touch, Christ's forgiveness. And children need our ministry too. A few verses after our text Jesus says, "Whoever causes one of these little ones who believe in me to sin, it would be better for him if a great millstone were hung around his neck and he were thrown into the sea."

Christ does not bid us idolize children, nor use children to justify our own failure to face problems, nor project our own fear and guilt on children by abusing them. We are to care for, to receive, to love, to nurture, to explain to, to strengthen children—all children, for the world's children are all in our midst. Mother Teresa, who is known to the world as one who receives children—and all the poor—for Christ's sake, asks us, "Why do you fear your children?"

229

The disciples received a simple, yet profound sign, a child. We who covet the promised freedom and power of adulthood might take another look at the goals of such pseudo-freedom by seeing the ways *adult* is used as an adjective, "adult entertainment," "adult movies," "adult bookstores." We even mark adulthood as the time one is old enough to die for one's country. Strange signs of adulthood!

A 1960s poster read, "War is not healthy for children and other living things." The truth of that is clear. Maybe it takes the child in our midst to finally see. Christ takes the child in our midst, the children here this day, and bids us look at them that we may not hide the truth from them, but more clearly see a new truth about what is healthy for us all. Christ takes the child and holds that child in his arms. He knows our fears; he is well acquainted with our distracting talk. He faces us squarely and says we can stop playing hide-and-don't-seek games. He, the one who was a child, who holds our children in his arms, reaches out to embrace us also, saying that we are on the road with him. We as disciples *will* be engaged in the decision making and in the suffering of this world. It is not a safe road ahead, but he is with us. Trust him, allow him to hold you and love you and empower you that you may feel safe enough, loved enough, full enough, and free enough for a new kind of servanthood.

NORMA J. EVERIST
Wartburg Theological Seminary
Dubuque, Iowa

NINETEENTH SUNDAY AFTER PENTECOST

The Dignity of Human Beings
Mark 9:38-50

As a theologian and teacher of the church, I have profound respect and love for historical dogma and orthodoxy; I also have a profound respect for the place of human experience. In this text Jesus gives us more than a little reason to think that radical attention to the person and situation is the highest form of orthodoxy. The picture we have before us is a paradigm that sees the human person as the highest form of God's created order—created in dignity, respect and, indeed, in the image of God. Therefore, our concern and focus today will be on a right

230

relationship with God as the power and strength for our right and active relationship with our neighbors—brothers and sisters—recognizing our dependence on God and our debt to God's mercy. We shall attempt with the aid of the Holy Spirit to reaffirm (1) our dignity created by God, (2) our dignity revealed by God in Christ, (3) our dignity shared in God's name.

Our Dignity Created by God

In the First Article of the Apostles' Creed we confess: "We believe in God the Father, Creator of heaven and earth." To make this confession with radical seriousness is to challenge with what set of eyes we see our neighbors. Do we see them as undesirables, poor, marginal, black, brown, women, communist? Or do we see them as created in dignity by God. Although humanity lost the image of God in sin, a God who created us in dignity was determined to redeem us to that dignity in Christ our God.

The way in which one thinks of humanity is, to be sure, always affected by the way one thinks of God. We hate to be told over and over again that we are sinners. Nothing so insults the pride of modern people. We have tried desperately to find other words—absence of good, falsehood, oppression, sickness, or error of nature. These however, only serve to remind us that surrounding human life is a tragic, threefold estrangement by which humanity is separated from self, neighbor, and God. The extent to which humanity is seen to be self-sufficient in resolving these estrangements is inversely proportional to the extent to which humanity needs God. Our Gospel for today says that those who would seem to be doing good and who are willing to meet on common ground of a sinned humanity are to be given the benefit of the doubt—for whoever is not against Christ is for Christ (truly a remarkable attitude toward marginal Christians and interested people).

Our Dignity Revealed by God in Christ

Therefore, it is the saving work of God in Christ that St. Augustine understood to be at stake in his controversy with Pelagius over the nature of humanity. This sense of utter dependence or the restoration of our dignity created by God along with the ordering of life is apparent in the Second Lesson for today. Human life becomes less than the dignity to which God created and therefore less than fully human when it is lived apart from a sense of God's presence. We are sinners in need of God's forgiving grace.

231

Moreover, we find that Jesus suffered, died, and rose again for our sins that we might have, through faith, life and dignity. As Martin Luther King Jr. put it in his book *Strength to Love*:

Where do we find this God? in a test tube? No. Where else except in Jesus Christ, the Lord of our lives? By knowing Him we know God. Christ is not only Godlike, but God is Christlike. Christ is the word made flesh. He is the language of eternity translated in the words of time. If we are to know what God likes and understand his purposes [for humankind], we must turn to Christ and his way, we will participate in that marvelous act of faith that will bring us to the true knowledge of God.

One of the great tragedies of life, is that we seldom bridge the gap between faith and practice, between doing and saying. But in the life and name of Jesus we find the separation is bridged. Never in history was there more a dynamic model of the consistency in word and deed. Jesus becomes all that we need to reveal to us what human life should resemble when Christian people close the gap between creed and daily activity. That is the activity expressed in our text from casting out demons to the picture of a cup of water passing from one human hand to another.

It is not so much our ability to articulate the faith that is our problem. God knows we spend enough hours in analyzing problems and editing our syntax. Rather, it is our failure to discern the human being as a *person*, which according to our text is at the root of almost every social problem.

For example, I believe that the conflict between races, classes, sexes, and nationalities is fundamentally centered in this: is the human being a person or a pawn? Segregation treats people as means rather than ends, reducing them to things rather than persons. A life is sacred as created by God and redeemed by Christ.

Our Identity Shared in God's Grace

In an industrialized, mass-production society, where people become "units" and one "unit" is interchangeable with another, it becomes even more important to reclaim the meaning of the dignity of personality and relationship to both God and humanity.

Perhaps the idea of a personal God that has arisen from the experience of a people who have endured the dehumanizing force of racism can speak to people who are enduring the dehumanizing forces of technology. The black Christian community (like other ethnic communities) is a *witness* and *testimony* to a life of peace, justice, hope, and faith in God, whose name is above all other names. The black Christian tradition

232

points to a relationship with a personal God who holds all creation in love, respect, and dignity. The songs of black people are an expression of the larger picture presented in our text of Christians sharing their peace and joy with others and their ability to survive in the name of Jesus. These songs typify what the Christian faith in Jesus' name has meant to black people. For example, the "Black National Anthem" (*LBW* 562) exhorts us to sing to the glory of God, to lift our voices until all creation sings. But how can we do more than the Israelites, who could not sing the Lord's song in a strange land? We sing because we are remembering that in a strange land nothing is really strange. For we remember that the earth does not belong to Egypt, Rome, Russia, nor the United States, but "the earth is the Lord's and the fulness thereof."

It has always been easy for the angels to sing praises to the Lord, because they have seen God in his *creative power*. And it takes the black preacher, out of the bowels of his imaginative experiences of suffering and oppression, to paint the picture in faith of what the angels saw with their naked eyes. For the old black preacher said that God stepped out of nowhere and stepped into nothing and reached back into nowhere, grabbed hold of nothing, and hung it out on nothing and told it to stay there. God took the hammer of his divine volition and struck it up against the anvil of his creative genius, and the sparks that flew he gathered on his fingertips and flung them into the far corners of the night and told them to shine for an eternity. No wonder the angels sang, "Glory to God!" No wonder we too can sing until all of nature "rings with harmonies of liberty."

We sing this song because we are exhorted to remember "the faith that the dark past has taught us." Martin Luther helped Christians of his day to remember that our faith is not in popes or councils, who have often contradicted themselves. We today can say that our faith is not in racism, but in Jesus Christ alone, who has brought us into one fellowship as his sons and daughters.

We can sing this song because we are exhorted by the Black Christian community to remember that the power of life and death is God's and God's only. For though we have come "through tears, and the blood of the slaughtered," yet through the might of God we will be led into the light—into the victory of the resurrection of Christ.

It is in this power of Jesus' name that we too are enabled to preach good news to the poor, proclaiming release to those in jail, liberating those who are oppressed and proclaiming the acceptable year of the Lord. For this mission we as the people of God need strength, forgiveness, and power from Christ, who freely gives it to us and his Word and sacraments. It is here that we meet the challenge of a new understanding of the church based on our text, a form-following-function approach, for the very being of the church is shaped by its missionary calling, its sentness, its function. The church without mission is as much of a contradiction as the mission without the church. This mission of love in behalf of our neighbor is of such importance to the glory of God and the dignity of all that the text exhorts us to usher it in at whatever length.

It is in this vein that I think Christians in established denominations must look for examples among marginalized Christians. I have specific references here to the civil rights movement of the 1960s. The movement had its basic orientation in the social action commission of the Black church. Its primary leaders were ministers, who were essentially attempting to make their faith relevant to the marketplace. When Dr. Martin Luther King Jr. emerged from his formal preparation for this Christian ministry, what was the good news that black people wanted to hear? Was it not that black people were to be freed in the name of Jesus from segregation? Was it not that blacks would be free in the name of Jesus to register to vote in every region in this nation, free in the name of Jesus from intimidation and fear and beatings and murders because of their attempts to exercise this basic right of Christian citizenship?

These are the kinds of social-action concerns that existed in the Black church at that time. Consequently, the Black church set out through the political process to change those conditions and to preach the good news to all of the people in the name of Jesus.

The late noted black scholar and theologian, Dr. Howard Thurman, provides us with a very meaningful definition of the Negro spiritual, which I think deepens our understanding of the roots of the mission orientation of the Black church. He describes the Negro spiritual as the "tools of the spirit by which our slave forebearers cut a path through the wilderness of their despair." We see therefore, in a Negro spiritual like "I Got Shoes, All God's Children Got Shoes" the expression of the black slaves' deep understanding of the relevance of Jesus Christ to the marketplace. They sang, "I got shoes, you got shoes, all God's children got shoes and walk all over God's heaven." With the knowledge, however, that religion is of no significance unless it expresses itself in everyday life, they also turn their eye to the big white house where the "master" lives and they sang about him, "Everybody talking about heaven, ain't going there."

Involvement on the part of the church does not mean that the church will forsake their religious functions and become agencies of the body politic. But it is unquestionably a part of the function of the church to influence the world and its affairs for the development of moral and a spiritual conscience.

Faith and Politics

The relevance of Christian faith to politics is deeply rooted in the gospel. It is not a new thing to find the church speaking to the issues of the day. Christ addressed the issues of his time, and, certainly he would be considered a revolutionary, a man who was feared and eventually crucified for his concern for the oppressed masses and the dignity of humanity. Had Christ abandoned his tasks, had the church not been a farsighted revolutionary institution, surely our world would be worse than it is today.

The Bible does not separate the sacred area of faith from secular life. It tells us that God is the God of all life. Throughout the Scriptures, God demonstrates a concern for the application of his will not only ecclesiastically but also secularly. Christianity is devoted then to freedom, love, and justice, and the Scriptures address themselves to how men and women love and respect each other in all places, including those where laws are made.

There is condemnation of those who make laws at the expense of human misery. Throughout the Old Testament, there are revelations of God's righteousness on behalf of the oppressed. Think of how revolutionary it must have been when a small band of Israelites from Egypt proclaimed their freedom and dignity, calling it the will of God, the will of a God in whom they had been forbidden to believe.

So, what then is the key to the dignity which all people possess? It is God's grace freely given in Christ, and once received by faith, shared in love with others. Thus, love is the means for the redemption of God's created world. We can only close the gap on broken community by meeting hate with love. Therefore the dignity of personality can only be fulfilled in the context of community.

The idea of community as the fulfillment of the dignity of personality is the goal of the text. Faith must accompany love if community is to be recreated and people enabled to respond to the exhortations of our text.

This text has raised a challenging question of whether we see people outside our group as people created and redeemed by God in dignity. I would like to answer that question with an illustration from Acts 16:30-31. The Philippian jailer raises the question, "What must I do to be saved?" The apostles answer "Believe in the Lord Jesus, and you will be saved, you and your household."

235

Perhaps there will come a time in the life of the nation and the church, as it was in the life of that jailer, when those who hold the keys to another's release will ask the ultimate question of salvation, liberation, healing, and wholeness. And if that ultimate question is asked in the presence of those who, though only recently out of chains, have not lost their spiritual sensitivity, perhaps a similar reply will be forthcoming: "Believe . . ." not in your two cars, money, tradition, rhetoric, nor in the compelling forces of your conception as a nation, but believe in him. Believe in Jesus whose presence even now has no business being here but is nevertheless, and thus must be dealt with by going to whatever lengths necessary in glorifying God for the dignity of humanity.

ALBERT PERO JR.
Lutheran School of Theology
Chicago, Illinois

Till Death Do Us Part?
Mark 10:2-16

There are times when I wish Jesus had said either more or less. If he did say more about certain subjects, I wish the gospel writers had recorded *all* that he said. Or if he didn't say more than they record, I wish they had helped us by telling us what they thought Jesus meant by what he said.

Today's text is a case in point. Jesus is talking about divorce. And he says either too much or too little so far as most of us are concerned.

He seems to say, in the first place, that there should never be divorce. God never intended it. When two people become one flesh, they are to remain as such. When they have been joined in oneness before God they have a relationship that should never be "put asunder," never be broken. And I can't think of many who would argue that point. We cling to it as the ideal. In spite of the fact that we know that many of them will not last, we keep inviting a man and a woman to make the promise to be faithful to one another "until death parts us."

But that's the *ideal*. Reality is such that many *do*, in fact, end up in the divorce courts, often sorrowfully and regretfully setting aside the promise made at the altar. Older cultural patterns tended to keep together

236

marriages that might otherwise have ended in separation and divorce. But with the breakup of those ethnic and community ties the divorce rate has skyrocketed. What was once rare and unusual in some communities has become quite normal and commonplace.

Jesus doesn't help us very much by what he says in the text: "Whoever divorces his wife and marries another, commits adultery against her; and if she divorces her husband and marries another, she commits adultery."

That may have worked well in Palestine of the first century. But how can we apply it to the 20th century in a modern and very complex society? All of the ethnic and cultural pressures that keep people together—even very unhappy people—are gone. Even in our most rural communities and churches divorce no longer carries the same stigma.

What Shall We Do with These Words of Jesus?

We could, of course, long for "the good old days." We could try to reconstruct a culture in which even the worst of marriages would be kept together by community pressure. We *could*—but only if we want to be hopelessly naive. Rail as we might against our changing and increasingly complex world, there is no way to return to "the good old days." Twentieth-century America is not first-century Palestine. Jesus spoke an important word about marriage and divorce. But we must ask how that word applies to our contemporary world. A basic tenet of our Lutheran heritage is that faith must be enlightened by reason. We begin with the Word of Scripture, asking, "What *did* God say?" But then we must carry that Word into our present setting and ask, "What *does* God say?"

The first word I hear him saying in this text is that we need to underscore the *sanctity* and the *permanence* of marriage. The pendulum has swung too far. We have become captivated by our culture, captivated to the point that the Word of God has been watered down and explained away until it has no force and no meaning for us. We need to say loudly, clearly, and firmly to those planning marriage and to those already married that vows taken at the altar are among the most serious promises we will make in the course of our lives.

Because we have weakened and explained away the seriousness of marriage vows, couples come to and leave the altar with almost no sense of long-term commitment. Instead of "till death parts us," the common mentality is "so long as I love you." And this often means: "I'll stay with you so long as I have a feeling of romantic love." "I'll stay with you so long as sex is fun." "I'll stay with you so long as you can provide an adequate life-style." "I'll stay with you so long as you let me have my full independence." "I'll stay with you so long as you agree to let me

237

have abortions." "I'll stay with you so long as you don't complain about how much I spend on my hobbies." Isn't it time—past time—for the pendulum to swing back? Isn't it time to talk again about *sanctity* and *permanence*?

Sanctity and Holiness

There is a certain God-given sanctity about marriage. It is a sanctity and a holiness that God gave to marriage from the beginning. Read Genesis 1 and 2 again. There you will find not one but two stories of creation. In the first we are told that marriage is meant for procreation. When possible, God intends that a man and a woman have children.

But Genesis 2 adds another dimension. Unlike animals, who can also procreate, God endows man and woman with one of his own God-like qualities—the potential to live in an emotional and a spiritual relationship with another person. In our Gospel for today, Jesus reaffirms that unique and God-endowed quality when he recalls the words of Genesis 2: "For this reason a man shall leave his father and mother and be joined to his wife, and the two shall become one."

"The two shall become one." The only other relationship that is described in terms anywhere close to this is the relationship between a believer and Jesus Christ. "It is no longer I who live," writes Paul, "but Christ who lives in me." There are many beautiful friendships that are described in Scripture—such as David and Jonathan, and Jesus and Lazarus, and Paul and Timothy—but of none of them is it said, "The two shall become one."

Because of its sanctity, the marriage relationship is also intended to be permanent. Yes, I know the pressures in our society are immense and intense. With the average family finding itself uprooted every six or seven years there is little wonder that some cannot endure the pressures. With extended family living hundreds and sometimes thousands of miles away, how can marriages survive? The very people who could help most to support and sustain a faltering marriage are seldom available when they are most needed.

In spite of these pressures and excuses, let me persevere in our insistence that marriage is meant to be permanent. All of us can conjure up images of that "ideal" marriage. We can think of couples who have stayed together 40 or 50 years with no apparent stress and strain. We envy them, wishing our own marriage could be as "successful."

But I challenge you to talk to that happily married couple. Ask them if its' been easy. Ask them if there were times in their marriage when it might have come apart at the seams. Ask them if the thought of separation and divorce ever entered their minds.

You may indeed find a rare couple who have sailed through untroubled marital waters, with not a single memory of a time when their marriage was in trouble. When you find that rare couple, please introduce them to the rest of us. Either we will meet two people who are indeed a rare and unusual pair who have much to teach the rest of us; or else we will meet a couple who are hopelessly naive and terribly dishonest about their marriage. I suspect the latter will be the case more often than the former.

Yes, even the couple who seem most happy and stable in their relationship will tell you very honestly that there have been times when their marriage might have fallen apart, times when the strain and anxiety nearly separated them, times when the forbidden thought of divorce crossed their minds.

But they will also tell you that somehow they survived. They should, and often will, give the major credit for their survival to the grace of God. But they will also tell you that it took a lot of hard work, a lot of painful honesty, and, at times, an act of stubborn determination: "We won't give up, no matter what. We made a promise and we'll stick to it." Those couples will tell you that the dark valleys of their marriage have actually drawn them closer together and that their life together has been enriched by the struggle.

So there you have it. A sermon that upholds the sanctity and permanence of marriage—just as it is envisioned in the words of Christ. We can all go home now, content that we have been true to the words of Christ and that I have spoken to the needs of the congregation.

Tragic Necessity

How I wish that were the case! And how I wish I didn't need to say a single word about what can only best be described as that "tragic necessity." Yes, there are indeed times when it is best for all concerned to go through with a divorce. We must fight it with every ounce of energy—and especially for the sake of the children who don't deserve the hell that comes with every divorce. But if an even worse hell results from staying together, then we must be reconciled to this "tragic necessity."

Our problem, of course, is to reconcile *any* divorce—even that rare "tragic necessity"—with these hard words of Christ. I confess to no easy answer. Years ago, when it was still the rare exception for people in the church to be divorced, Dr. Elton Trueblood struggled with this complex question. And this Quaker theologian gave an answer that is as good as any I have found since. Appealing to the deeper currents of the New Testament, Trueblood asked the question: "What would Jesus do if he were living today? How would he deal with marriage in our complex

239

20th century? Would he insist that we apply the same rules today as was the case in first-century Palestine?"

Trueblood warned against watering down the words of Christ so as to make them completely invalid for today. Yet, he felt just as certain that Christ would recognize that there may be those times—exceptional times—when we should say, "It is better for these two that there be separation and divorce."

The deepest current in the message of Christ is a message of grace, forgiveness, and hope for the worst sin and for the worst sinner. Divorce is indeed a sin. It is a broken covenant, a shattered promise, a fractured relationship. And when it happens to those who confess to be Christian, it is a sad witness to the world.

But there *is* grace! And grace is often heard and experienced most fully by those who know brokenness at its very worst. Out of the tears and remorse of divorce can come hope. God can heal even the most wounded and bleeding heart. And he can even open the door to a new relationship of love and commitment that could not have been known with the first partner.

The key in all of this is that we must never give up easily on any relationship. If we are to accept divorce as a "tragic necessity," it must only be chosen after every possible alternative has been exhausted.

Surely those who have kept their vows will not sit in judgment over those who have had to choose the "tragic necessity." Instead, we will all acknowledge our brokenness and we will reach out to one another, joining hands and voices in the prayer from the Service for Marriage:

> Gracious Father, you bless the family and renew your people. Enrich husbands and wives, parents and children more and more with your grace, that, strengthening and supporting each other, they may serve those in need and be a sign of the fulfillment of your perfect kingdom, where, with your Son Jesus Christ and the Holy Spirit, you live and reign, one God through all ages of ages. Amen (© 1978 *LBW*).

HERBERT W. CHILSTROM, BISHOP
Minnesota Synod—LCA

How To Be an Exceptional Christian
Mark 10:17-27[28-30]

Benjamin's father was a shepherd. His grandfather had been a shepherd. When Benjamin announced he was leaving home to open a bagel shop in downtown Jerusalem, the news shocked his family. If Benjamin had not been an outstanding son, his father might have forbidden him to leave home. "Let the boy try it. He'll have his fling in the business world and be home soon," Benjamin's father told his mother.

But it was not long before the shop on the corner of Samuel and Saul streets spawned another at the intersection of Rebecca and Rachel Avenues. Soon a chain of "Benjamin's Bagel Shops" dotted the streets and suburbs of Jerusalem. From that humble beginning, fast-food restaurants were added. Then a "Benjamin's Bed and Board" hotel chain became popular. Finally, he acquired a contract to provide the meals for all the camel caravans leaving from Jerusalem, Jericho, and other major cities of Israel.

But the most exceptional thing that happened during the time Benjamin achieved success as a businessman was that he kept his marriage strong and became a good father. He stole from no one, resisted the temptation to run down the reputation of his competitors, treated his employees fairly, and worked at healing the disappointment of his parents that he abandoned the traditional occupation of the family.

An Exceptional Encounter

It was an exceptional event when a person of Benjamin's stature traveled to meet Jesus, who was on his way to Jerusalem. Even more surprising was the way Benjamin greeted Jesus. He fell on his knees and called Jesus, "Good Teacher." The uniqueness of the meeting is apparent from the fact that Mark commented, "And looking upon him, Jesus loved him." While Jesus loved everyone in general, I can think only of two other people specially loved by Jesus—his friend Lazarus and the disciple John.

Even the conversation was exceptional. Jesus appeared to reject the title "Good" which Benjamin applied to him. I think Jesus did that because he wanted to shake Benjamin's confidence in himself. Convinced that he had kept the commandments, Benjamin probably thought he

241

was about to begin a conversation as one good person talking to another good person.

Of course the whole idea Jesus voiced, that one could achieve eternal life through keeping the commandments or even by selling all one's possessions and giving them to the poor is also shocking—is it not? If one of our eighth-grade confirmands answered the question, "What must I do to inherit eternal life?" the way Jesus answered it, I would immediately demote that student to the seventh-grade confirmation class and ask him or her to make a new beginning.

But the most exceptional thing of all was the mumbling chagrined statement of Jesus as Benjamin walked away: "How hard it will be for those who have riches to enter the kingdom of God!" The disciples were amazed and astonished at such a comment. They couldn't believe their ears when they heard Jesus say it was easier for a camel to go through the eye of a needle than for a rich man to enter the kingdom of heaven.

"Then who can be saved?" they asked disbelieving. They had been raised to believe that most prosperous people were godly people. That is when they learned that every person who enters the kingdom of God does so by divine exception.

We Are Exceptions to the Rule

"Nice guys run last," is a rather well-established worldly rule. Yet Benjamin was a living demonstration of the fact that there are exceptions to that generality. "For the wages of sin is death, but the free gift of God is eternal life in Christ Jesus our Lord," Paul wrote (Rom. 6:23). To that rule there are no exceptions. Since all of us have sinned and earned eternal death, only God can give us the kingdom and the gift of eternal life. Whenever he calls people to faith in Jesus Christ, God makes a gracious exception to his own rule that all who sin deserve eternal death.

The Gospel for today teaches us that even the best of us do not *deserve* eternal life, but a gracious and loving God *gives* eternal life—even to the worst of us. And because that is true, to question God's grace in any Christian's life is to run the risk of losing it for ourselves.

This Gospel also tells us that wealth is not the only obstacle to entering the kingdom of God. None of the disciples were affluent people, yet they felt themselves indicted by what happened in the encounter between Jesus and the man of great possessions.

"Children, how hard it is to enter the kingdom of God!" Christ remarked, and with shocked minds the disciples asked, "Then who can be saved?" That is when Jesus told them about the impossible possibility: that God saves people graciously. Make no mistake about it. If the wealthy man had sold all his goods to follow Jesus, that act of self-sacrifice would not have qualified him for entrance into the kingdom of heaven as an act of merit.

To people discussing the misfortune of those killed by cruel Pilate, Jesus remarked, "Unless you repent, you will all likewise perish" (Luke 13:5). The people who questioned Jesus about the Galilean tragedy were not necessarily wealthy individuals, but they were people who presumed upon God's goodness because of their religious preference, their social status, and their good fortune. Repentance involves no longer relying on any possession, any privilege, any deeds of piety for salvation. Repentance means turning wholly toward God for salvation. Repentance frees us from being possessed by our possessions and teaches us to lay claim on one priceless possession as greatest gift of all—Jesus Christ.

The New Rule

The fact that we are saved by God freely rather than by the success we have achieved at keeping the Ten Commandments does not mean that we can or should be indifferent to God's will for our daily living or that the manner in which we use our possessions is unimportant. While writing to the Romans and stressing that where sin abounded grace abounded all the more, Paul made this point several times: "What shall we say then? Are we to continue in sin that grace may abound?" (Rom. 6:1, 15). The answer to that question is always an emphatic *no!*

The good news that we are saved in spite of what we have achieved professionally, theologically, psychologically, allows us to possess our possessions in a new and free manner. Knowing that God freely gives us the most important gift we need—salvation—inspires us to work for justice and equality for all. The prophet Amos and the ministry of Jesus both remind us that we cannot be the people God intends us to be if we are indifferent to the needs of the poor or if we use our good fortune for personal advantage at the expense of those less fortunate than ourselves.

The Second Lesson for today speaks of our heavenly calling. God has graciously called us to be his "house in the world." Health, wealth, wisdom, social standing, our position in society—all can be used as tools through which God can do exceptionally good things for people. As a matter of fact, if we faithfully communicate the good news that God loved us enough to send Jesus Christ to die for our sin, to rise for our salvation, to pour out the Holy Spirit on people, our lives can become

243

the instruments through which God performs his impossible possibility—channels through which God gives entrance to the kingdom to fellow human beings. To live in that spirit, making personal sacrifices for the sake of Jesus and for the gospel's sake (Mark 10:29-30), is to joyfully possess everything we have and all that we are. To live in that spirit is to discover the blessing in our possessions.

The New Viewpoint

Once we have learned to think of ourselves as exceptional people and when we marvel at the impossibility which has become possible for us in Jesus Christ, surely we will have a new appreciation for one another and for all those for whom Christ lived and died and rose again. Both the Lord's Supper and Baptism unite us to each other at the same time that they bring us the benefits of Christ's life.

Christians are a unique group of people. Each of us has something they did not deserve—entrance into the kingdom of God. That makes us exceptional people. By God's grace we can live exceptionally Christian lives.

GEORGE F. LOBIEN
St. Andrew Lutheran Church
Silver Spring, Maryland

TWENTY-SECOND SUNDAY AFTER PENTECOST

To Live Is to Die
Mark 10:35-45

In that unenlightened world before Kübler-Ross, nobody talked about death and dying. People just lived until they died in ignorance. Well, not quite. Jesus knew something about dying that he was anxious to share with his disciples. In this text, in fact, he was teaching them how to die in the midst of life, how to die as a style of life. For his followers, then and now, the implication is clear: to live in Christ is to die.

Suffering without Glory

Three times Jesus had told his friends where they were going and why they were going there. They were going to Jerusalem, where he

244

would suffer and be put to death by the religious authorities and rise again on the third day.

Three times the disciples didn't hear or chose not to hear that shattering message. We would call it "denial." The Gospels prefer "little faith" or even "hardness of heart." The disciples may have thought of it simply as "positive thinking." Let's go back to the word of God's Kingdom. Now there's something to get excited about and discuss and even argue over! Forget about death and dying. Concentrate on the glory which will soon be ours.

So right on the heels of Jesus' third passion warning, James and John came to him with their unrelated—but oh so urgent—request. "Master," they said, "we'd like you to do us a favor."

"Yes, what is it?"

"Grant us the right to sit in glory with you in positions of authority— one at your right hand and the other at your left."

It was almost as if they hadn't heard Jesus at all. But if they hadn't heard him, he emphatically had heard their request, as unreasonable as it was. "You don't know what you're asking" he replied in one of the classic understatements of all time.

Indeed, they did not know, but they would soon find out. Oh, the test seemed easy enough: "Can you drink the cup I drink or be baptized with the baptism with which I am baptized?"

A piece of cake. "We can," they quickly responded, again without realizing exactly what they were affirming. For the baptism that Jesus mentioned here was not the one in the River Jordan. This one would be more like a deluge—a torrent rushing over and submerging him in chaos, darkness, and destruction. And the cup was not for a champagne toast. It was a cup of suffering and woe which had to be endured to save the world he had come to save.

Not a piece of cake at all, but bread and body broken. Not champagne, but wine and blood shed. It wouldn't be nearly so easy as they had supposed. But by God's grace, yes they would. James would be slain by the sword as a martyr; John, according to tradition, would endure a long, lonely exile. But even then, they didn't get what they asked for. That had been prepared for two others, who didn't enjoy the privilege very much. For on either side of Jesus when he entered his glory were two criminals, one crucified on his right and the other on his left.

Suffering without glory—that's the promise James received. It's the promise all disciples receive. Baptism still carries with it the imagery of drowning, death, and burial as we are joined to Jesus' death and resurrection. The sign of the cross was placed on our forehead as a visible reminder that we follow the crucified Lord. And the cup we receive not only proclaims his sacrifice, it sends us out to share that sacrifice with others by word and deed. And that may well cause us some pain and hurt. Nor is there any guarantee that we'll ever get a reward—or even be appreciated.

Rough? Of course. It's part of dying. In Christ, to live is to die.

Serving without Power

The 10 other disciples were furious when they discovered what James and John had done. How could these brothers have so completely misunderstood Jesus' teaching and mission? Alas, that's not why the others were angry. They were upset simply because they had been outhustled and outmaneuvered. Actually, they may have considered the same request for themselves. The two brothers were just bold enough to put it into words.

For a moment it appeared that a power struggle might develop among the disciples. As a matter of fact, they had previously argued about which of them was the greatest. Jesus, however, quickly silenced their grumbling. "That's how it is," he said, "in the world—people scheming and vying with one another for positions of power and influence. And once you get ahold of that power, you don't let go. You use it to put others in their place, to let them know who's boss, and to keep yourself on top. But that's not the way it is in God's family. There greatness is measured not by control over others, but by humility and service to others. Among you, whoever would be great must be your servant, and whoever would be first must be slave of all."

Is that still a valid word for disciples today? When the world holds before our eyes examples of power most frequently expressed in brute force, organizational skill, subtle manipulation, or even more crassly, in the massive stockpiling of weapons systems capable of destroying all life on this planet—against that background, does the role of servant have any meaning or significance at all?

The church still confesses that it does. In feeding the hungry, in visiting the sick, in spending time with the lonely, in nurturing children, in advocacy for the poor and oppressed, in pleading for justice and peace, in sharing the good news by word and deed, God's people continue to affirm Jesus' directive.

And that's no piece of cake either. It means sharing bread—daily bread and the Bread of Life—without first taking our slice off the top. It means giving up claims of power and the urge to control others. It

246

means giving rather than hoarding. And because the world is in op- position to such a threatening way of living, it usually means a cross in one shape or another.

In short, servanthood is a form of dying while we're still alive. And it's the kind of dying Jesus still calls and equips disciples to do. For in him to live is to die.

Believing without Seeing

But where is the payoff? Or is there one? The usual payoffs which the world looks for (indeed, which disciples were and too often still are looking for) power and glory, have been excluded. So have riches. Of course, there is the final payoff, the great feast in God's kingdom, but that's not really a payoff. That's a gift, pure and simple, a gift that is ours because the Lord of all came to serve and suffer and give his life as a ransom for many. Good Lutherans should never confuse a payoff with grace!

And yet there may be a payoff after all. It just may happen that a life of serving and, if need be, suffering for others and for the sake of the gospel is its own reward. Perhaps such a life has significance and au- thenticity that a life of grasping, achieving, possessing, controlling, ma- nipulating, and notoriety can never approach. There just may be a fruitfulness and abundance in Jesus' style of living and dying that leave all other styles sterile by contrast.

Of course, such assertions can never be proved, and they certainly aren't self-evident. Indeed they can be recognized only through eyes of faith. Sometimes they're even difficult for faithful Christians to recognize. I suspect we all at times can identify with James and John. We don't have to sit in positions of authority with the Lord, but a little recogni- tion—even a thank-you once in a while—would surely be helpful.

And yet, there are some faith-pointers along the way to direct us to what Jesus was saying. The Catechism reminds us that implicit in our Baptism is the call daily to drown our "old sinful selves." It invites us to die every day. "The cloud of witnesses" assures us we're not alone. James and John, after all, eventually did follow their Lord—and will- ingly. So have many others down through the years: Peter and Paul and Francis and Martin of Tours, and Thomas More and Martin Luther and John Wesley and Albert Schweitzer and Martin Luther King Jr. and Mother Teresa. All in various ways have underscored the validity of the Gospel. Most of all, there's Jesus' own life. He lived what he taught. He embodied the Suffering Servant of today's First Lesson as he served and suffered and gave to the limit—without holding anything back.

247

In faith—without seeing—we proclaim that his living and dying have ultimate significance for us. In faith—without seeing—we proclaim that our living and dying also have significance, for "in the Lord your labor is not in vain."

In Jesus Christ, to live is to die. But that's OK, because he goes one step beyond Kübler-Ross. He, not death, has the last word; he is the resurrection and the life. In Christ, then, ultimately, to die is to live.

DAVID B. KAPLAN
St. Luke's Evangelical Lutheran Church
Baltimore, Maryland

To See and Follow

Mark 10:46-52

Mark wrote his gospel shortly after the destruction of Jerusalem, which occurred in A.D. 70. He wrote for the churches in Galilee (today's Golan Heights), Lebanon, and southern Syria. His goal was to reinterpret the Jesus of history for the people of his day only 40 years after Jesus' death and resurrection. Unless Jesus is reinterpreted in each generation he ceases to be a live option. In the same spirit we must attempt to make the message and memory of Jesus meaningful and intelligible for people of our own day.

The central section of Mark's gospel (8:22—10:52) has been the source of our Gospel readings since the Seventeenth Sunday after Pentecost. This sort of piecemeal reading can be detrimental to a total comprehension of Mark's gospel. As a result we need to think about the whole occasionally—or at least about the section of the whole from which today's reading has been isolated.

In this central section the author traces Jesus' journey with his disciples from Caesarea Philippi in Galilee of the north to Jericho on the southern outskirts of Jerusalem. While traveling on this way, Jesus prepared his disciples for what was to happen after their arrival in Jerusalem. As a result we gain deeper insight into both the person of Jesus and the nature of discipleship.

248

Eyes to See

Mark has placed a frame around this central section of his gospel. At the beginning he reported the healing of one blind man (8:22-26), and at the end, the healing of another (10:46-52). The section is thus framed by two stories each of which describes the opening of the eyes of a blind man. In doing this Mark has given these events a distinct interpretation. The opening of eyes he says is what characterizes Jesus' relation with his disciples along the way from Galilee to Jerusalem. What Jesus did for the two blind men is what he was trying to do for the disciples on their journey—open their eyes.

What does Jesus want the disciples to see according to Mark? There is one statement that Jesus repeats three times in this section, namely, that he is going to Jerusalem to suffer, die, and be raised again. In all three of these sayings there is great emphasis on Jesus' suffering—his being rejected, delivered up into the hands of the authorities, tortured, and killed. Jesus spares no effort to open the eyes of the disciples and make them see the meaning of his life. He is going to be a suffering and rejected person, tormented, spat upon, and killed. But he will overcome death and be raised after three days. By the time they got to Jerusalem, the disciples should have been prepared for what would happen. Jesus had made every effort to open their eyes, but they remained blind.

This blindness of the disciples is seen in their responses to Jesus' words about his suffering and death. In response to the first passion prediction, Peter calls Jesus the Messiah. This is not a satisfactory answer (for Mark at least) because the Messiah in Jewish thought was the one who would conquer the enemies of God by force. And this notion Jesus rejected over and over. After the second prediction of his passion and the transfiguration, the disciples admitted their inability to cast out a demon. This tells us that they saw Jesus as a miracle worker who would redeem God's people with magic. And after the third passion prediction, James and John argued about who would be first in the kingdom of God. The implication is that Jesus would claim his right as Son of God when he came before the Jerusalem authorities. And Jesus (or at least Mark) rejected this understanding also.

Perhaps these three temptations to which the disciples succumbed sound familiar to you. They should because they are the ones rejected by Jesus in the wilderness when Satan tempted him as told by Matthew and Luke. Mark tells us that the disciples, unlike their Lord, fell for the temptations.

249

Even in our Gospel reading for today there is not total vision. Bartimaeus is given sight, right enough. But how does he understand Jesus? He calls him "Son of David." The title implies the nationalistic hope, which centered on a Davidic king. And this, too, Jesus denied. However, Jesus does not therefore refuse to heal Bartimaeus. And Mark tells us that after being healed Bartimaeus followed Jesus "on the way." Thus, Mark tells us that the disciples who were on the inside and received Jesus' private instruction failed to see, while the two on the outside did see and follow on the way.

Misunderstanding Jesus

Mark thus conveys a disturbing but profound truth: those who are closest to Jesus and claim to know him best of all, may be farthest from the truth, while those who are spatially and temporally removed from Jesus may be very close to him spiritually and in the conduct of their lives.

There are some indications that many people do misunderstand Jesus, even people who are committed churchgoers. One hint about this misunderstanding is the attitude of some people toward a crucifix. Many Christians feel this is too "Roman Catholic" and therefore must be false. Mark the author of the Gospel, I suspect, would have been quite comfortable with a crucifix, because it would have reminded him that Jesus did indeed suffer cruelly on the cross. After all, Mark's understanding of Jesus was that he was the Suffering Servant—and the greatest evidence of his suffering was his crucifixion. So, our rejection of anything that reminds us too clearly of Jesus' suffering may indicate a misunderstanding of Jesus among us.

Another suggestion of misunderstanding is the notion so frequently expressed that Jesus' purpose was to do good. They understand Jesus as a worker of miracles, who did what he did when he healed or cast out demons because he felt sorry for the victims. Mark would not have been very pleased with such an understanding of Jesus. Of course, Mark would not have denied that Jesus did heal and cast out demons. But Jesus did not do these things because he felt sorry for people—though he felt sorry for them too. Rather, he did that in order that people might know that he was the Suffering Servant of God, who came into this world to serve rather than to be served.

It is also true to say that many people understand Jesus primarily as a great teacher. Bartimaeus in our reading today, called Jesus "rabbi." And indeed Jesus was a rabbi, that is a teacher. However, this was not the most important thing that one can say about Jesus, from Mark's point of view. Jesus taught his disciples because he wanted them to know what it meant to be a disciple. To follow Jesus means to deny oneself, to be the first in service and the last in power, to show a willingness to suffer— even to the point of losing one's life and drinking the cup that Jesus drinks.

There is another misunderstanding of Jesus in our day that probably was not a problem in the day of Mark. It is so subtle that to mention it seems crass. However, it is fatal to true discipleship as Mark would say if he were here today. The misunderstanding of which I speak is that Jesus came to found the church and that the task of his disciples is to perpetuate the church. Again, Mark would not deny that Jesus founded the church. But he would object strenuously to the notion that the purpose of the Christian life was to perpetuate the church. We have often fallen prey to this temptation. We think that our task is to bring members into the church, when it really is to make disciples. Disciples are persons who deny self, serve others, and suffer willingly for others. We have concluded that only those who belong to the institutional church can be disciples, but neither Jesus nor Mark would agree with that.

Discipleship of Suffering

The story of Bartimaeus and his healing spell out for us the nature and conditions of discipleship in unequivocally plain words. Provided the disciples understand the mission of Jesus, his discipleship message will also make sense to them, because discipleship in Mark is closely fashioned after the model of the suffering Jesus. If this is understood, then the gist of the discipleship message does not come as a surprise. There can be little doubt regarding the essence of discipleship, as far as Mark is concerned.

It is sometimes claimed that religion is a classic case of an escape from the realities of life, a denial of the brutalities of suffering and of our common destiny of death. Whoever makes such claims must not be familiar with the Scriptures. They deal extensively with the suffering of the people of God, the death of the just and the seeming triumph of evil. Many of the biblical traditions in Judaism and Christianity struggle with the fundamental issues of human life: the suffering of the innocent, the destruction of individual and collective life, the annihilation of cities and civilizations, the overpowering force of evil, and man's alienation from himself and from God.

The story of Bartimaeus serves as an example of deliberate integration of the realities of suffering and death. There is no reward without toil and pain, and there can be no success without the suffering that precedes

251

it. It may well be the single most important message that Mark conveys: there is no life without death, there is no Easter without crucifixion. To be a Christian means to follow Jesus on the way, to drink the cup of suffering, to be concerned with the salvation of others, and less—if at all—with one's own life and well-being.

It is my prayer that we will not be blind to what Jesus says and that we will follow in his way.

BRYCE W. SHOEMAKER
St. Mark Lutheran Church
Baltimore, Maryland

TWENTY-FOURTH SUNDAY AFTER PENTECOST

Stewards of Love
Mark 12:28-34[35-37]

One of the lingering disappointments in my life, which should be forgotten, happened in college. It was the final audition for the St. Olaf Choir. Some colleges are known for their football team, or science faculty. My alma mater has long been known for its famous choir. I wanted very badly to make it!

There were about 30 of us on the recall list for a dozen places in the bass section. Eleven were chosen by the director, leaving two of us still competing for the one remaining spot. Afterward, a friend said to me, "You almost made it." Yeah, almost!

Almost There

Almost has to be the most frustrating word in human language. Often it is used in encouragement: "You almost passed the test," or "You almost got the job." Nicodemus was almost there, but he had to be born again. The rich young ruler was so near, but gave up and went home. Today we meet a good and sincere man, a scribe, with whom, frankly, I have a lot of sympathy.

He asks, "What's the key? What's the center? What matters most?" He seems to want to know. He's open to the insights of Jesus, not like others in the story, who are trying to trap the Master. And he almost made it with Jesus. How disappointing! He's a sincere seeker, no smart

252

aleck, no phony, no "I dare-you-to-teach-me-anything" type. His sincerity brings him to the door, but not through it.

What Is Most Important

This pious Jew likes the way Jesus simplifies the law. He knows his Bible. He understands that God wants right hearts, not right liturgies. He sees the promised land, but he does not enter. What more could Jesus expect, anyway? If you mean well, are open to learn, agree with the truth, what more can there be?

Is that a smile on our Lord's face, a wink in his eye, when he says, "You're almost there?" Almost there? What more? What's the next step? The text doesn't say. Unless the secret lies in connecting the two commandments into one. It is an answer that provides a question for many in the church today. What is most important? Some people say, "Love God." Others insist, "No, it's love for justice and our neighbor." The answer Jesus gives dissolves both. He forces each to face the other, and he drives the uncommitted among us from the cover of our labels. The answer is so simple. It is neither "Love God," nor "Love your neighbor." It is both. We must love both, equally and intensely. One has no priority over the other.

Here is the secret. You may fall in love with God by loving your neighbor. Or you may fall in love with your neighbor by loving God. Which comes first does not matter. To love God and one another with everything we are and have is a vision-altering, life-changing experience.

In Touch with the Kingdom

Jesus seems to be inviting the scribe to be his disciple. Gently, indirectly, he says, "You've come to me for the truth, now join me." In other words, "You are as close to the kingdom as you are close to me."

But this is the most frustrating thing of all. Jesus is not merely smiling and winking; he's holding out his arms with compassion. He wants to embrace him and kiss him. You are almost there! What Jesus means is this: if you will reach out and grasp his hand, you will be in touch with the kingdom of God. If you will listen to the gospel, you are in. Whoever is not offended by carpenter's overalls can know the secret: that God is in disguise, that God is incognito, that God is reconciling the world to himself.

But how does a person get there? When I feel like I almost have it, what can I do? "Love God with all my heart, soul, mind, and strength . . . and my neighbor as my own self." But how do I do that?

Welcome Home

Someone says, "Surrender." But, what do I surrender? The preacher says, "Repent!" Repent of what? Another says, "Decide." Decide about what? Such searching brings us to take the step that lands us in the kingdom. Frustrated, almost there, we sigh, we sob, we say, "Lord, I can't love you as I ought. I'm afraid to. Lord, I don't love my neighbor, and I don't really want to." Then Jesus says, "Welcome home. Now you are in my kingdom. It has been as near for you as this all the time."

Love in Action

When the gospel of Luke tells this same story, the main character is a lawyer, not a scribe. His question to Jesus is, "How can I get eternal life?" Our Lord's answer is the same: love God and love your neighbor. Then Jesus tells the story about the good Samaritan.

Of course, the figure of the good Samaritan fits Jesus perfectly. The lawyer missed that. So did the scribe. I hope we don't miss it, too. God doesn't simply "feel" love for his rebel earth-children. Neither does he blare out the message in heavenly stereophonics. No, his love is acted out in the living and dying, the saying and doing of Jesus.

Jesus came to a broken and helpless humanity. He brought healing, excitement, and hope; he brought life and love. He was and is neighbor to the millions of us who would be lost without him.

Gracious Love

Jesus is also gracious love. We have no claims on him. There is no way we can earn his favor or deserve his blessing. He comes neighboring because his love is gracious. The love he pours out for us is our beginning and end, our hope and salvation.

The love of Jesus is always breaking down walls of estrangement between heart and heart. His love went out to all without distinctions. He rejected no one on grounds of race, color, sex, or national origin. For 2000 years his Spirit has been softening the hearts of cantankerous, class-conscious people. Now and then he wins some notable battles among us.

Costly Love

Calvary's cross is a constant reminder of the costly character of Christ's love. He knew rejection, hatred, brutality, suffering, and death, because

254

he loved. He knew the danger of being neighbor to a sinful, thoughtless, fast-forgetting people. Nothing in his example suggests that being a neighbor is easy. Everything in his example tells us being a neighbor is costly. But it is fulfilling and right.

So Luke helps us see what Mark may have left us puzzled about. What is the great commandment? It comes down to this: let God's reconciling act in Jesus turn your heart and mind to him and to each other.

New Energy

What will happen if you take that step, if you are not happy with almost being there, if you let God's reconciling action turn your heart to him and to your beaten, bewildered sisters and brothers? I believe life will become suddenly full for you. Life will become suddenly rich beyond words to express it. As the Psalm says, "My cup spills over."

Here is the origin and power of the Christian life. We are energized by the merciful, forgiving, bridge-building love of God as it reaches us in Jesus. Is that energizing power intended to simply recreate in us a mood of adoring Jesus? No! This new energy restlessly seeks an object. There's a magnetism here. And what other object than your neighbor?

A 70-year-old brother in our company said, "I can't retire. I've got to help my children and my grandchildren. And I'm glad to do it." You know what it is like to be loved, to be reenergized by the love and concern someone has for you. Why is it so invigorating? Why is it driving you to seek larger meaning? Because the goodness of your neighbor is a living expression of God's loving heart.

A Love Affair

This commandment is not meant for the secular population in general. It is given to the Christian church. God's New Testament people are intended to be a radically new human species. The distinctiveness of Christian sisters and brothers is that we belong to God as loved ones and lovers.

Now let's take a different track for a moment. Why should we love the Lord God? Because he needs our love. Why does Jesus ask Peter repeatedly, "Do you love me?" To Peter and us he would say, "I need to hear that you love me. I don't need to know if you've got the answers right to the questions of creed and conduct. No, do you love me?" G. K. Chesterton said, "Let your religion be less of a theory and more of

255

a love affair." The Gospel doesn't give us an *-ology* or an *-ism,* but a living person, a living Lord to love and be loved by forever.

We are reminded constantly of our neighbor's need to be loved. And it's true. A lot of needy, suffering people are not going to make it without us. So many are only half-alive; they need our help and healing. But we need their love also. The deeper and more terrible truth is this: to be really alive, not simply half-alive, we need to be healers and helpers. It's not just for the sake of the neighbor that we come to the rescue. It's also for our own sakes. Neither we nor our neighbors can really be human, really alive, without the other. Every time we pass by our suffering neighbors, leaving them in their own misery, we suffer for it. Unless we live for each other, no one can live very well. Life can only be real where there is love.

JACK F. HUSTAD
First Lutheran Church of Richmond Beach
Seattle, Washington

TWENTY-FIFTH SUNDAY AFTER PENTECOST

Giving Up Our Last Penny
Mark 12:41-44

This is a familiar and simple scene in the gospel of Mark. It is the season of Passover. From cities all around the ancient world the children of Israel are going to Jerusalem to celebrate this great festival. The city is filled with people. The focus of worship is the great temple on Mount Zion, which overshadows the rest of the city. Jesus also enters that city with his disciples. As he comes down the road, crowds gather around him. They have heard about him, this rabbi from Nazareth. Now he comes to that city, the center of religious and political power. Each day he teaches in the temple. Much of his teaching is in the courtyard of the Gentiles, the outer precinct of the temple. There the sellers of sacrifices and the changers of money create a swirl of activity surrounding the temple.

A Scene in the Temple

One day Jesus stepped into the next court, the court of the women, where Israelite women were permitted to worship. He looks around this

256

courtyard and sees 13 chests scattered about the area. Each of them is a large receptacle with a trumpet-shaped opening on top called the *shofar* chest, the trumpet chest. One is for the temple dues that are overdue. The one next to it is for temple dues for this year. If you want to add to the gold on the mercy seat, which sits secluded in the most holy place, you can put something in the box for the mercy seat. If you would like to offer a sacrifice, there is a box for that. If you would like to add to the supply of wood, you may give to that. And if you would like to buy some incense to be used in the temple, there is still another box for that. The other six chests are labeled "Free Will Offering" and are used by the temple officials to help the needy in Jerusalem and the land of Israel.

Because this is an annual pilgrimage for most of the Israelites, there is a steady stream of pilgrims going to this place, selecting the chests and placing their large offerings for the year in the boxes. Amid this turbulent scene there comes a woman in the ordinary garb of a Palestinian peasant. Quietly and imperceptibly she falls into the stream of moving people. She reaches a box labeled "Free Will Offering" and holds out her hand containing two thinly shaved copper coins, each worth about one-eighth of a cent. She turns her hand over and drops these two coins into the neck of the trumpet. She might have continued her journey unnoticed had not our Lord said something. He called his disciples together. He said, "I have something very important to tell you. That woman has given more than all of the other people you have seen streaming out of the temple."

I'm sure the disciples were amazed, as you and I would have been. Jesus' words don't compute in our accounting system. Two thinly shaved pieces of copper worth about a fourth of a cent are more than all the other coins in the box? God's accounting is certainly different from ours. The point of the story is obvious, and Jesus goes on to make it. An old English version puts it in such an interesting way. He said that everybody else gave "out of their superfluity." Do we have superfluity? We do. We tuck it away in the closet, down in the basement, and up in the attic. It is made up of all those things we really don't need. Another name for it is "stuff." Everyone else gave from the resources of their superfluous stuff. "But this woman gave all her assets," says Jesus. It was all there in the palm of her hand, everything she owned, all her living. She turned it upside down and dropped it into the *shofar* chest. The greatest gift is the gift that costs us the most. And by those standards Jesus' accounting was correct.

The point of the story is obvious. The application to our lives is more difficult. How can we become more like her? As we think of its meaning for us, one of our questions is what motivated this woman? What made

257

her that kind of giving person? If we can learn the secret of her freedom to give, then we might become God's giving people.

An Understanding Mind

This morning we focus our attention on three aspects of this woman's life which might help us understand her. First of all, to be a giving person we must have a level of understanding of the needs of other people. This woman was a widow. In Jesus' day there were no survivor benefits, pension plans, or Social Security. In the Old Testament widows and orphans were particularly protected by the law. Israel was reminded to remember them and not forget their needs. She was a person who understood what it meant to be a widow in need. Now, that may sound unnecessarily obvious to us who are not widowed. But those who experience it remind us that without facing it we can't fully understand it. That is true of many of our human situations. We can talk about facing surgery or facing a family crisis, but living through it is another matter.

To be a giving person requires a certain level of experience and maturity. If you and I are having trouble becoming giving persons, perhaps it is because we are immature. Perhaps it is because we are still little children emotionally who think that life owes us only pleasure and happiness without any pain. This woman was a giving person because she understood what it means to be in need.

A Compassionate Heart

However, understanding is not enough. We have all known people who have gone through tough times and have become cynical and bitter. They wrap themselves in a mantle of self-pity and take out their bitterness on other people. Their hearts can become like stone. It takes more than an understanding mind to be a giving person. It is obvious from this story that this woman also had a heart of compassion. The word *compassion* is one that is used frequently in the teaching of Jesus. In the Hebrew culture they believed that your emotions were in your stomach. That is where you felt, they thought. When the Old Testament talked about people who felt for others, they spoke of "the bowels of compassion," in the very center of our being. Today we use the term *heart*. For us it is the symbolic center of compassion. If you and I are struggling with stone hearts and wondering if it is possible in a cynical, self-centered world to feel any kind of compassion, we can turn to the Scriptures and discover where our hearts can find compassion.

258

Children learn from their parents, for better or worse. And there are clever commercials that remind us that boys and girls look up to their parents and often do what they do and live as they live. In a similar and yet more profound way, we Christians have a model for the compassionate heart in the Father who loves us in Jesus Christ.

One time Jesus' disciples came to him and asked him what is the limit? "How many times do I have to forgive my brother? Is seven times enough?" Jesus said, "Seventy times seven." That is God's strange mathematics. We wonder where such thoughts come from. The answer Jesus gives us is a parable about the king who forgave a great debt, pointing to the God who has taken away the sin of the world. In the cross and resurrection of his Son, he offers us his heart of compassion. He knows we have nothing to offer to him. He doesn't sit there with his celestial computer adding up the good things we have done or subtracting the bad things. He simply says, "I love you. I love the world so much that I gave my only Son." It is that heart of the compassionate Father that enables us to have hearts of compassion. God does not create such hearts with the harsh wind of his threats, but he lets the bright sun of his love and forgiveness shine upon us. Our hearts of stone are warmed and they become flesh again. Like the widow, not only do we understand the needs of others, but we begin to care.

A Helping Hand

Finally, there is that third essential element. This widow could well have understood the needs of others, she could well have felt compassion for them, but she still had to walk over, open her hand and let all her assets go. That, of course, is the final step—a mind that understands, a heart that cares, and a hand that gives.

Could we have done what she did? Do we still believe that the abundance of our lives somehow can be measured in the things we possess? If we do, then a tragedy touches us. As long as my hand holds tightly to the things that I possess as if they were my own, there is another hand that reaches from these possessions and holds my heart tightly. The hand of an Ebenezer Scrooge that grasps selfishly at all he possesses produces the heart of an Ebenezer Scrooge that is gripped by the things that possess him.

Some years ago I spoke to a man who had left eastern Europe as a refugee. He described his experience of locking the door of his home and taking only the key with him. That was all. He knew that once he crossed the border, he would lose everything he owned. Can we even imagine what kind of action that must have been? Yet in a real sense

259

we can't be giving persons until, with this widow, we put everything into the hands of him who really does own them. For we are not owners; we are caretakers. We move these things around and rearrange them. We put them away and take them out for 70 or 80 years. Then our treasures become someone else's trash. Life moves on. When we open our hands as the widow did and let go, then the hand of our possessions begins to loosen its grip on our hearts. We can begin to make choices and decisions with people in mind, rather than things. We can respond to the needs of others. We can discover the purpose of our lives as God's people.

The invitation of God is full and free. He is eager to give us understanding, compassion, and the freedom to give. Lord, renew our minds, our hearts, and our hands.

RICHARD J. GOTSCH
Grace Lutheran Church
Northbrook, Illinois

Excuse Me for Interrupting
Mark 13:1-13

No one that I know of has ever written a theology of interruptions, but there's a ready market for such a tract in the pastoral ministry. Every so often my date book shows a blank page—no appointments or meetings from dawn to dusk. What a great opportunity to work nonstop on those towering piles called "overdue assignments"! But within 15 minutes the door bangs, the phone rings, the mail arrives. Something goes wrong at home, snafus multiply—and before I can say "Hosanna!" it's another day past.

Interruptions can be annoying. A friend of mine used to rise at 4:30 A.M. and take a portable typewriter out to a picnic grove on the edge of town. There he could write his sermons from start to "amen" without interruptions. If there is any one item that wrecks my week, it's a phone call between the third point and conclusion of my Saturday afternoon sermon spinning.

Interruptions can be occasions for creative response. One day in the middle of a pastors' committee meeting at the local youth center, the

260

phone rang. Since the center's director was heaven knows where—I picked it up. On the other end was a young lad who had decided to take his own life. He decided to give someone, anyone, one last chance at arguing for going on living. I'll never forget how I felt. The rest of the group carried on with their agenda (I think it was frustrations in the ministry) while I grew increasingly wide-eyed and uptight! The interruption was a matter of life and death to a 16-year-old. It was a mild annoyance to my peers, who had no way of knowing why I stayed on the phone for 20 minutes.

The whole Bible story could be looked at from the viewpoint of interruptions. Creation is interrupted when God's evening stroll through the orchard called Eden reveals one less apple, one vanished snake, and one guilt-ridden couple. That peaceful harmony and sweet communion with God is forever interrupted by our age-old rebellion. Sin interrupts God's plan, so *he* interrupts sin by being born as a human being who lives among us filled with grace and truth.

Interrupted Jesus

Yet Jesus comes to us in stories that were sparked by interruptions, interruptions, interruptions! A sermon is interrupted by a demoniac. The sermon gives way to something most of our sermon hearers would give anything to see this morning—the power of God which can cast out Satan and his legions with one word!

A friendly chat as the disciples and Christ stroll into Nain is loudly interrupted by the grief and mourning of a funeral procession crowding through the gates. Death is always a potent interruption into our plans for the day. Yet a widow's grief interrupting Christ's walkabout triggers a miracle of life restored and a promise of our own resurrection.

Jesus' sleep is interrupted by a frightened fisherman who shakes our Lord out of a refreshing nap into a howling marine gale. This storm soon becomes a bit player in a cosmic drama as the Creator of the oceans and the tamer of primeval monsters shouts a loud "Hush up!" to the winds and the waves, leaving several stunned young men to ask that most necessary of all questions for those seeking faith: "What manner of man is this . . . ?"

For Jesus the great festival of Passover is interrupted by the need to arrange a banquet hall on the sly, by a traitorous friend who sells him out for the price of a slave, and by his ultimate rejection at the hands of those whose whole duty was to represent the salvation of God. His death becomes an annoying bother to those who want to go on enjoying their limited freedom to celebrate their religious heritage. Even that

261

unsteady calm of Friday afternoon is interrupted by news of an empty tomb, of unsealed stones, and of a Christ who won't stay dead!

The Interruptions in Our Lives

Perhaps we can handle the interruptions that intrude into our lives a little better when we see that *all* interruptions are life events that cannot be fenced out anymore than the Pacific can be kept three feet off the California shoreline.

That's not to say they'll be easier to handle. But like life itself, interruptions are what happens while we wait for something else.

I remember how my parents always felt they had been robbed of something every young couple should have—a time to meet and fall in love and enjoy each other. That little interruption which put a damper on their plans was called World War II. Nothing like a three-year sidetrack to really interrupt a courtship!

Then there was the sweet, almost-spring day back in the late 1960s. The first crocuses were peeping through the snow. Baseball would soon be underway again, and for five days each week there were jobs to get to, and then weekends to enjoy. There were letters to write, routines to get through, lives to live. But all these ended when a phone call told me that my best friend up the street had just been killed in an auto crash. How quickly, and how often since then, have I seen the unstoppable brute force of death interrupting family circles and tearing apart plans and friendships and expectations.

Or how mindlessly crippling disease can invade and interrupt a promising athletic career, or as happened once in my parish, come as a death sentence to a young mother of two. Family life-styles can be interrupted and thrown into shambles by a sudden announcement that one's job is no more. Churches can be fatally interrupted and even wounded unto death by mass migrations and and demographic shifts, as a little country church building with its weed-choked cemetery so eloquently bears witness. They say, in effect, that all life, all community, is subject to the unexpected interruptions of war, discord, change, upheavals, death.

But to these interruptions about us cries from human hearts arise, interrupting God and his eternal aloneness. "Abba, Father," we cry. "Excuse me for interrupting, but if it be possible, let this cup, this telegram from the Defense Department, this closed-down mine, this divorce my parents have told me about, this towering cross of pain, pass from me. Nevertheless, not my will, but yours be done, even if it means my life will have to be picked up from dust and ashes and even death."

262

Interrupting Prayer

Surely any theology of interruptions must deal with this: if God allows so much to interrupt our Eden, just as surely he waits for us to interrupt him with our cries and prayers! And no more heartfelt prayer comes to us in all our liturgies and prayer books than our plea that our Father in heaven will interrupt our pain with his presence: "Lord, have mercy on me a sinner. Maranatha! Our Lord, come!"

Today's difficult text makes us see that the whole world will feel the nails of its tailor-made cross. Everything we cherish, everyone we love, every built-up institution and tradition and counted-upon treasure will be interrupted by a force that will tear it from us. Sometimes that force will be Brother War, and sometimes Sister Anger, and sometimes Cousin Death. Mostly it will be Father Sin. And sometimes it will be just plain old Grandfather Time and Grandmother Change. Everything preliminary, even our own baby, will be torn from us and cast away. Only the ultimate will last: only our relationship with our Father in heaven cannot be interrupted by heights and depths and forces and powers and principalities—indeed, no power in all creation can tear us from God's love! Whoever holds on to the Good Shepherd's hand will be saved whole for the pastures eternal, and whoever cries out to this world's Savior will have life when the whole world passes away. Every party, every kingdom will cease: but God's kingdom is citizenship unending and unlimited.

The very ground under our feet was once ocean floor. Only the spiritually short-sighted refuse to read this truth in the masterpieces of geology. God casts down the mighty mountains and raises up the silt beds, just as he will throw down the nuclear-tipped empires to raise up refugees from the slave pens for his own special people.

Surely, only one prayer is worth praying by the whole world:

> Savior of our falling apart world, who died on a cross even as our whole world will someday die, pardon us for interrupting you with our sin, but while we have your attention, have mercy on us and bring us home.

And until our Lord does interrupt our wars and our crumbling societies and our religious divisions when he comes to answer that prayer once and for all, let's think about three teens who upset their canoe near our church camp: they were two miles from shore, the water was cold, the wind was picking up and blowing them apart from each other and from me. I had to right their canoe before I could rescue them: meanwhile they were starting to get frantic. One by one I threw them a length of rope and hauled them over to my canoe, where I told them to hold on until I could lift them back into their bailed out boat. Well, until the

263

end, let's all *hold tight* to the rope our God has thrown us—our faith, and let's *stay* in the boat he's sent us—his church, and let's learn how to be like Christ and help him save those who are sinking around us.

BARRY E. BENCE
Church of the Cross
Lac Du Bonnet, Manitoba

TWENTY-SEVENTH SUNDAY AFTER PENTECOST

Pessimistic or Optimistic?

Mark 13:24-31

Some stories begin with optimism and hope. Take the musical *Camelot*. Here is a drama which explores the Arthurian myth. It begins with King Arthur, Guinevere, and Lancelot optimistic and hopeful about society, relationships, and moral achievement. They all appear on the scene with a clean slate. The future is open. Tomorrow is theirs!

But sometimes a story that begins in such a hopeful way may not end that way. And so, as the players in this drama act and interact, their dreams fade; their hopes collapse; their optimism dies. And in the end, the lives of these people lie as broken as the Round Table itself. The "brief shining moment" that was once Camelot, proves to be only that. Utopia is lost, and with it chivalry, relationships, and social order. At the end only war seems inevitable.

By contrast, other stories begin just the opposite. Other stories begin rather gloomily and end on a note of optimism and triumph. Let's take another mythical story, C.S. Lewis' tale of *The Lion, the Witch, and the Wardrobe*. This story tells of four children: Peter, Susan, Edmund, and Lucy, and of the adventure they have in a magical land called Narnia. They discover Narnia by entering a wardrobe in an old English country house. As they walk deeper and deeper into the wardrobe, they find that the fur coats of the closet soon turn into fir trees. The fir trees are covered with snow, because this magical land is under an evil curse. Narnia is a place where it is always winter and never Christmas, let alone spring. The only thing that can break this spell is the appearance of Aslan, the great lion and lord of the entire wood. For when Aslan comes, as the little creatures of Narnia believed, he would set everything right. And that is exactly what happens. The great day finally arrives. Aslan appears.

264

Spring cannot be put off any longer. In the end, Aslan triumphs over death and the wicked witch herself; her spell is broken. And all the little creatures that have been turned into stone by her magic are set free and brought back to life.

Another Story

Today's Gospel is a story, too, or more accurately, part of a story. This story begins with the first verse of Chapter 13 in Mark's Gospel. It is a story which, like *The Lion, the Witch, and the Wardrobe*, begins in pessimism and gloom. For the backdrop of this story lies in the terrible ":Day of the Lord," the day on which God would directly intervene in history, judging all people. Our First Lesson from Daniel tells of this time when the Ancient of Days would sit in judgment on his throne, and the account books would be opened.

But before that day, there would be a period of terror and tribulation that the earth has never seen. Jesus mentions some of these things to his disciples early in Chapter 13: wars and rumors of wars, earthquakes in various places, famines, persecutions, and even the destruction and the desecration of the temple itself.

But the story does not end in pessimism. "The bottom line," as we Americans like to put it, is that the gloom and doom that begins this chapter does not conclude it.

Two Parts

This Gospel text has traditionally been divided into two parts. The first part has to do with the coming of the Son of man. Here Jesus speaks *apocalyptically*. That is to say, he *unveils* what is to happen in the future. This should not be understood in a literal way, as an exact time line of future events. Rather these are dreams and visions of what will come to pass. It is poetry and not prose. And in a sense, like the other stories I have discussed, this is myth. Now myth has not so much to do with logic as it has to do with reality. Here in this passage, Jesus expresses the reality of his return in word pictures that the people of ancient Palestine would understand. The words are meant to impress upon the hearers the greatness of the event that could overtake any of them at any time and become fact. Such a passage describes the indescribable; it captures in words something beyond our comprehension. And such a passage conveys great truth: the truth that Jesus will someday return in "power and glory" and that his elect will be gathered "from the ends of the earth."

The second part of the text has to do with the lesson of the fig tree. Now in some ways, the fig tree in Mark's gospel is a puzzling symbol.

265

You may recall how Jesus cursed a fig tree earlier in this gospel (11:12-14,20-21), and it withered. It could be that the fig tree symbolizes the nation of Israel (cf. Luke 13:1-9). And so when Jesus curses the fig tree, he is acting out what he teaches—namely, a call for national repentance. Here, though, the lesson is more clear. The lesson of this fig tree is that its tender branches and young leaves are analogous to the signs of the times. Just as you know that *summer is near* when you see these things occurring on a fig tree, so you will know that *he is near* when you see things occurring in historical events. And note how optimistic that is. Summer is the time of fruition for a fig tree. And so in history, when these terrible events happen, one should not despair and be consumed with worry and doubt. For all these events, as terrible as they may look on the surface, are really the necessary indications that all of history will reach its fulfillment in the coming of Christ.

But Didn't Jesus Get It Wrong?

But didn't Jesus get it wrong? Wasn't he ultimately mistaken about his return? For after all, he goes on to state in the very next verse, "This generation will not pass away before all these things take place." I don't think that Jesus was mistaken. The reason I don't is because of two things. First, remember that the entire 13th chapter of Mark is preoccupied with the destruction of the Jerusalem temple. And its destruction did occur in A.D. 70, or within the lifetime of the generation who heard Jesus' prediction. Thus the things that Jesus described did take place during that generation. And secondly, Jesus goes on in the next verses following today's Gospel to say that not even he knows when that day will come. Thus the emphasis is more on *what* will happen in the future than on *when* it will happen.

We should keep in mind that Jesus' words about the end times convey the underlying assurance of the fulfillment of history. The people of Jesus' times had a gnawing feeling of imminent doom. Likewise, Luther, during the Middle Ages, felt that the end was at hand. Similarly today, many feel, and for good reason, that what Jesus once predicted will come to pass in our lifetimes. The threat of national and world destruction, the rise of false teachers and cults, the abundance of wars, the commonality of natural disasters, the multitude of persecutions, and the problems of our natural environment—all combine to paint a pessimistic picture about the shape our world is in and the direction we are going. Winter is here. Wickedness is the order of the day. But the point is that when you see these terrible things happening in history, paradoxically summer is near as well, because he is near, at the very gates.

God's Story Is Forever

I love a good story. I love a story like *Camelot*, which begins with optimism and ends pessimistically, because above all the story is a good one. It tells the enduring tale of human ambition and human fault. Truth is to be found here; the story is good.

And I love a story like *The Lion, the Witch, and the Wardrobe*, which begins pessimistically and ends optimistically, because this is a good story too. It tells of a reality basic to, and yet beyond human experience. Truth is to be found here; the story is good.

But the story I love most of all is God's own story, the story written on the pages of human history and on our lives. Jesus tells us this story today. The Gospel lesson is such a story. It begins in pessimism, the pessimism of a world about to collapse, of a history gone awry, of a winter with no spring. And it ends with optimism, eternal optimism, the optimism of a gathered elect, of a summer that is near, and of the one who is near.

All of history is moving toward fulfillment. For Christian believers this will take place when God once again breaks into history. And so we should not become so immersed in daily work and become so burdened down with all the bad news and become so preoccupied with the things of this earth that we fail to look up. God's story is forever! If we live in that hope, if our hearts are captured by that story, if our imaginations long for such an ending, we will not be disappointed.

Things will look up, if only you and I will look up. Your ending is to be joy and not judgment, delight and not despair, gladness and not gloom. Christ the Lord is at the gates! Can't you hear his footsteps? Can't you feel his presence? Can't you sense his hand on the lock? Summer is near. Winter will soon be over. The spell will be broken forever!

WILLIAM R. BRAGSTAD
Messiah Lutheran Church
Hayward, California

CHRIST THE KING—LAST SUNDAY AFTER PENTECOST

The King of Truth
John 18:33-37

A great study in contrast took place between Pilate and the prisoner, Jesus. Pilate shuffled back and forth as he listened to what the accusing priests and people had to say. His ears were picking up the crucifying chant of the crowd. All the cries catapulted around him, and Pilate became a figure of bewilderment. He was losing control of the situation.

Pilate asks Jesus, "Are you the King of the Jews?" In essence Jesus replies that he is, but not in the sense in which Pilate uses the word. His kingdom is not a dominion over people's bodies but over their minds and souls. This kingdom is not maintained by force but by the persuasion of love and truth. Pilate is baffled so he blurts out, "What is truth?" Pilate becomes a picture of a man who is unsure of himself. No guiding principle is undergirding him. He was guided only by expediency and the fear for his own position. This ruler was reeling around the ring like a punch-drunk fighter. Confidence was waning.

In striking contrast, Christ stood calm and collected before him. He was unafraid. In spite of the denunciation Jesus' dignity was never darkened. He knew that for which he was born; his mission was well-defined; his loins were girded with truth. His words to Pilate were simply, "for this I was born . . . to bear witness to the truth."

What is truth? A parade of past philosophers would give us varied answers. Some would say that truth is a statement that agrees with the facts. Others would inform us that something is true only when it is compatible with a system of other truths. Then, some would tell us that truth is more pragmatic. If a statement is acted upon and the results are good for you, then it's true. Trying to define truth is no easy task.

In Scripture Jesus says, "If you continue in my word, you are truly my disciples, and you will know the truth and the truth will make you free" (John 8:31-32). God's Word is thus authority and truth. As a boy I remember the preachers always using the phrase, after reading Scripture, "These are thy words, Heavenly Father. Sanctify us in the truth, for thy words are truth."

The Source of Truth

Yet there is another kind of truth that I believe is more important than philosophical or theological statements. It is the truth of the person. John says, "And the Word became flesh and dwelt among us, full of grace and truth" (John 1:14). Truth was wrapped up in a person. Jesus said, "I am . . . the truth" (John 14:6). Truth is something you should be. Jesus was the embodiment of all truth. Truth as absolute honesty and perfect integrity—the kind of truth we are called to be—was contained in the very core of Jesus' being.

Paul Tillich said, "In [Jesus] the true, the genuine, the ultimate reality is present, unveiled, undistorted in his infinite depth, in his magnificent mystery." William Temple made this declaration, "The ultimate truth is not a system of propositions grasped by perfect intelligence but a Personal Being apprehended by love."

Jesus is the source of all truth. In that truth comes our freedom to be. In relationship to the grace and truth of Jesus we are set free from guilt, sin, insecurity, and legions of fear.

The Openness of Truth

There are two main words in Scripture used for truth. In the New Testament the word is *aletheia*. The basic meaning is "nonconcealment" or "unhiddenness." Truth is open to view. It is expressed rather than suppressed. It is the opposite of a cover-up. Jesus talks about this aspect of truth when he said to his disciples, "All that I have heard from the Father I have made known to you" (John 15:15). Jesus did not have a hidden agenda. He made no fake passes.

Falseness is an intent to deceive. It can be done by words that mislead, by the glance of an eye, by an expression of the countenance. Satan is the arch deceiver. Jesus is the light in whom there is no darkness of deception.

The person of truth walks in the light. There is no fear of being transparent. But because we have not really made friends with truth, many folks stay buttoned-up. We want our flaws and faults to remain under wraps. We forfeit closeness with anyone, because we are afraid of being exposed.

So games of deception continue to be played. If a boss does not want to talk with a disagreeable client, he merely tells his secretary to tell him that he is not in. Expense accounts are exaggerated to accumulate a little more pocket money. Tracks leading to secret trysts are covered over with plausible explanations that hide the truth.

If we identify with Christ and let him free us, we will be given the courage to be open and honest to family and friends. We will not have to babysit our reputations. We will be able to accept either failure or success in stride. The honest person does not have to live on cloud nine every day and pretend that everything is just dandy. He or she can admit it openly when something is botched up.

There was a little fellow who bragged constantly. He told his father that he was a great hitter in baseball. They went out to the back yard and his father stood to the side as the boy threw the ball into the air and then swung the bat with all his might. "Strike one," said the boy as he missed completely. "Strike two," as he missed again. The third time he again hit nothing but air as he called out, "Strike three." Then he turned to his father with a determined glow on his face. "Dad, it just goes to show that I am a great pitcher!"

We are tempted to deal with life that way. Reality is never confronted. Deception destroys the truth and damns the soul. Open up the door and let the fresh air of truth clean out the musty corners of life. There is a freshness in the freedom of openness.

The Reliability of Truth

In the Old Testament the word for truth is *emeth*. It comes from a verb that means "to be firm, solid, sure," and its basic meaning is "reliability" or "faithfulness." Ellen G. White wrote: "The greatest want of the world is the want of men—men who will not be bought or sold, men who in their inmost souls are true and honest, men who do not fear to call sin by its right name, men whose conscience is as true to duty as the needle to the pole, men who will stand for right though the heavens fall." Reliability sometimes means speaking up and sometimes will mean keeping the mouth shut. The reliable person is a dependable person. Truth is not tucked away in a safe place. It takes on flesh and gets up and walks around.

You can bank on Jesus. What he said, he would do. Standing before Pilate, listening to the angry mob was not easy. He could have packed his bags and run for his life. He could have called in the legions of heaven to deliver him. But Jesus refused to escape. He said he came to give his life as a ransom for many. Nothing would sidetrack him from completing his mission.

Scripture depicts our God as one whose word will stand forever. The psalmist sings, "Thy faithfulness endures to all generations" (Ps. 119:20). Paul says, "If we are faithless, he remains faithful" (2 Tim. 2:13). Sweeping across Germany at the end of World War II, Allied forces searched farms and houses looking for snipers. At one abandoned house, almost a heap of rubble, searchers with flashlights found their way to the basement. There, on the crumbling wall, a victim of the Holocaust had scratched a Star of David. Beneath it, in rough lettering, was this message:

> I believe in the sun—even when it does not shine.
> I believe in love—even when it is not shown.
> I believe in God—even when he does not speak.

That is faith in the faithfulness of God at its finest.

For you and me truthfulness means that we will attempt to be the kind of people who others can always count on. Assignments that we undertake will be carried out to completion. When we give our word,

270

there will be no backing out. Truth will be our rudder, so that we will not be subject to every shift of wind or tide. Just as God's grip won't slip, we too, will give permanence and security to those around us.

A man had fallen off a fishing pier into deep water. He could not swim. He hollered for help. Another fisherman came running and asked what he could do. The drowning man cried out, "Give me something to hold on to!" May our words and our life be just that.

At the end of another church year let us thank King Jesus that he has the power to produce everything he has promised. Paul shouts: "For all the promises of God find their Yes in him. That is why we utter the Amen through him, to the glory of God" (2 Cor. 1:20). Let us "continue in his Word so we shall know the truth and the truth will make us free." Let us see that truth is something we are. If Pilate had sat at the feet of Jesus, he would have found truth. Then he would not have been a pawn pushed to and fro on the day Jesus was delivered to be crucified.

JAMES R. BJORGE
First Lutheran Church
Fargo, North Dakota

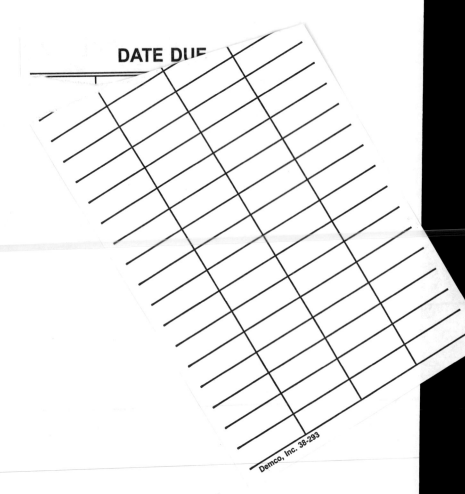

DATE DUE

Demco, Inc. 38-293